PENGUIN BOOKS

OIL AND ICE

Peter Nichols is the author of the national bestseller *A Voyage for Madmen*, as well as three other books. He has appeared on CNN, NPR, PBS, and regional network and cable programs promoting his work. He spent ten years working as a professional yachting captain, sailed across the Atlantic Ocean three times (once completely alone), and worked in the film industry as both a screenwriter and union "Ship Wrangler" (he once spent six months in Borneo outfitting a native cargo vessel as a pirate ship for the film *Cutthroat Island*). He has taught creative writing at NYU, Georgetown University, and Bowdoin College and currently teaches at the University of Arizona. He splits his time between Camden, Maine, and Europe.

OIL AND ICE

*A Story of Arctic Disaster and the Rise and Fall
of America's Last Whaling Dynasty*

PETER NICHOLS

PENGUIN BOOKS

Previously published as *Final Voyage*

PENGUIN BOOKS

Published by the Penguin Group

Penguin Group (USA) Inc., 375 Hudson Street, New York, New York 10014, U.S.A.

Penguin Group (Canada), 90 Eglinton Avenue East, Suite 700, Toronto,
Ontario, Canada M4P 2Y3 (a division of Pearson Penguin Canada Inc.)

Penguin Books Ltd, 80 Strand, London WC2R 0RL, England

Penguin Ireland, 25 St Stephen's Green, Dublin 2, Ireland (a division of Penguin Books Ltd)

Penguin Group (Australia), 250 Camberwell Road, Camberwell,
Victoria 3124, Australia (a division of Pearson Australia Group Pty Ltd)

Penguin Books India Pvt Ltd, 11 Community Centre, Panchsheel Park, New Delhi – 110 017, India

Penguin Group (NZ), 67 Apollo Drive, Rosedale, North Shore 0632,
New Zealand (a division of Pearson New Zealand Ltd)

Penguin Books (South Africa) (Pty) Ltd, 24 Sturdee Avenue,
Rosebank, Johannesburg 2196, South Africa

Penguin Books Ltd, Registered Offices:
80 Strand, London WC2R 0RL, England

First published in the United States of America as *Final Voyage* by G. P. Putnam's Sons,
a member of Penguin Group (USA) Inc. 2009
Published in Penguin Books 2010

1 3 5 7 9 10 8 6 4 2

THE LIBRARY OF CONGRESS HAS CATALOGED THE HARDCOVER EDITION AS FOLLOWS:
Nichols, Peter, date.
Final voyage : a story of Arctic disaster and one fateful whaling season / Peter Nichols.
p. cm.
Includes bibliographical references.
ISBN 978-0-399-15602-1 (hc.)
ISBN 978-0-14-311836-7 (pbk.)
1. Whaling—Arctic regions—History—19th century. 2. Marine accidents—Arctic regions—History—
19th century. 3. Whaling—Economic aspects—Massachusetts—New Bedford—History—19th century.
4. Seafaring life—Massachusetts—New Bedford—History—19th century. 5. New Bedford (Mass.)—
Economic conditions—19th century. 6. New Bedford (Mass.)—Biography. I. Title.
SH383.2.N53   2009   2009023057
338.3'72950974485—dc22

Printed in the United States of America
DESIGNED BY NICOLE LAROCHE

This book is for Gus,
my son, Augustus Paris Nichols.

OIL AND ICE

Prologue

After surging to an all-time peak, oil prices were falling, despite the depletion of fields around the world. Oil itself was talked about as an outmoded commodity, soon to be relegated to the past as cheaper, inexhaustible, emerging energy sources were being developed.

Oil barons and financiers were suddenly facing the loss of an industry that had supported them and supplied the world's needs for generations. Banks and hitherto bedrock-solid financial institutions were foundering.

Wealthy men were ruined overnight, stunned that they had not seen what was coming, that everything they had believed in and counted upon lay in ruins.

The old paradigm was broken and a new one was overtaking the world.

This, then, was the state of the whale-oil industry 140 years ago.

One

Alaska, June 1871

Early in June 1871, as the whaling bark *John Wells*, of New Bedford, Massachusetts, approached the snow- and fog-shrouded Siberian shore at the southern entrance to the Bering Strait, the ship was intercepted by a small boat full of wild-looking, fur-clad men. At first the whalemen on the *Wells*'s deck mistook them for Eskimos, natives of this coast. For the most part, New Englanders found the Eskimos, with occasional female exceptions, repellent-looking (made more so by the chin tattoos of the women, and the holes men bored in their cheeks around their mouths, then plugged with ornamental pieces of bone), but these creatures, as they drew closer, looked particularly wretched. All were bearded, their long hair matted, their faces smeared with grease and blackened from crouching over smoky fires. They appeared out of the cold, vaporous air like spectral phantoms, waving and calling, their voices thin and imploring. But their cries were in everyday English. The boat was soon alongside the *John Wells*, and its ripe-smelling occupants were helped aboard the ship.

One of them introduced himself as Captain Frederick Barker and explained that he and the men with him were the surviving crew of the whaling ship *Japan*, which had driven ashore on the nearby coast in a storm eight months before. Barker and his men were taken below, where they bathed, shaved, and were given clean clothes. Finally, over a seaman's meal of beef, pork, beans, and bread—Christian food they had not tasted for eight months—they told their story to the *Wells's* captain, Aaron Dean, and his officers.

They had enjoyed an exceptionally fortunate season's whaling the previous year, in the summer of 1870. The *Japan* had pushed through the ice in the Bering Strait and reached the Arctic Ocean whaling grounds by the unusually early date of March 10—it was normally July before ice conditions allowed whaleships north of the strait. Their good luck had continued throughout the summer and into the fall. Because of mercurial changes of weather at the season's close, when summer might be replaced by winter in the space of twenty-four hours, most whaling captains normally started heading south from the Arctic by early September. Lulled by continued fine conditions and an abundance of bowhead whales—and mindful of the injunction given by all whaling ship owners to their captains: "You are not to omit taking a whale when you can"—Captain Barker delayed his departure by a full month. He continued taking whales even as the autumn rime coated the shore, the true barometer of what was coming.

Early in October, Barker finally turned his ship south. On October 4, a heavy gale struck the *Japan*, and with it came the full, brutal, change of season. In driving snow, with ice forming in the rigging, Barker and his crew attempted to work the ship through the fast-disappearing channel between the coast and the solidifying ice pack that the storm was hourly driving closer to shore. With the ice and the storm came snow squalls, and between the squalls, the air was filled with a dense, disorienting fog. When even the roughly level plane of the sea beyond the decks became invisible, Barker's world was reduced to an icy, disorienting cloud. Without visual or celestial aids, his navigation exponentially veered toward guesswork as he aimed the *Japan* for the eye of a geographic needle, the sixty-mile-wide Bering Strait, beyond which lay the open waters of the Bering Sea and the North Pacific.

The benign season had also seduced other whaling captains into postponing their departure from the Arctic, and these ships were now sailing through this same storm. The New Bedford whaleship *Elizabeth Swift* was not far away. *"This day blowing a terible gale from the N,"* noted the *Swift*'s logkeeper on October 5. Waves continually broke aboard the *Swift*, filling her with water, keeping her men laboring at her pumps. The oar-powered whaleboats carried in davits high above the decks were swept away. As the storm went on, the height of the waves and the force and weight of the water crashing aboard increased. On October 6, a great wave smashed into the ship's side and *"stove our starboard bulwarks all to atoms."* Sails blew to ribbons. Another New Bedford whaleship, the *Seneca*, was seen working heavily through the seas not far away. Neither ship knew its position with any certainty. *"Dont know whare we are,"* wrote the *Swift*'s logkeeper. *"Vary cold. So ends this day."*

On October 8, the men aboard the *Japan* sighted another whaleship through the snow, the *Massachusetts*, of New Bedford, also running south at speed. The *Japan* made signals to the other ship, hoping to stay in company with her, for Barker feared the *Japan* might not weather the storm. But the *Massachusetts* either did not see the signals or could do little about them, and disappeared into the spumy air.

At the same time, the *Champion*, of Martha's Vineyard, lay about sixty miles to the north, behind the *Japan*. She had recently caught and cut up four whales, but there hadn't been time before the storm struck to boil the blubber from these into oil and stow the barrels below. Large chunks of whale meat and blubber, called "horse pieces," 500 barrels' worth, were now stored "between decks," the space between the upper deck and the ship's hold. This constituted a danger almost as great as the storm, for such deadweight, forty or fifty tons of it, sliding around with every roll and pitch, made the ship dangerously top-heavy, more likely than ever to slew around out of control before the wind and capsize. The *Champion*'s captain, Henry Pease, later described the circumstances aboard his ship as it headed for the Bering Strait:

> . . . ship covered with ice and oil; could only muster four men in a watch, decks flooded with water all the time; no fire to cook with or to warm by, made it the most anxious and miserable time I ever experienced in all my sea-service. During the night shipped a heavy sea, which took off bow and waist boats, davits, slide-boards, and everything attached, staving about 20 barrels of oil.

With the coming of a bleak daylight, the *Champion*'s crew lowered the lead line (a lead weight on the end of a rope) in an attempt to get some idea of where they were. They found seventeen fathoms of water beneath the ship and concluded that they had passed through the Bering Strait during the night and were now headed for the rocks of St. Lawrence Island, directly ahead. By then the storm moderated enough to allow them to raise two small sails and haul the ship away from the island, saving themselves from certain shipwreck.

Barker and his crew were not so lucky. On the morning of October 9, running at "racehorse speed" before the wind, in "such blinding snow that we could not see half a ship's length," the *Japan* drove like a runaway train onto the rocky shore at the western side of the strait. All of her crew were miraculously unhurt in the wreck. Most of them immediately jumped overboard and waded a quarter of a mile through the pounding surf to the shore. The water temperature was at, or only a little above, freezing. Barker went below to gather his ship's papers and logbook, but as he emerged from the cabin, a breaking wave swept over the deck and tore everything from his arms. Drenched, in clothes instantly growing stiff with ice, he descended to his cabin, again to change. Although the *Japan* was now pounding in the shallows, the ship's position had stabilized somewhat. Knowing he would probably not have another chance, Barker spent a further three hours belowdecks, attempting to collect clothing and provisions for his men.

Meanwhile, two of the *Japan*'s crewmen, who had reached dry land and started running up and down the shore to restore their frozen circulation, spotted fresh dog prints in the snow. They followed these to an Eskimo village, whose inhabitants immediately returned with them to the shore to help the sailors.

The Eskimos met Barker staggering out of the surf. They put him on a sled and began pulling him toward their village. On the way, he saw the bodies of many of his men, who, after safely reaching the shore, had collapsed on the ground and frozen to death. He imagined that he, too, was dying.

The air was piercing cold. . . . I thought my teeth would freeze off. . . . I supposed I was freezing to death. In a short time we reached the huts and I was carried in like a clod of earth, as I could not move hand or foot. The chief's wife, in whose hut I was, pulled off my boots and stockings and placed my frozen feet against her naked bosom to restore warmth.

But there were no hot meals for the survivors. Raw walrus meat and blubber, much of it putrid and rotting, was the only food, and it was days before the whalemen could bring themselves to eat it. "Hunger at last compelled me, and strange as it may appear, it tasted good to me."

The *Japan* had wrecked on East Cape, Siberia, the easternmost point of mainland Asia, at the top of the Bering Strait. After two months of the native diet, Barker and the healthier members of his remaining crew (others were too weak to travel) set out along the now solidly frozen shore for Plover Bay, several hundred miles away, at the southern end of the strait. This deep, protected harbor was well known to arctic whaling and trading vessels, and was the site of several large Eskimo settlements. Barker hoped he might still find a ship there that could carry him and the rest of his crew away before the onset of the long winter, or at least find better food if they could not get away. The white men had already traded their stiff salt- and ice-sodden pea-coats, canvas foul-weather clothing, wool pants, and boots to the natives, who coveted these smart outfits, for warm fur and skin Eskimo garments and boots, and these served Barker and his men well on their ten-day tramp over ice and rock.[1] At Plover Bay they found the San Francisco whaler *Hannah B. Bowen*, which was wintering over in the bay. They were taken on board and made comfortable, but four days after they arrived, the *Bowen* sprang a leak as ice thickened around her waterline and stove in some planks, forcing all hands to move ashore. They fixed up a small hut and remained there through the winter, eating the *Bowen*'s more civilized rations. Three times over the next few months, Barker made trips overland through the brief hours of faint

---

1. Early in his career, the Norwegian polar explorer Roald Amundsen learned the great advantage of Eskimo clothing in such conditions, and this was a factor in his success in reaching, and surviving, the South Pole ahead of the doomed, wool- and canvas-clad English party led by Robert Falcon Scott.

daylight to bring provisions to the thirteen men who remained at East Cape. Although the Eskimos there continued to show every kindness to the wrecked sailors, all but one of them, Lewis Kennedy, who was too sick to move, finally could no longer bear the grim austerity of native life and attempted to make the trek south through the strait. They got as far as Indian Point, thirty miles from Barker's quarters in Plover Bay. One of them froze to death on the way. There they remained.

BARKER AND HIS FIRST MATE, E. W. Irving, told this tale to Captain Dean and the officers of the *John Wells*. The next afternoon, June 6, 1871, they boarded another New Bedford whaler, the *Henry Taber*, which had arrived in Plover Bay, and repeated their story. Both ships then sailed around the coast to Indian Point, where a third New Bedford whaler, the *Contest*, had found and taken aboard the *Japan*'s eleven crewmembers camped there. Ten days later, on June 17, the *Wells* and the *Taber* reached "Owalin" (the present-day Russian settlement of Uelen) near East Cape, where the *Japan* had wrecked, and the ship's last shipwrecked sailor, twenty-four-year-old Lewis Kennedy, an Englishman, was taken aboard the *Taber*. Kennedy had been one of the men who had safely reached shore, and then almost died of hypothermia on the beach. He had never recovered enough to make the trek south, and had remained in the Eskimo settlement, where, despite the best attention and food the Eskimos could give him, he was still unwell. "We've now 15 of the japan's men aboard including Captain & second mate," wrote the *Wells*'s logkeeper, second mate Nathaniel Ransom, who hailed from New Bedford's neighboring town of Mattapoisett. At most times, Ransom's log entries were the usual for ships' logs: dry, essential details of weather, course, location, and ship's business; but on this Saturday evening, after hearing of the *Japan*'s ill-fortune, his thoughts flew to the comfort of home, and he added, "Wrote a few lines to my darling wife."

Abram Briggs, logkeeper aboard the *Henry Taber*, was more forthcoming:

> *Now, I am glad to state here that all of the survivors of the Ill fated Ship (Japan) are kindly cared for, as circumstances will admit and distributed among several of the fleet. From the time of her stranding, up to the present day, they lost 9 of the ships company & let us all trust they are far better off then In this World of Trouble, and let us hope the (all wise being) will permit the rescued ones to return to there friends no more to pertake of the trials & troubles of The Arctic Ocean.*

The two young logkeepers, like every other whaleman in the Arctic, readily saw themselves in the *Japan*'s luckless and lucky crew. They were not inured to the prospects that lay beyond a moment's bad luck, and keenly understood the peril of their situation. They were almost constantly afraid, like men in combat, and devoutly believed that, but for the grace of God, any one of them might find himself shipwrecked in the same unforgivable circumstances, facing a numbing or painfully lingering death, or, at best, a season in icy hell on an Eskimo diet. They put their lives and faith almost equally in the hands of God and His closest proxy in their world, their ships' captains.

THE *JOHN WELLS*, the *Henry Taber*, and the *Contest* were in the vanguard of a fleet of forty whaling vessels then nosing through the melting ice in the Bering Strait. Most were from New Bedford. Others had sailed from Sag Harbor, New York; New London, Connecticut; and

Edgartown, Massachusetts; several were registered in Honolulu; and one ship sailed annually to the Arctic from Sydney, Australia. The ships' captains and crews fully expected to encounter one another, to see perhaps ten, twenty, even thirty other whaling vessels at a time in good weather, wherever they sailed during the season. But even amid such fierce competition, there was, by 1871, no better place on earth for finding whales.

High in the Arctic Ocean, roughly 300 miles south of the permanent polar ice pack (only 1,200 miles south of the North Pole itself), these "Arctic grounds" opened only for a few months every summer. They comprised a narrow channel that ran along the Alaskan coast from the Bering Strait to Point Barrow, Alaska's northernmost tip of land, in the shallow water between the shore and the temporarily retreating ice pack. Then, as now, a powerful ocean current pumped northward through the Bering Strait out of the North Pacific, rising from abyssal depths and sweeping over the undersea continental shelf, stirring up and carrying a rich sediment of nitrates, phosphates, and other minerals into the Arctic Ocean. In spring, as the days lengthened toward twenty-four hours of chlorophyll-producing sunlight, this earthy undersea stream mixed with the oxygen-rich surface water at the edge of the melting ice pack to produce a dense, unparalleled efflorescence of plankton in the shallow water off the Alaskan shore. And as the ice melted, the arctic bowhead whales, whose diet consisted of plankton (filtered out of the water by the fronds of baleen that filled their great mouths), came here to feed on this rich soup. And the whalemen came for the whales.

As more ships gathered and nosed through the retreating edge of the ice pack in the strait, captains and crews went visiting. They rowed about in their small whaleboats for "gams"—social visits—aboard other vessels. Barker and first mate Irving accompanied Captain Dean, of the

Wells, and often remained for several days as guests of other captains, telling again the story of the *Japan* and her crew's long winter in the Arctic.

One of these ships was the *Monticello*, of New London, Connecticut. Her captain, Thomas William Williams, was one of a number of whaling ship masters who sailed with his wife and children aboard his ship.

Captain Williams's youngest son, William Fish Williams, was twelve years old when Captain Barker came aboard for a meal in the *Monticello*'s saloon in June 1871. The food served to visitors was always the ship's finest, yet it was plain. Sailors were not adventurous eaters. Despite the monotony of scanning the horizons for whale spouts for years at a stretch, they wanted dependability in their shipboard diet. Beef, pork, codfish, cheese, bread, and coffee they consumed daily with a relish undiminished by repetition. They were not bold experimenters when it came to the exotic foodstuffs to be found ashore—except for fruit, which, like children, they prized most for its color and sweetness. (One youthful seaman, who had never in his life seen or tasted tomatoes, bought a bag in Japan. Their "sourness" was so surprising that he threw the bag away.)

What young Willie Williams remembered most from his meeting with Barker was the captain's revolting account of going hungry and eating tallow candles salvaged from his ship's wreckage before succumbing to the natives' diet of raw and rotting walrus blubber and meat with the hair still on it.

This also made the profoundest impression upon the captains of the other whaleships: the threat of starvation, the unsustainability of life ashore along this coast in the event of a shipwreck. A scenario that would determine the fate of every man, woman, and child in the fleet at the end of this summer.

NINETEENTH-CENTURY SHIPOWNERS, whale-oil refiners and dealers, whale-product merchants, ship captains, harpooners, whaleboat crews, coopers, and the common seamen who sailed aboard whaleships, their families, and the communities they returned home to, felt little of the Melvillean romance, of the environmental concerns, and nothing of the abhorrence that have since attached themselves to the enterprise of whaling. True, museums are full of scrimshaw carvings made by common seamen who were affected in an aesthetic way by the elemental, primordial struggle they experienced and witnessed in their work; some were genuinely enthralled by what they saw, though most of this work was occupational therapy, to stave off the stultifying boredom of life aboard a whaleship. Herman Melville's dark, rapturous vision did not resonate with the readers of his day. His greatest book was a critical and commercial flop on publication, marking the end of his career as a popular novelist. There weren't many fanciful types who held romantic notions about life aboard whaling ships. A shelf or two of memoirists of small or no literary merit tried (usually many years later, after the quotidian normalcy of shipboard life had given way to marveling at what they had once done in their heedless youth in the pursuit of a very few dollars) to express the astonishing, unquestioning audacity of pursuing a great whale in a small rowboat, to catch it with a hand-thrown hook, stab it to death, haul it back to a small, rolling ship, and there chop it up and melt it down for its oil. Why, what an idea.

For most of its practitioners, at every level, whaling was a rational, workaday endeavor, no more romantic than house carpentry, and far more dangerous and unpleasant. For the businessmen at the top of the trade it could mean phenomenal wealth; for the seaman in the cramped fo'c'sle, whose pay would often amount to no more than pennies a day, it was employment where none existed ashore, a path off the farm, or out of the slum, an opportunity of last resort. Very few young men, mainly delusional misfits, would have seen it as a tempting way of driving off the spleen, addressing a damp, drizzly November of the soul—Melville's existential getaway. Life aboard a whaleship was too brutal and too dull for sensitive souls. Even Melville jumped ship, deserting the whaler *Acushnet* after only eighteen months—his only experience of whaling.

But for many, particularly those from New Bedford, there was a central tenet of whaling behind the economic rationale, an imperative that grew the industry from a part-time fishery to a holy calling, a belief that Melville nailed with bravura satire in chapter 9 of *Moby-Dick*, "The Sermon":

"Beloved Shipmates," cries Father Mapple, from the lofty prow of his pulpit, fashioned to resemble the bow of a whaleship,

"clinch the last verse of the first chapter of Jonah—'And God had prepared a great fish to swallow up Jonah.' Shipmates, this book, containing only four chapters—four yarns—is one of the smallest strands in the mighty cable of the Scriptures. Yet what depths of the soul does Jonah's deep sea-line sound! what a pregnant lesson to us is this prophet! What a noble thing is that canticle in the fish's belly! How billow-like and boisterously grand! We feel the floods surging over us; we sound with him to the kelpy bottom of the waters; sea weed and all the slime of the sea is about us!"

Melville cleverly appropriated Jonah, perfect for his story, but one may wonder what other tales from the mighty cable of the Scriptures Father Mapple would have read from on the remaining fifty-one Sundays of the year. He would soon have turned to the Book of Isaiah, which proclaimed, with less of a fish story, a truth that everyone in New Bedford held sacred: they were doing the Lord's work. The slaying of whales was a holy directive, unambiguously ordered by God Himself in Isaiah 27:1–6:

> In that day the Lord with his sore and great and strong sword shall punish leviathan the piercing serpent, even leviathan that crooked serpent; and he shall slay the dragon that is in the sea. . . . He shall cause them that come of Jacob to take root: Israel shall blossom and bud, and fill the face of the world with fruit.

The message was clear: slay whales and prosper. Every man, woman, and child in New Bedford knew that the whale was a divinely created oil reserve, placed floating in the sea by God so that His Children might secure it for themselves. And in so doing, whaling had anointed its practitioners with unmistakable signs of the Lord's blessings. The merchants who controlled the whaling industry in New Bedford in the mid–nineteenth century had grown wealthy to the point of embarrassment, beyond what appeared seemly. The only possible conclusion they could draw was that they were doing the Lord's work, His pleasure evinced by the otherworldly scale of their rewards, which they struggled to accept with modesty and disperse with responsibility. And the sailors who etched scenes, on sperm whales' teeth, of men battling the leviathan in small boats, were responding to the same urge that led early man to draw scenes of the hunt on cave walls: they believed they had experienced a partnership with the divine. God had given them dominion over the earth and all it contained. Father Mapple and all New Bedford knew the truth in Psalms 107:23–24: "They that go down to the sea in ships, that do business in great waters; these see the works of the Lord, and his wonders in the deep."

. . .

WHILE HERMAN MELVILLE'S TALE was too gothic and obscure for his contemporaries, the popular imagination of his day was thoroughly hooked by the money to be made in what was universally known as the "whale fishery." This first industrialized oil business found its most successful form as a paradigm evolved by a tightly knit cult of religious fundamentalists on Quaker Nantucket. It realized its apotheosis of worldly reward when this paradigm was enlarged in Quaker New Bedford, which became the world's first oil hegemony, the Houston and finally the Saudi Arabia of its day. Yet so fanatically and narrowly held—by some—was the religious faith that powered this great design, that it could not countenance or accommodate change, diversification, reappraisal, or compromise. The oil business of the second half of the nineteenth century was overtaken so swiftly by new paradigms created in the petroleum industry that New Bedford's most hidebound merchant tycoons, and the world they had created, were swept away like sand castles in a hurricane. They vanished as fast as the new oil barons appeared to replace them. And New Bedford lost its preeminence as God's Little Acre for merchant princes, though it would rediscover itself in the less exalted role of a Massachusetts mill town where the flotsam and jetsam of the whaling business—Azorean and Hawaiian seamen, freed and runaway black harpooners and their families, and poor young men and women from all over New England who had come to New Bedford to find a place aboard its ships and in its ropewalks and oil refineries—found steadier and far safer employment as cotton mill workers.

The rise and fall of the American whale fishery in New Bedford is a classic Darwinian story of the fitness of a group for a specific environment; of the failure by some of that group to adapt when their world changed, and how they withered and disappeared from the world, while others evolved and lived on.

That change was most abrupt for the 1,219 men, women, and children aboard the fleet of whaleships in the Arctic that summer of 1871. For them it would be a season of unparalleled catastrophe.

For the oil merchants and shipowners back in New Bedford, the change that overtook their lives would be more profound and longer-lasting.

Two

"The Dearest Place in All New England"

Seven years earlier, on September 14, 1864, New Bedford's preeminent whaling merchant, George Howland, Jr., then fifty-eight years old, gave a speech to an assembly of citizens and merchants on the two hundredth anniversary of the incorporation of the town of Dartmouth, Massachusetts, of which New Bedford had once been a part. The whaling business was still suffering the depredations of the Civil War, which had seen the loss of many whaleships and severely affected the town's economy; quantities of whale oil brought home by whaling voyages had fallen in recent years, and the market price of whale oil was softening. Yet Howland's message was unequivocally optimistic:

> When I look over our city, and see the improvements which have taken place within my time, and over the territory represented by you, my fellow citizens and neighbors, and then go further, and

embrace the whole country, I sometimes ask myself the question, "Can these improvements continue? And will science and art make the same rapid strides for the next fifty or one hundred years?" The only answer I can make is the real Yankee one: why not?

Howland's boosterism was genetic. His father, George Howland, had made a fortune in the whale fishery. When he died, in 1852, he left an estate including: $615,000 in cash; a fleet of nine whaling vessels; a wharf with a countinghouse sitting on it; a candle factory; property and acreage in New Bedford, Maine, western New York, Michigan, and Illinois; an island in Pacific; and charitable bequests of $70,000. This was great wealth in the mid–nineteenth century, the highest tier of any Fortune 500 equivalency of the day. Yet Howland's success had been duplicated forty or fifty times over by other New Bedford whaling merchants during his lifetime. Half of these successes had been forged by men named Howland, descendants of Henry Howland, brother of John Howland, who had arrived in America aboard the *Mayflower*. There were at least twenty Howland millionaires in New Bedford during George Howland's lifetime, close and distant cousins. Most of them, like George, were devout Quakers.

His sons, George Howland, Jr., and George Jr.'s half brother Matthew, inherited their father's ships, wharf, countinghouse, candle factory, and whaling business. In 1866, a year after the end of the Civil War, two of their ships, the *Corinthian* and the *George Howland*, returned to their wharf in New Bedford with a total of 930 barrels of sperm oil (from the head "case," or reservoir, of sperm whales) and 8,100 barrels of whale oil (the lesser quality made from boiling down blubber). The gross return from these two voyages was $383,433, from which George Jr. and Matthew first paid themselves back the $50,000 invested in outfitting the ships. Half of the remaining $333,433 went to the captains and crews as their share of the profits; $166,716 was the two Howland brothers' net profit on these two voyages alone. They received additional income from their candle-making and oil-refining factories and other related businesses. Undoubtedly most of it went back into the business, for as Quakers the Howlands lived simply and modestly, but at a time when a common workingman's annual earnings might be between $50 and $300, when a federal district judge in the East earned between $2,000 and $3,700 per year, and the president of the United States earned $25,000, the Howland brothers were netting annually around $100,000 each—with no income tax to pay.

It's understandable if George Howland, Jr., looking back over the improvements made to his city during his own and his father's lifetimes, could not—or would not—see beyond the incontrovertible facts of his own circumstances. During the previous one hundred years, the town had grown from a scattering of smallholdings along a riverbank to arguably the richest town in America. His father had ridden that growth to unprecedented wealth and passed it on to him and his brother, and at any time before the summer of 1871, George Jr. and Matthew could point only to the continued improvement of their personal wealth and business.

George Jr.'s walk home from anywhere in New Bedford, climbing the gentle hill that rose from the harbor, would have underscored this steadfast belief, for down the hill and as far as he could see in any direction, in tangible brick, wood, iron, and seething human endeavor, lay the whole of reality as he had always known it. Below him spread the waterfront, lined with warehouses, ship chandlers, thousands of barrels of oil, and the countinghouses of merchants whose names had been well known a century earlier. Every foot of wharf up and down both riverbanks was jammed with moored whaling ships; others lay at anchor in the river waiting for dock space to unload their cargoes, or to refit and load supplies for another voyage. By any route home, Howland passed the substantial houses of other merchants and ships' captains who had grown rich on whaling. The town was "perhaps the dearest place in all New England," Melville had written in *Moby-Dick*. "Nowhere in all America will you find more patrician-like houses, parks and gardens more opulent than in New Bedford. Whence came they? All these brave houses and flowery gardens came from the Atlantic, Pacific, and Indian Oceans. One and all, they were harpooned and dragged up hither from the bottom of the sea."

George Jr.'s own four-story brick mansion and carriage house on Sixth Street, occupying an entire east-west block, and half a block north-south between Bush and Walnut streets (where it still stands today), was the most solid, unassailable measure of his substance, and of the permanence of his business. He had designed the house himself, had it built in 1834, and had lived in it for more than thirty years. Barrels of whale oil and bricks and mortar were equally solid to George Howland, Jr., and his sense of security about his business and the business of New Bedford was unshakably strong. How could he not think so?

The smart money agreed with him. R. G. Dun & Co., the early credit-reporting and business-information agency, described and rated George Jr. and Matthew Howland in 1856 as being: "of the middle age both of them, men of good character and habits, and of business capacity; each with several hundred thousand dollars—ship owners, dealers and oil manufacturers. Good and safe."

George Howland, Jr., married Sylvia Allen, a distant cousin, the grandchild of another Howland. They had three sons, but two died in infancy, and the third at the age of twenty-eight. Perhaps grief propelled him out of his house to lose himself in service to his community. A family biographer writing in 1885, when George Jr. was seventy-nine years old, noted that "he has been frequently sought for to fill public positions of trust." He was a member of the town's school committee; he represented New Bedford at the General Court of Massachusetts; he was twice the city's mayor; a member of the State Senate; a trustee of the New Bedford Institution for Savings and of the Five Cent Savings Bank; a trustee of the State Lunatic Hospital; a trustee of Brown University; a trustee of the New Bedford Public Library, to which he donated his first two years' salary as mayor ($1,600); and in 1870 he was one of the commissioners appointed by President Grant to visit the Osage Indians in Oklahoma, where he spent a few weeks living in a tepee. In New Bedford, George Howland, Jr.'s, pronouncements were as good as the Delphic Oracle's. If he said business was good, it must be so.

Laboring in the shadow of his older half brother's eminence, Matthew Howland maintained far less of a public profile. He was at times a director on several bank boards, and an active member, elder, and clerk of the New Bedford Monthly Meeting of the Society of Friends, but he wasn't a statesman or a dignitary or a great traveler. Almost every day of his life after the age of fourteen, he walked downhill to the Howland countinghouse on the waterfront, where he busied himself primarily with the daily management of the family whaling business. While George was about great civic deeds, it was Matthew who oversaw the fitting out and repair of vessels at the Howland wharf, the sale and shipment of oil to many foreign ports, the running of the candle-making factory, the hiring of captains and crews. It was Matthew who wrote to his shipmasters a long letter at the commencement of each voyage: "We give thee the following orders and instructions which thou will attend to during the present voyage. . . ."

Matthew's home was four deep blocks farther inland from George Jr.'s and the grander mansions on the hill above the harbor. The homes along

County Street, which rode the crest of the hill north and south, and those immediately below it on its eastern flank, where George Jr.'s sat, looked down over the harbor and the Acushnet River, and were in turn seen by those below. Matthew's house on Hawthorn and South Cottage streets offered no view and occupied an unobtrusive position in a flat, leafy neighborhood of solid but not grand houses. (It, too, is still there, today housing medical offices.)

But Matthew made the showier of the two brothers' marriages, landing what could only be called a trophy wife in terms of the Quaker community. Rachel Collins Smith was a great beauty—dark hair, a pale complexion, fine features, and huge dark eyes, "wondrous beautiful" according to Massachusetts governor John Andrew, who met her at a reception in New Bedford during the Civil War—and of significant pedigree: she was related to William Penn, the Quaker founder of Pennsylvania, and came from a family that was much concerned with politics and the abolition movement. "The Smiths were a contentious family—" wrote Rachel and Matthew's descendant Llewellyn Howland III, a hundred years later in a family history, "evangelists, crackpots, faddists." They were also fighters for just causes. This energy was a marked contrast to Matthew's plain, insular lifestyle, and the narrow focus of his concerns. Rachel, too, presumed she had made a stellar connection: a fabulously rich Howland brother, of a most pious, observant line. Until she married him, Rachel did not know that Matthew was an epileptic, and probably a depressive. There must have been a considerable curve of adjustment early on in the marriage, but it became a strong one. Matthew continued in his stolid, almost shut-in habits, the daily commute to and immersion in the Howland counting-house, a preoccupation with prices, barrels of oil, pounds of whalebone. Rachel, a strident woman who was "inclined to tyranny," according to Llewellyn Howland III, became a firebrand Quaker minister, the queen of New Bedford society, a mover and shaker pushing for social improvement and charitable causes throughout the American Quaker community, and one of the most powerful women in the country. She was intelligent—probably much more so than Matthew—and passionately outspoken. She fought against slavery with her contemporary and friend Harriet Beecher Stowe, and, when she felt it necessary, visited President Lincoln in the White House to offer him her views on the subject.

Matthew's fortune was the earning machine and springboard for Rachel's social works, and her philanthropic deployment of the prodigious wealth generated by whaling.

EVIDENTLY, the precise and careful numbers from Matthew's counting-house were in line with George Jr.'s bully optimism. In 1866, after the return to port of the *Corinthian* and the *George Howland*, R. G. Dun noted that they had "made money very fast lately in the whaling business." So confident were the two brothers that year of the long-term prospects for the whaling industry that they decided to add a tenth vessel to their fleet of whaleships. They commissioned the shipyard of Josiah Holmes and Brother, of neighboring Mattapoisett, with the building of the new ship. The selection of the Holmes brothers by the Howland brothers says everything about the quality of product expected from them. "The bark's frame is of pine and oak . . . all timbers carefully selected and cut in the vicinity of Mattapoisett," reported the *New Bedford Mercury*. The Holmeses, or their master carpenters, would have spent considerable time in the woods looking at great numbers of trees, observing their aspect to the sun and the prevailing winds and the winter cold—all of which affected the density of the cellulose—noting the health of the bark, examining the crooks of the boughs that would make the knees that would knit together deck and hull. Such men saw in a tree what a sculptor sees in a piece of marble, knowing the shape he wants to bring out of it and how the material's grain and properties will help or hinder him. The shipbuilders were keenly aware of the stresses and hardship their vessels would be subjected to, and every aspect and detail of the ship's construction was given the highest degree of forethought and artisanal craftsmanship. The shipbuilding businesses that had developed around New Bedford during a century of continued growth of the whale fishery had been like the concentrated tooling-up of industry that comes with a great war—and the heyday of whaling was indeed a hundred years' holy war that saw untold losses of men's lives. The men building the ships they sailed off in understood this. Shipbuilding techniques were developed, improved, and refined with economy and ingenuity. Whaling historian Everett S. Allen wrote this about the whaleship builder's method of fastening plank on frame:

> The trunnel [a contraction of "tree nail"] was a superlative device, an ingeniously contrived wooden nail, usually of white oak or locust. It was square on one end, gradually turning to round at the other; it was driven into the plank far enough so that the square portion was embedded and thus would not turn or loosen. The trunnel head was sawed off flush with the plank, split slightly with a chisel, and a wooden wedge driven in. This fastening was more durable than iron and could only be removed by boring it out. . . . Leave it to the Yankee Quaker to find a use for a square peg in a round hole.

The Howlands' new ship was christened *Concordia*. At $100,000, when fitted out, it was the most expensive whaleship, then and later, ever built for the New Bedford fishery. It was "bark-rigged": square sails on the fore- and mainmasts, while setting fore and aft sails on the mizzenmast, making it more close-winded than fully square-rigged ships, and more maneuverable. At 128 and a half feet long, she was average-sized for a larger whaleship, but unusually fine in the appointments, with decorative faux graining of the pine paneling below to make it resemble curled maple, rosewood, and satinwood. This was a rare touch on a Quaker-owned vessel, including those owned by the Howland brothers, who eschewed ostentation and generally saw their ships' interiors painted and finished in the plainest utilitarian manner. But something about the Howlands' commitment to the building of the *Concordia* brought out a rare fulsomeness of attitude toward the endeavor. She was a beautiful ship, unlike most whalers, which were square and boxy. "She did not have to be so un-Quakerishly pretty," wrote Everett S. Allen, "yet she was." Never again would such prettiness or care be lavished upon the shapeliness and decoration—the unpractical, irrelevant aspects—of a whaleship.

The brothers' plan for the lovely new ship was, however, nothing but pragmatic: she would be sent to the unforgiving Arctic, the only remaining spot on earth where such an expensive ship—or any ship in the late 1860s—might have a chance of a profitable voyage.

The Howlands built the *Concordia* with the same faith that had set Noah to building his ark. The concord between them and their God had taken George Howland, Sr., his Quaker merchant contemporaries, and all their Quaker ancestors very far. There was no basis for George Jr. and Matthew to question Him.

The *Concordia* was launched on November 7, 1867. With routine care and refurbishment, she might have lasted forever. She would have a life of only four years.

Three

A Nursery and a Kindergarten

Born aboard a whaleship in the stormy Tasman Sea in 1859, twelve-year-old William Fish Williams was on his third whaling voyage with his parents as the *Monticello* sailed north in the summer of 1871.

He was three years old before he began to live ashore in San Francisco during the Civil War. Until then, land was a distant, occasional novelty, strange and wondrous as a carnival attraction, and never the same. As a baby and toddler, he was handed by strong whalemen down to his mother, who sat in a rocking boat, and rowed ashore at Russell in the Bay of Islands, New Zealand, at Guam, Honolulu, Hakodate in Japan, and Okhotsk on the Siberian coast—all were brief sideshows to the little boy, whose truest home was the cramped rear cabin of a rolling, pitching whaleship and the surrounding sea in all its moods and conditions from the latitudes of New Zealand to the Arctic. His most common spectacle, and the abiding ethos of his world, was the pursuit, capture, and dismemberment of great whales.

His father, Thomas William Williams, and his family had come to America from Hay-on-Wye, the ancient border town between England and Wales, as steerage passengers in 1829, when Thomas was nine. After a year on Long Island, they moved and settled in Wethersfield, Connecticut. The family, including young Thomas, found work in local wool mills. But this was grueling indoor labor, and Thomas's mother, worried about his health, got him apprenticed to a Wethersfield blacksmith to learn the toolmaker's trade. However, when he was twenty, something inside Thomas—perhaps the impression made by a transatlantic voyage on a nine-year-old boy[1]—made him lift his sights beyond the claustrophobic insularity of village life. "My father's case was typical," wrote his son William many years later. "I recall the stories of the captains when gamming with our ship or calling at our home in Oakland, California, they all ran away from home to make their first voyage." These future-captain boys had a streak of ambition or a lust for adventure, and from the tidy and constrained village life of the early nineteenth century there were only two kinds of territory to light out to: the undeveloped West, or the sea. Thomas didn't run away—he was twenty and had completed his apprenticeship when he told his mother he was going to sea—but his departure greatly alarmed his family. The sailors the Williamses had known in small towns in England were generally retirees from Napoleonic-era sea battles, contemporaries of Nelson and the fictional Jack Aubrey, whose limbs had been blown off by cannonballs and flying shards of ship timber. Thomas's parents and grandparents were horrified and fully expected him to return, if at all, minus an arm or leg. He traveled to New Bedford in 1840, near the peak of the American whale fishery, as many other young men did, and

---

1. I crossed the Atlantic myself at nine. Only five days on a Cunard liner, but the impressions made by both the ship and the sea were indelible, certainly a germinative factor in my later interest in the sea. Nine-year-old Thomas would have been at sea for four to six weeks.

shipped as a "green hand" aboard the whaleship *Albion*. Andrew Potter, the shipping agent who hired him, was impressed by the tall—six-foot-three in his socks—capable-looking youth. When Potter boarded the *Albion* on its return to New Bedford two years later, he again met Thomas, who was apparently suffering from "moon blindness" from sleeping on deck in the tropics beneath the full light of the moon. The young man was eager to get home to see his mother, and Potter lent him traveling money so he could leave before the voyage's accounts were settled and the men paid off. Thomas sent Potter back his money by mail from Wethersfield. The two men were to become lifelong friends. After a month at home, his eyes healed, Thomas returned to New Bedford, and Potter found him a job as a blacksmith and "boat-steerer" (harpooner) aboard the whaleship *South Carolina*. When that ship discharged its crew in Lahaina in 1843, Thomas shipped as boat-steerer again aboard the *Gideon Howland*, which brought him back to New Bedford in 1844. From there, he sailed as second mate aboard the whaleship *Chili*; subsequently as second mate, and eventually first mate, of the *South Boston*.

In April 1851, Thomas married Eliza Azelia Griswold at Wethersfield. Three months later he sailed as captain of the *South Boston*. He was away for three years and returned to meet his two-year-old son, Thomas Stancel. His voyage aboard the *South Boston* had earned the ship's owners $140,000, a great success, making Williams highly sought after as a captain for hire; but he might have tried to give up the sea then, to stay home with his young family, for he purchased a one-hundred-acre farm in Wethersfield, and a herd of cattle that he drove himself from Vermont to Connecticut. Yet he was back aboard a ship later that same year, in October 1854, as captain of the whaleship *Florida*. He was away on this voyage for three and a half years, returning again to meet his second son, Henry, then almost three years old.

Thomas's wife, Eliza Williams, was born in 1826, in Wethersfield, where her family, the Griswolds, had lived and farmed since 1645. She was a small woman, weighing less than a hundred pounds, and could stand erect under her husband's outstretched arm. Her retiring character was unsuited to the job of tending to her husband's affairs in his absence, collecting the interest on his investments, and dealing with Thomas's brother-in-law, who was a sharecropper on their farm and unpleasant to her. Like many whalemen's wives, she tried at some point to get her husband to give up the sea, which may explain the purchase of the farm. Some wives prevailed, like Jane Courtney, who persuaded her husband, whaling captain Leonard Courtney of Edgartown, Martha's Vineyard, to try his hand at some land-based venture in the expanding west of New York or Ohio. Whaling captains often found themselves surprisingly vulnerable outside their chosen element: on their way west, in April 1847, Captain Courtney, who had sailed hundreds of thousand of miles, driven his ship around Cape Horn, and taken many whales from small tossing boats, was killed in a stagecoach accident.

Most captains and their wives were resigned to long separations. Such men, by temperament or long habit, were not always skilled at navigating the more democratic environment of home; and his absence from it, and mutual longing between husband and wife, often kept a whaler's marriage fresh, or allowed it to endure. Probably just as often, it made the whaleman, of any rank, a bemused stranger in his own home and propelled him to sea again.

Eliza and Thomas were an unusually devoted couple—their letters while he was away from her at sea frequently expressed how greatly they missed each other. But Thomas Williams had become a confirmed and exceptionally skilled whaleman (he tried numerous speculative ventures ashore, but none proved successful), so Eliza instead sailed with him on his next voyage. The degree of her longing to be with her husband is evident by the fact that she was somehow able to leave the two boys, ages six and three, with her family in Wethersfield.

Eliza was five months pregnant with their third child when she sailed from New Bedford with her husband aboard the *Florida* on September 7, 1858. From the first moments of the voyage—even before, on the pilot boat sailing out to the ship, hove to below Clark's Point— she kept a journal. Her impressions were plainly and frankly recorded, yet her essentially uninvolved, supernumerary, fly-on-the-bulkhead observations of all that was new to her, and the accretion of minutiae that filled her pages over the course of three years, make for some of the most vivid and accurate descriptions to come down to us of the life and work aboard a whaleship:

> *In company with my Husband, I stept on board the Pilot Boat, about 9 o'clock the morning of the 7th of Sept. 1858, to proceed to the Ship Florida, that will take us out to Sea far from Friends and home, for a long time to come.... The men have lifted me up the high side in an arm chair, quite a novel way it seemed to me. Now I am in the place that is to be my home, posibly for 3 or 4 years; but I can not make it appear to me so yet it all seems so strange, so many Men and not one Woman beside myself.*

The small aft cabin was furnished with a geranium and a pet kitten. The food at her first meal aboard was *"a good deal like a dinner at home"* except for the universally disliked, rock-hard ship's biscuit. But as the boat that brought her out to the ship headed back to shore, Eliza found herself miserably awash with "tender associations" of home and thoughts of *"Dear Friends, Parents, and Children, Brothers and Sisters, all near and dear to us. But I will drop the subject; it is too gloomy to contemplate."*

And she did thereafter almost completely drop the fulsome lamentations for home and family. Her entries were confined to the world of the ship and its business. At first she didn't know enough about that world to write about it, and could only focus on the misery of her own condition:

SEPTEMBER 8TH.

There is nothing of importance to write about today; nothing but the vast deep about us; as far as the eye can stretch here is nothing to be seen but sky and water, and the Ship we are in. It is all a strange sight to me. The Men are all busy; as for me, I think I am getting Sea sick.

While Eliza lay sick in her bed, Captain Williams was going through the procedures accompanying the commencement of a whaleship voyage. On the first day out, the crew were mustered in the "waist," the clear area of the main deck forward of the mainmast where the drawing of the boat crews—the men who would actually go out in the small whaleboats after whales—took place. These boats were usually commanded by the first, second, third, and fourth mates, but aboard the *Florida* and all the ships of which he was the captain, Thomas Williams, a large, powerful man who had been a successful boatsteerer, always "lowered" in his own boat to chase after whales himself, unless weather conditions or the close presence of land made it imprudent for him to leave the ship. So, in turn, the first, second, third mates, and finally Williams, sang out names from the crew gathered before them until five men, in addition to the mate or captain, had been chosen for each boat. The crews of the captain's and the second mate's boats stepped to the starboard side of the ship, and became the starboard watch; the men of the first and third mates' boats stepped to port and became the port watch. The men not selected in the draw were divided between the two watches. Then Williams explained (for the green hands) that watches were four hours long, starting at midnight. While one watch was on deck, running the ship, the other was off watch, below, sleeping if at night. From four to eight p.m. daily, the "dogwatch," all hands remained on deck working the ship, then the order of watches—the next watch to go below—changed from the preceding twenty-four hours. Every man was to learn to steer and take his two-hour "trick" at the wheel. The ship's cooper, cook, steward, and cabin boy were exempt from watches and rarely went off in the boats after whales, as they had regular duties and rested at night when not engaged at these.

SEPTEMBER 10TH.

It is quite rugged today, and I have been quite sick; these 3 or 4 words I write in bed.

SEPTEMBER 11TH.

It remains rugged and I remain Sea sick. I call it a gale, but my Husband laughs at me, and tells me that I have not seen a gale yet.

When better weather returned, Eliza got up and began to explore. Her first impressions of the activities aboard ship were strange and baffling, as the coopers, carpenters, blacksmiths worked away and the officers bawled orders to the men, who tried to obey them.

More quiet days followed, helping Eliza to get her sea legs, with several *"beutiful moonshiny evenings"* during which *"one of the boat steerers, a colored Man, has a violin, and we have some musick occationaly which makes it pleasant these nice evenings. There is a splendid comet to be seen."*

On another clement day, she did some sewing, helping Thomas make a new sail for his whaleboat.

On Sundays, unless whales were spotted and chased, all work was laid aside and Eliza was surprised, after the bellowed orders that accompanied every heave of the ship, at the solemn peace aboard the ship. Many of the men read their Bibles, or worked at some piece of carving or scrimshaw. *"It is the Sabbath, and all is orderly and quiet on board; much more so than I expected among so many Men between 30 and 40 . . . nothing done on Sunday but what is necessary."*

Three weeks after leaving New Bedford, when the ship was close to the mid-Atlantic islands of the Azores, sperm whales were spotted. Though it was late in the day, boats were lowered, including the captain's, and rowed off into the twilight that was deepening across the ocean. It was night when the second and third mates' boats returned, without whales, and Eliza grew worried about Thomas, who, like the first mate, was still out on the water, fighting whales in the dark. *"My anxiety increases with the darkness. . . . The Men have put lanterns in the rigging to help them see the Ship."* The mates' and Thomas's boats eventually returned with a catch. *"All is confution now to get the whale fast alongside. . . . I am quite anxious to see how [the] fish looks, but it is too dark."*

She got her first look at a sperm whale the next morning. The mate's whale was a calf, but it looked enormous to Eliza. She groped to describe it:

SEPTEMBER 29TH.

My Husband has called me on deck to see the whale. . . . It is a queer looking fish. . . . There is not much form, but a mass of flesh. . . . They are about a mouse color. . . . [The men] first take the blubber off with spades with verry long handles; they are quite sharp, and they cut places and peel it off in great strips. It looks like very thick fat pork, it is quite white.

Eliza was still seasick when she recorded that first sight of a whale. As she got her sea legs and the men caught more whales, her interest

in the endeavor—the primary focus of all activity aboard the *Florida*—
and her ability to describe what she saw quickly sharpened:

NOVEMBER 8TH.

*. . . The welcome cry of "There blows" came from aloft before breakfast
this morning; then all was bustle. . . . Two boats were lowered and pulled
lustily for them. The movements of the boats were watched from the Ship
with great interest. . . . Some of the time [the whales] went a good ways
off. It also takes a good while to wait for them to come up after they go
down. Then they come up in quite a different place. On board the Ship,
they place signals to mast head in different places, and different shaped
ones, made from blue and white cloth, to let those in the boats know in
what direction the whales are and whether they are up or down, as it is
difficult sometimes for the Men in the boats to tell, they are so low on the
water and the whales change their position so often. . . .*

*The Mate finally got fast to one. . . . It looked queer to me to see those
three little boats, attached together with ropes, towing the whale
along. . . .*

*[Finally, the whale is alongside the hull.] There are ridges all over the
back, which I should think must be from age. . . . There were a great many
marks on the back, caused, my Husband said, from fighting. They are a
much handsomer fish than I had an idea they were. . . .*

*It must be quite an art, as well as a good deal of work to cut in the
whale. . . . The Men . . . seem to know exactly where to cut. They begin
to cut a great strip. The hook is put through a hole that is cut in the end
of this piece . . . then it is drawn up by the tackle as they cut. They do not
stop till the piece goes clear round. Then it comes clear up and is let down
into the blubber room where it is afterward cut in pieces suitable for the
mincing machine. . . . The head they cut off and take on board in the same
way. . . . It was singular to me to see how well they could part the head*

from the body and find the joint so nicely. When it came on deck, it was such a large head, it swung against the side of the Ship till it seemed to me to shake with the weight of it.

It was all done and I was glad for the Men. . . . It made me tremble to see them stand there on that narow staging, with a rope passed around their bodies . . . to keep them from going over, while they leaned forward to cut. Every Man was at work, from the foremast hand to the Captain. The sharks were around the Ship and I saw one fellow, more bold than the rest, I suppose, venture almost to the whale to get a bit. The huge carcass floated away, and they had it all to themselves.

The next day more whales were spotted, and boats lowered to give chase. Eliza stood at the ship's rail and avidly followed the pursuit with everyone else aboard. *"Though they were a good way off, we could tell when the iron was thrown, for the whale spouted blood and we could see it plain."* It was a "cow" that had been trying to protect its calf. *"The poor little thing could not keep up with the rest, the mother would not leave it and lost her life. [The mate] says they exhibit the most affection for their young of any dumb animal he ever saw."*

By the next day, four dead sperm whales were lying alongside the *Florida*, making much work aboard. The first mate took Eliza down to the "reception room, as he termed it," the "tween-decks" blubber room immediately beneath the main deck, in the middle of the ship, where the great peeled strips of blubber were chopped up for the "try-pots" (great cauldrons placed in the "tryworks"—brick fireplaces—in which the blubber was melted to oil). The men were waist-deep in "horse pieces" of blubber, coated with oil, but all of them "laughing and having a good deal of fun." Intensive activity aboard a whaleship meant money for all hands. "Greasy work" always put the entire crew in a happy mood.

Eliza became fascinated: *"It is truly wonderful to me, the whole process, from the taking of the great, and truly wonderful monster of the deep till the oil is in the casks."* Several months later, after a night of watching the crew cutting in and trying out an enormous right whale, she wrote: *"It is certainly the greatest sight I ever saw in my life."*

Yet with the excitement came the frequent anxiety for the safety of the men, sometimes gone all night in the boats after whales, and, on more than one occasion, real fear for her husband's life. This episode came in the foggy and ice-strewn (even in July) Sea of Okhotsk, off the Siberian coast:

JULY 21st.

. . . I have passed a very unhappy night. My Husband was away all night. . . . I was frightened when I heard them lower [his] boat, for I did not suppose he would go at all—or anyone go alone in such a foggy night. I worried all night long and did not sleep at all. The time seemed very, very long, every minute thinking, and hoping that he would come back, until I was very much afraid his boat had been stoven and no one to assist him. . . . The thought was awful to me and the night a long one. . . . The Officer said that he was sure he was fast to a whale and as he had no anchor in the boat, had to lay by him. It proved to be so. We had sent two boats off to look for him quite early. They found him and towed the Whale back to the Ship. I saw him coming about 8 o'clock. He had had good luck in taking the Whale, but the unpleasant job of laying by him all night. He will make about 60 bbls [barrels of oil].

I was overjoyed to see my Husband coming. I was much afraid that something had happened to him.

Her fears had been amply fueled by the news a few weeks earlier of *"Capt. Palmer being killed by a Whale, or rather he got fast in the line and was taken down by the Whale and never seen again. His poor Wife and three Children are at Hilo, and will not hear about it till fall."*

And death came to the *Florida* in the Sea of Okhotsk just three weeks later. Tim, the black boatsteerer who had a violin and made the "musick" Eliza liked, had, like Captain Palmer, been caught in a line attached to a whale and dragged out of the boat into the water. The whale was later caught and Tim's body recovered, *"bruised a good deal by being dragged on the bottom."*

Though she wrote openly of her fears, Eliza was, with the sensibility of her time, conspicuously reticent about certain things. The lead in this entry is buried amid whaleship minutiae:

[FEBRUARY 4, 1859.]

It is now about a month since I have written any in my Journal and many things have transpired since then.

The 10th of January we had a gale of wind that lasted till the 12th, the heaviest gale we have had since we left home. On the 11th, the fore sail was carried away. We spoke [to] the Whale Ship Rodman, Capt. Babcock, on the 11th, bound home. Did not exchange many words, it was blowing so hard. They had Pigeons on board and four of them flew on board of us. They are very pretty and my Husband has had a nice house made for them. We have a fine healthy Boy, born on the 12th, five days before we got into Port.

There is no mention anywhere in Eliza's journal of her pregnancy, how it made her feel, any difficulty that moving about a tossing ship in her condition might have created for her, or the contribution this might have made to her seasickness; there is only this briefly noted fact: the boy, born in that *"heaviest gale we have had since we left home"* in the notoriously stormy Tasman Sea, between Australia and New Zealand, was William Fish Williams (Fish was the name of one of the *Florida*'s New Bedford owners).

Eliza was fortunate in being so close to New Zealand at the time of Willie's birth, rather than far out on the Pacific. Thomas sailed his ship into the port of Manganui, on New Zealand's North Island, where he knew they would find an oasis of sailorly and, paradoxically, womanly society. As soon as the *Florida* anchored, the harbormaster, Captain Butler, sent his wife on board, who returned every day until Eliza could leave her bed, and then she and the baby moved ashore to the Butlers' house. The British Butler family was large: eight children, three of them grown women, who, with Mrs. Butler, enveloped Eliza and her baby in feminine care. *"They are a nice Family, extremely kind and affectionate, and every one of them seemed to try to see which could pay me the most attention. . . . They all sing, dance, and play on the piano. They are quite a lively Family and one of the young Boys plays on the violin."*

There were eight other ships in port at the time, and their captains, who used the Butler residence as an informal clubhouse, visited her and the baby and brought gifts: *"Oranges, Lemons, several kinds of Preserved Fruits, some Arrowroot, a nice Fan made on one of the Islands . . . and a bottle of currant wine."* Several of the captains had their wives and children with them, one of these a ten-month-old boy who had been born in the Butlers' house. Eliza was also comforted by the piety of the Butler household. Captain Butler was an Episcopal minister and conducted daily services in his house.

She spent only two weeks ashore before the *Florida* left New Zealand for the "Japan grounds."

It was almost a year before Eliza referred to her son by his name in her journal. Until then, he remained "the Baby," a noun, like "my

Husband," whose small adventures were duly recorded. *"The Baby is well and healthy and sleeps a good deal,"* she wrote on February 24, 1859. *"He is a very pleasant Baby."*

In addition to mastering the pull of gravity, like all babies, Willie had to acquire gyroscopic skills to accommodate the nearly constant roll and pitch of a ship through his first years.

> *It has been a very unpleasant day, blowing a gale all day and the Ship rolling very badly. I can't keep the Baby in one place, and he gets a good many bumps. . . . The Baby likes to be on deck most all day. He goes about the deck by taking hold of things but does not go alone yet. . . . He will climb a good deal for such a little fellow. . . . We have been making a real Sailor's Cot [hammock] for the Baby to sleep in. The motion of the Ship keeps it in motion all the time. The Baby is delighted with it. . . . Willie [past his second birthday now] has met with a bad accident this afternoon. He was playing in one of the Staterooms and fell off from a Chest and cut his lip open very badly—with his teeth, we suppose. It bled a good deal. His Pa sewed it up. The poor little Fellow bore it better than I thought he would.*

Melville's Ishmael said that "a whale ship was my Yale college and my Harvard." For Willie it was his nursery and his kindergarten.

THOUGH THE *FLORIDA* SET OFF from New Zealand, heading for the remotest regions of the globe, Eliza was to find more female company wherever they went. Whaleships invariably sailed the same routes from commercial hubs like New Zealand or the Hawaiian (then the Sandwich) Islands to the whaling grounds, and from one whaling "ground" to another, and there they would find other whaleships, increasingly in greater numbers, all competing for the same whale stocks. Far out in the lonely, still primitive, barely discovered, and to a large extent still unspoiled Pacific, along routes as well defined as air routes 150 years later, whaleships would routinely see and often "speak"—sail within speaking range of—other ships. On the Brazil Banks, in the Seas of Japan and Okhotsk, and crowding the narrow channels between ice and land in the Arctic, whaleships met other whaleships. A small number of these were, like the *Florida*, "lady ships," which carried a captain's wife and sometimes their children aboard. These supernumerary passengers formed a floating community that preserved a strong fabric of home. Wives and children visited other wives and children as they might have on any afternoon in New Bedford, except that here they were rowed back and forth by whaleboat crews instead of traveling by carriage. They gathered aboard nearby ships for Sunday services. An active social life, which included cultural and religious visits, was a vital part of what made an isolated life at sea bearable.

The journals kept by some of these captains' wives give an indication of this cozy society of satellites, virtually a floating annex of New Bedford neighbors and their families that existed wherever whaleships sailed.

In the Sea of Japan, Eliza wrote:

APRIL 23RD.

This morning it rained quite hard and was rather foggy. As soon as I was up, I heard that there was a Ship ahead, and I was in hopes that it was the South Boston. . . . To my Joy it proved to be. My Husband came to the skylight and told me that I might expect to see Mrs Randolph, for he was going to speak the Ship in a few moments. Very soon he came down and told me to hurry and get ready to go on board. I was not long getting Willie and myself ready. We went aboard before breakfast and stayed till evening. We had a nice gam and spent the day very pleasantly.

The *South Boston* also had letters for the Williamses, picked up in Hawaii five months earlier, but written six months before that: *"We got our letters—one of them from home—and feel very thankful to hear that our Dear little Boys, Father, Mother and all were well at that time, which was in June."*

The very next day, the whaleship *Harvest* hove in sight close to the *Florida* and the *South Boston*, all of them cruising the "Japan grounds," and Eliza and Mrs. Randolph were rowed to the *Harvest* to spend the day with Mrs. Manchester.

Such visits offered a respite from the constant claustrophobia of the close quarters aboard ship. In June, the *Florida* passed through La Pérouse Strait into the Sea of Okhotsk. The whaling was slow, and the weather for the next week was rainy, snowy, or foggy, keeping the family cooped up in their small cabin.

"It is very dull on deck," wrote Eliza, with uncharacteristic complaint. *"I have been ironing for one thing and doing other little things too numerous to mention. Thomas [a rare use of his name] has been reading a good part of the day, and Willie has been through his usual course of mischief."* A week later, Eliza sounded positively peevish: *"Have not seen a Whale and scarcely a Bird. It is dull—very dull. We have not seen a Ship since we were in the Straits [nine days earlier]."* In the same seas the previous year, Eliza had counted nineteen whaleships in one day. But soon enough company hove in sight again: *"This afternoon have been on board the John P. West and spent the afternoon very pleasantly with Mrs Tinker . . . [and] their little Boy. He is about 2 years old and a fat little fellow. . . . Capt. Tinker's Wife and little Boy have been on board and spent the afternoon. We enjoyed it much—the Children in particular."*

THESE WHALING WIVES developed a keen, sometimes intense interest in the taking of whales, which had a direct bearing on their husbands' fortunes. Eliza found "that odor with the smoke that comes below from the try works is quite unpleasant, but I can bear it all first rate when I consider that it is filling our ship all the time and by and by it will all be over and we will go home."

Mary Chipman Lawrence, of Falmouth, Massachusetts, sailing with her husband, Captain Samuel Lawrence, and their daughter Minnie, aboard the New Bedford whaleship *Addison*, became obsessively involved with the ship's search for whales. *"A whale, a whale, a kingdom for a whale!"* she moaned to her journal in July 1858, during a dismal summer of arctic whaling:

> *We have looked and searched in vain. . . . If we cannot find the whales, we cannot get the oil. . . . [The captain of the* Dromo*] had been to Cape Lisburne and as far north as the barrier of ice and had not seen a spout. . . . Captain Bryant came on board and stopped until dinner. He has been as far as the ice barrier . . . and has seen ne'er a whale. If we cannot get ourselves, it is a great satisfaction to know that others are not taking it in great quantities. . . . Oh, where shall whales be found?*

Mrs. Lawrence recorded that her *"sorrow found vent in tears,"* until finally, *"Eureka! Eureka! We have got a bowhead at last."* And then: *"We have been eating bowhead meat for several days. . . . It is really good eating, far before salt pork in my estimation."*

In July 1859, when she learned that a few lucky ships had, just one month earlier, found a great pod of whales and scored an enormous windfall of oil off Cape Thaddeus, where the *Addison* had cruised so fruitlessly the year before, Mary Lawrence was sick with envy:

> *Imagine our feelings when we were told there had been a grand cut taken off Cape Thaddeus by a few ships in June, where thirty or forty ships were*

hanging about for weeks in the ice last season and not a whale to be seen. . . . The Mary and Susan took 1,600 barrels, the Eliza Adams 1,400, Nassau seven whales, Omega seven, Mary six, William C. Nye six. Those are all the ships we have heard of that were there. I never felt so heartsick in my life. . . . Why couldn't we have been one of the number? Because it was not for us, I suppose.

In the late fall, when the weather turned cold off Siberia, Captain Williams turned the *Florida* east and sailed his ship across the entire Pacific Ocean for a winter's whaling off the Mexican coast of Baja California. This was a seasonal migration for many whaleships, and the wide bays and lagoons north of Cabo San Lucas had all the social attractions of a riviera for whaling wives and families.

At Turtle Bay, the Williamses' *Florida* shared an anchorage with four other ships, another *Florida* among them:

DECEMBER 9TH.

It has been a splendid day, and my Husband, Willie and I have been aboard of the Florida, to see Capt. Fish and Wife, and spent the day very pleasantly. They have a little Son with them, 6 years old. . . .

DECEMBER 23RD.

It has been a very fine day. My Husband, Willie and I have been aboard of the Florida and spent the day very pleasantly with Capt. Fish and his Wife. Captain Hempstead and his Wife were there. I like them very much. Mrs H. is a little, small Woman and quite pretty.

Cruising along this same coast two years earlier in the *Addison*, Mary Lawrence, her husband Samuel, and their eight-year-old daughter Minnie joined a picnic in progress:

Saw a tent with flags flying onshore; concluded they were having a picnic. Soon after we were anchored, a boat came off to us with an invitation to us to unite with them, which invitation we cordially accepted. On our arrival there we found Captain Willis, wife, and three children; Captain Weeks, wife and two children . . . Captain Ashley, wife and one child of the Reindeer; Captain May of the Dromo . . . and Captain Lawrence, wife, and one child of the Addison. Made ten captains, four ladies, and seven children. We could hardly realize that we were whaling. Had a nice chowder, coffee, cold ham, cake, bread, crackers, and cookies. We also roasted plenty of oysters.

Through the winter, Thomas, Eliza, and Willie socialized their way down the Mexican coast. Eliza was still ready to party on February 26: *"I am going on board [the Cambria] to see Mrs Pease this evening."*

The next day—no mention of the approaching event appears in her journal—Eliza again gave birth. *"We have had an addition to the Florida's Crew in the form of a little Daughter,"* she recorded, a full month later, as the ship rolled west again across the Pacific toward the Hawaiian Islands, *"born on the 27th of February in Banderas Bay on the Coast of Mexico. She weighed 6-3/4 pounds, is now one month old and weighs 9 pounds. . . . Willie is much pleased with his little Sister."*

IN THE PROCESS OF SAILING up and down and across the length and breadth of the Pacific—in some cases entirely around the world through the Roaring Forties by way of Cape Horn—Eliza, Mary Lawrence, and the other whaling wives became, each in her own fashion, champion tourists.

"It will be a pleasant sight to me to see land, even though it be a bleak, foreighn Island of the Sea," Eliza had written in October 1858, as the

Florida approached the first landfall after leaving New Bedford. It was the island of Brava, one of the Portuguese Cape Verde Islands, off the coast of Africa. After weeks aboard ship, and in complete ignorance of what it would take to get there, Eliza agreed to accompany Thomas ashore. It was no pleasure trip:

OCTOBER 12TH [1858].

The wind not fair to get the Ship in to the harbor; concluded to row there in one of the small boats. My Husband said I could go with him, but I most repented it before we got there. It got quite rugged, and they had to go some ten miles to get into harbor—

Any sailor will appreciate that "rugged" would be an understatement to describe a ten-mile upwind row and sail in a light whaleboat off an Atlantic island. The small boat was frequently swamped with waves that drenched Eliza, the captain, and the crew. Eliza was frightened, but Thomas told her there was no danger, and the she believed him.

They had stopped at Brava to buy food and supplies, and to recruit additional crewmen from among the fishermen in the port where their boat landed, but business kept them there overnight. The only accommodations were in "the city," a three-mile ride by donkey up a steep mountain trail. At times on the way up, Eliza *"could hardly refrain from screaming, for it seemed to me that the poor faithful animal must fall."* But her terror was relieved by the sight of her husband close behind: *"I would look at him once in a while and laugh in spite of my fear, for he looked so comical on that little Jackass and he so tall, with his long legs coming most to the ground."*

Eliza's gaze at the islanders, and her description of their clothing, were clear and—rare for a New England whaling wife—without any kind of censuring prejudice. She was even capable of seeing herself through native eyes: *"I suppose we looked as strange to them as they did to us, dressed so different as we were."*

Mary Lawrence's attitude toward natives everywhere was framed by a rigid Christian superiority. She could not see a people and their culture, only a substandard race of creatures that needed uplifting: "I confess that I am disappointed in the appearance of the natives," she wrote from Lahaina, in the Sandwich (Hawaiian) Islands, in 1857.

> They are not nearly so far advanced in civilization as I had supposed. Why, the good folks at home pretend to hold them up as a model from which we would do well to copy. I do not doubt but that there has been a great deal done for them, but there is a vast deal more to be done to raise them very high in the scale of morals. From what I saw and heard of them (and I made many enquiries) they are a low, degraded, indolent set. They have no apartments in their houses; all huddle in together. Many of them go without clothing; both sexes bathe in the water entirely naked, unabashed. As I am writing, two men are close by my door without an article of clothing.

(Mary Lawrence's first view of the edenic island of Maui and the mountain slope rising through the clouds behind Lahaina was just as blinkered: "I looked in vain for a resemblance to my own dear native land.")

This was the normal, accepted Victorian perception, which, even after the publication of Darwin's *On the Origin of Species,* tended to see Adam and Eve as rather Teutonic-looking northern Europeans, and everyone else, particularly darker races, as benighted, fallen versions of the Scripture-credentialed ideal. A view easy to take issue with 150 years later, but it underscores the freshness and open-mindedness with which Eliza Williams saw the world. In Hakodate, Japan, Eliza described Japanese harbor officials as *"dressed nicely though quite singularly, to me. Their dress is quite loose and slouching, very loose pants if they can be called such, and a kind of loose cloak with very large sleeves."* She and Thomas admired the sheathed samurai sword and knife each man wore in his belt, and an interpreter explained the use of each, which Eliza wrote down without comment: *"They struck with the sword . . . and they cut off the head with the knife, which it seems they do for a small offence."* She and Thomas watched a funeral procession and visited a temple. She found Japanese workmanship "exquisite" and the word "beautiful" is used repeatedly in her descriptions of Japan. She tried some of their food, commenting that the *"Pears and Oranges are poor"* but *"they have a kind of Fig that is very good."*

Eliza and Willie went ashore with Thomas and some of his men in Okhotsk, Siberia, where they experienced the sort of hospitality that was only shown when the world was a much younger, less jaded place:

SEPTEMBER 8TH [1859].

. . . They appear to be a very nice, kind People and did everything for us that they could. They would take all the care of the Baby, hardly giving me time to nurse him. They took me to all the biggest Families and they all wanted me to stop all night, but the first Family claimed the privilege of keeping us. . . . They had everything nice that could be obtained . . . nice butter, and milk. They make very good tarts but no cake. . . . They have nice berries of several kinds. They treated us to wine, tea, and coffee which they make very nicely. . . . I liked them very much.

Between such Marco Polo adventures, there was the sea in all its states to contend with, ice, storms, the ship and its bits and pieces, and Eliza soon wrote about all this and the business of whaling with the fluency of a seaman; hearing of these things spoken only by whalemen, she knew no other way of describing them. The sights Eliza saw—*"the Bears come down from the mountains every night for [stranded] Whale meat"* on the Siberian shore, waterspouts, ice floes, tropical islands—and the people she met—the Japanese, Russians, Eskimos, Pacific island kings and queens (*"The King has a nice new house . . . in the centre of the ground was the place for fire"*), British and American settlers and missionaries, and the common people everywhere—all became the ambient features of Eliza's, and Willie's, everyday lives, and she put it all down in her journal without a shred of judgment.

Willie saw all this at close hand and learned much of life from his mother's example. "I often marveled at my mother's courage and control of her nerves under real danger or trying conditions," he wrote, "because in small matters she was timid and dreaded the sight of blood. . . . But when a situation arose that called for the kind of courage that sweeps away all evidences of fear and leaves the mind in calm control, she was superb." When the lance from a bomb harpoon gun exploded by accident in a whaleboat, it sliced across the face of a mate, James Green:

His wound was sewed up by my father without anesthetic or antiseptics, as they had none, and first, officers and finally my mother held his head while this sewing was done. . . . I cannot overlook . . . the nerve and grit of one little woman compared to the big strong men. First one officer and then another, as they gave up sickened by the sight of blood, held Mr. Green's head while my father took the stitches but my mother had to take over and finish the job. . . . In my experience, a woman can be depended upon to show true nerves and grit at the crucial moment better than a man.

Willie's experience of women began with an unusual example, and one wonders what he found later that could have measured up to it.

Willie's father, whom he idolized, provided an equally high standard of manhood:

I had an intense respect for my father; he has always been to me the finest type of man I have ever known. He stood six feet three inches in his stockings, was broad shouldered, straight as an arrow, blue eyes, black hair, large and fine-shaped head, and weighed over two hundred pounds with no superfluous flesh. He was a natural leader and commander of men, being utterly fearless but not reckless, and a thorough master of his profession. Like most men who follow an outdoor life, of a more or less hazardous nature, he was reserved. He was always ready to enforce an order by physical means, if necessary, but he was not a bully or a boaster.

Eliza, too, surely saw a hero in her husband. No captain could be fairly judged by his neighbors or even family members during the relatively short periods he spent at home, where he was perhaps ill-at-ease, or inept, in social settings, on hiatus from his work and what it was that most truly defined him. The conditions of life aboard a whaleship—or any ship—provided extraordinary opportunities for revealing a person's true nature—to oneself and everyone else aboard. Joseph Conrad liked setting his stories aboard ships because they were entire hermetic worlds: "The ship, a fragment detached from the earth, went on lonely and swift like a small planet. Round her the abysses of sky and sea met in an unattainable frontier . . . she was alive with the lives of those beings who trod her decks; like that earth which had given her up to the sea, she had an intolerable load of regrets and hopes."[2] A ship was a crucible holding a packed cargo of human material, and the conditions

2. Joseph Conrad, *The Nigger of the Narcissus*.

of life at sea—weather, whaling, and other men—were like a flame that unraveled personalities to their discrete strands.

Mary Chipman Lawrence, in her acutest insight, realized this early on as she saw her husband, Samuel Lawrence, respond to the demands of captaincy aboard a whaleship: "I never should have known what a great man he was if I had not accompanied him. I might never have found it out at home."

Yet even the greatest of whaling captains, and Thomas Williams was certainly one of them, could be overcome by adverse circumstances—it was a lesson the best of them learned firsthand. On August 28, 1870, then in command of the whaleship *Hibernia*, with his family aboard as usual, Williams was sailing through a driving snowstorm toward another ship that appeared to be in distress (the signal for which was the national flag flown upside down) when the *Hibernia* collided with a large chunk of ice. Water began pouring into the hull immediately. No longer in a position to help anybody, Williams turned his ship toward the shore. He anchored in shallow water and with the help of crews from several other vessels set men to pumping and bailing throughout the night, but by the next day the *Hibernia* had settled into the mud and was declared a loss. Williams sold the wreck and its cargo of 500 barrels of oil and 3,000 pounds of whale "bone" (baleen) to another captain for $150 at an impromptu auction held on the ship's heeled deck. Williams and his family and crew were taken aboard the whaleship *Josephine* and sailed to Hawaii.

Thomas Williams's reputation was strong enough to weather the loss of several ships, for the risks of an arctic voyage were well understood, while the skill of a competent captain in those waters was prized. Williams immediately found another ship, whose owners were happy for him to assume command. On November 24, 1870, within three weeks of landing in Honolulu, the entire Williams family again put to sea, this time aboard the *Monticello*. They sailed for the South Pacific whaling grounds, the "between season cruise." In early spring they sailed north once more to the Japan grounds, and from there to the Siberian coast off Okhotsk, and finally, during the long days of June, to the Arctic.

Four

The Crucible of Deviancy

George Jr. and Matthew Howland and their Quaker contemporaries who constituted the world's first oil oligarchy also represented an American aristocracy of the first water. There was no more esteemed or solid organization of merchants in America than these whaling Quakers of New Bedford, no group more venerated for their business acumen and their unswerving religious devotion—two attributes that had dovetailed into an apotheosis of wealth, social station, and worldwide fame.

The position had been hard won: an evolution of two centuries of obdurate adherence, by a once tiny band of societal renegades, to a singular code of living, in the face of persistent, often savage persecution by America's founding authorities. The hounding and marginalization of the early Quakers case-hardened them into the tightly knit, clannish society of mutual reliance and unyielding stubbornness that produced this seemingly impregnable plutocracy.

The New England Puritans who fled to the New World because of religious intolerance in England were aware that history was watching them.

"We must consider that we shall be as a City upon a Hill," John Winthrop, the second governor of Massachusetts, told them. "The eyes of all people are upon us, so that if we deal falsely with our god in this work we have undertaken and so cause him to withdraw his present help from us, we shall be made a story and a by-word through the world."

But by crossing an ocean and setting up a new society on its other side, the Puritans metamorphosed from a band of deviants into a state authority more fanatical and uncompromising than the one they had fled. Their heretical beliefs became the new state's religious orthodoxy, and the new Massachusetts Bay Colony demanded an unyielding conformity to the state religion.

One of their early problems was Anne Hutchinson. The wife of the Bostonian William Hutchinson, she struck Winthrop as "a woman of haughty and fierce carriage, of a nimble wit and active spirit, and a very voluble tongue." Mrs. Hutchinson enjoyed the company of ministers, the social luminaries of her day, and her parlor was a popular gathering place for discussions of theological scholarship—a religious salon. She had her favorites among Boston's ministers and wasn't timid about suggesting that others lacked a sufficient "covenant of grace" to lead their congregations. At first this was simply talk emanating from the Hutchinson home, but it grew into feuding factions that polarized around Anne Hutchinson.

Part of what rankled her opponents was the fact that she was a woman. John Winthrop, like most men—and hence, the authorities—of his time, believed that women could become mentally ill and stray from the proper direction God had set for them in life as a result of reading books. As the strength of her challenge to the colony's ruling and religious leaders grew, Anne Hutchinson was brought to trial on charges of sedition and blasphemy, and also of lewd conduct, for the mingling of so many men and women in her home at one time. At her trial, her skill at antagonizing her interlocutors, and her belief that her own communion with God was "as true as the Scriptures," were plainly demonstrated. Court testimony shows that she had no problem or hesitation puncturing the strained arguments laid against her. A historian writing of the trial two centuries later described it as "one more example of the childish excitement over trifles by which people everywhere and at all times are liable to be swept away from the moorings of common sense."

In 1638, Anne Hutchinson was found guilty and banished from the Massachusetts Bay Colony. "After she was excommunicated," wrote Winthrop, "her spirits, which seemed before to be somewhat dejected, revived again, and she gloried in her sufferings, saying, that it was the greatest happiness, next to Christ, that ever befell her." Hutchinson, along with her husband and a group of followers, moved to the more tolerant wilderness of Rhode Island, where they founded the town of Portsmouth. After her husband died, Anne moved to New Netherland, now Pelham Bay, on Long Island, where she was killed in an Indian attack in 1643. (The Hutchinson River Parkway—the "Hutch" to its users—running through Westchester County and the Bronx in New York City, is named after her.)

Between the unmooring of common sense over Anne Hutchinson and the long-brewing hysteria about witches that would culminate in Salem in 1692, Massachusetts Bay Colony discovered another threat to its society, and its reaction was unwise, intemperate, and violent.

In July 1656, an elderly woman, Mary Fisher, and her maid, Ann Austin, arrived in Boston aboard a trading ship, the *Swallow*, from

England via Barbados. The more than one hundred books in their luggage (the seventeenth-century equivalent of a suitcase full of Semtex) raised an immediate alarm. Most of the volumes, upon inspection, were determined to be heretical and, with the stridency that marked every aspect of the authorities' approach to perceived threats to the status quo, were burned in the public marketplace by the colony's hangman. The women were meanwhile stripped naked and examined for "evidences of witchcraft." Such signs could be, most manifestly, "witchmarks"—unusual-looking moles or birthmarks—but also anything out of the ordinary that might raise the hackles of a knowing examiner. (When suspected witch Bridget Bishop was examined in Salem in 1692, her clothing indicated unnatural aberrations: "I always thought there was something questionable about the quality and style of those laces," noted a witness, observing that some of the laces were so small he could not see any practical use for them.)

No sign of witchery was found on the two women, but when interviewed by magistrates they were discovered "to hold very dangerous, heretical, and blasphemous opinions; and they do also acknowledge that they came here purposely to propagate their said errors and heresies, bringing with them and spreading here sundry books, wherein are contained most corrupt, heretical, and blasphemous doctrines contrary to the truth of the gospel here professed amongst us."

The two women were Quakers, the first to reach the Massachusetts Bay Colony. One of them had recently been whipped in England for her beliefs, and, like other pilgrims, they had sailed to the New World in the hope of finding greater freedom of religious expression. They were misinformed. After being imprisoned for five weeks, allowed no light, books, or writing materials in their cell, they were shipped back to Barbados. Soon eight more Quakers arrived in Boston on a ship from London. They, too, were imprisoned, put on trial, and eventually shipped back to London. A year later, a group of Quakers landed in Rhode Island, whose government was more tolerant: "As concerning these quakers (so called), which are now among us, we have no law among us, whereby to punish any for only declaring by words, &c., theire mindes and understandings concerning the things and ways of God."

The Quakers were the mildest of anarchists. George Bishop, at one time an English soldier in Oliver Cromwell's New Model Army, and a contemporary of Fisher and Austin, who became a Quaker himself, wrote a scathing denunciation of the Massachusetts Bay Colony's response to these pilgrims: "Why was it that the coming of two women so shook ye, as if a formidable army had invaded your borders?" But the Quakers were formidable in their gentle resolve; and they kept coming. In Rhode Island, where they were tolerated and largely ignored, they wanted only to travel to Massachusetts, where they provoked and were rewarded with hysteria, which they embraced with an appetite for martyrdom. This was keenly understood in Rhode Island, where the authorities had shrewdly taken the measure of the Quakers:

In those places where these people ... in this colony, are most of all suffered to declare themselves freely, and are only opposed by arguments in discourse, there they least of all desire to come ... for ... they are not opposed by the civill authority, but with all patience and meekness are suffered to say over their pretended revelations and admonitions. . . . We find that they delight to be persecuted by civill powers, and when they are soe, they are like to gain more adherents by the [sight] of their patient sufferings, than by consent to their pernicious sayings.

Yet few could articulate what these pernicious, heretical doctrines were. They were poorly understood, if at all, by the bristling paranoiacs in power in Massachusetts. In truth, the Quakers resembled no one so much as the Puritans themselves in their earlier, purer, condition. Like them, the Quakers had resisted the formal doctrines and rituals of the Church of England as a path to God. They sought the divine illumination of Christ in the individual's heart. "Believe in the Light, that ye may become Children of the Light," urged George Fox, the founder of the Society of Friends, as they called themselves. Fox's words led to their being frequently referred to as the Children of the Light.

Born in Leicestershire, England, in 1624, Fox—like the *Mayflower* Puritans who predated him—espoused a simpler, more austere, more personal relationship with God, without the muddying mediation of a minister or a church. He got into trouble everywhere and was continually being brought before judges and jailed for blasphemy. One judge, ridiculing Fox's instruction to his followers to "tremble at the word of the Lord," called them "quakers." Mary Fisher, Ann Austin, and the Quakers who followed them were, in fact, almost indistinguishable from the original Puritans who voyaged to America. But they came in small groups, without the municipalizing quorum and financial backing that had launched the Massachusetts Bay Colony. And Quakers exhibited two conspicuous behavioral trademarks that readily enabled the authorities to identify them and brand them as deviants. They held strong egalitarian beliefs, and, following the custom set by George Fox, they doffed their hats to no man, including magistrates. And they peppered their speech with the quaint biblical pronouns, already old-fashioned in the seventeenth century, "thee" and "thou."

Mary Fisher and Ann Austin were inspected for witchcraft and interviewed for hours, and their books were examined, yet none of the damning proofs (if any) was needed when they were finally brought before Deputy Governor Richard Bellingham. The moment one of the ladies uttered the word "thee," Bellingham turned to his constable and said, "I need no more, now I see they are Quakers." When a later Quaker trial bogged down in legal abstruseness (for it proved difficult to both level and defend against poorly defined charges), Boston magistrate Simon Bradstreet cut in: "The court will find an easier way to find out a Quaker than by blasphemy—the not putting off the hat."

When Quaker convert Edward Wharton was brought before a magistrate, he asked, "Friends, what is the cause and wherefore have I been fetched from my habitation, where I was following my honest calling, and here laid up as an evil-doer?"

The magistrate replied, "Your hair is too long and you are disobedient to that commandment which saith, 'Honor thy mother and father.'" (The "mother" and "father" of the Fifth Commandment were routinely employed by the courts as metaphorical stand-ins for a local authority; the accusation of Anne Hutchinson's civil disobedience had also been supported by the Fifth Commandment.)

"Wherein?" answered the baffled Wharton.

"In that you will not put off your hat before the magistrates."

Such disrespect may have been proof of a mild social disobedience, but it didn't illuminate the nature of Wharton's, or any other Quaker's, blasphemy. Nevertheless, it was sufficient for the magistrates, and the public, to indicate guilt of more nebulous evildoing.

In 1656, the General Court of Massachusetts Bay Colony passed laws stipulating steep fines for ship captains who brought Quakers into the colony, steeper fines for those who sheltered them, and for "what person or persons soever shall revile the office or persons of magistrates or ministers [i.e., by not removing their hats], as is usual with the Quakers, such persons shall be severely whipped or pay the sum of five pounds." The Quakers of course refused to pay the fines, embraced the opportunity to make public spectacles of their persecution, and were routinely flogged, eliciting sympathy and often converts. And so, in 1657 the court got tougher:

> If any Quaker or Quakers shall presume, after they have once suffered what the law requireth, to come into this jurisdiction, every such male Quaker shall for the first offense have one of his ears cut off, and be kept at work in the house of correction till he can be sent away at his own charge, and for the second offense shall have his other ear cut off, and kept in the house of correction, as aforesaid; and every woman Quaker that hath suffered the law here and shall presume to come into this jurisdiction shall be severly whipped, and kept at the house of correction at work till she be sent away at her own charge, and so for her coming again she shall be alike used as aforesaid; and for every Quaker, he or she, that shall a third time herein again offend, they shall have their tongues bored through with a hot iron, and kept at the house of correction, close to work, till they be sent away at their own charge.

The court now also made provisions aimed at the growing trend of local converts: "And it is further ordered, that all and every Quaker arising from amongst ourselves shall be dealt with and suffer the like punishment as the law provides against foreign Quakers."

But, as the Rhode Island authorities had well understood, these measures were simply red flags to Quakers. After being punished and banished to Rhode Island, three persistent Quaker offenders, Mary Dyer, William Robinson, and Marmaduke Stevenson, returned to Massachusetts in 1659 and were sentenced to be hanged. When asked for her feelings as she was walking to the gallows, Mary Dyer replied, "It is an hour of the greatest joy I can enjoy in this world. No eye can see, no ear can hear, no tongue can speak, no heart can understand, the sweet incomes and refreshing of the spirit of the Lord which I now enjoy." On the scaffold, Robinson declared more prosaically, "Mind you, it is for the not putting off the hat that we are put to death."

Mary Dyer was reprieved after the two men had been hanged, and again sent away to Rhode Island. So profound was her disappointment, and determination, that she returned to Massachusetts and succeeded in getting herself hanged in 1660.

But many Quakers were less fanatical. They wanted more from life than a martyr's death. In both the Plymouth and Massachusetts Bay colonies, groups of Quakers—and others who felt oppressed, if less physically threatened, by these fascist regimes and such interference in their daily lives—began to think of moving away from populated centers: not outside the colonies, for beyond their borders lay an outer space of wilderness, but away from the nosy neighborhoods of towns, toward remoter areas where they might practice religion, dress, and speech to their own tastes and pursue peaceful lives.

In between cannily tolerant Rhode Island and hyperreactionary Massachusetts Bay Colony lay comparatively mild-mannered Plymouth Colony. There, Quakers were dealt with less hysterically, if not actually embraced by the aging *Mayflower* Pilgrims and their multiplying children. Quakerish delinquency was seen as a cranky misdemeanor rather than a high crime in Plymouth; fines were levied where ears were severed in Massachusetts; there were whippings instead of hangings for persistent offenders. In 1658, one Humphrey Norton behaved "turbulently" when brought before the court in Plymouth as a Quaker, saying to the governor, "Thy clamorous tongue I regard no more than the dust under my feet and thou art like a scolding woman." This got him fined and whipped, but it would have been worse for him north of Plymouth's border.

Another fractious Quaker was Arthur Howland, who had been born in Fenstanton, in Huntingdonshire, England. Arthur and his younger brothers, Henry and John, were among the Puritan separatists, also including William Brewster and William Bradford, who had worshipped in secret in Scrooby, Nottinghamshire, on before relocating to Leiden, in Holland, from where some eventually sailed to America on the *Mayflower* in 1620. John Howland, the first of the brothers to reach the New World, achieved a small measure of lasting fame by sailing with this group as an indentured servant. Plymouth's governor, William Bradford, described John as a "lusty younge man," referring to his strength and staying power. He had been washed overboard from the *Mayflower*'s deck during a storm at sea—a near-certain death sentence—yet managed to grab and retain a tenacious grip on a rope as the ship lurched and plunged in the icy Atlantic until he was pulled aboard. He proved as indomitable during their first winter ashore, when a number of "Saints," as the Pilgrims called themselves, and their hired crew died of cold and disease. Howland was indentured to John Carver, a deacon who had been elected the colony's first governor. Both Carver and his wife, Katherine, died in the spring after the colony's first winter, and John Howland is thought to have inherited much of their property and land. Clearly, he was made for the New World, and he must have sent word of the opportunities there back to his two brothers, Arthur and Henry, for they both followed him to Plymouth in either 1621 or 1623.

John Howland was and remained a Presbyterian Puritan, but Arthur and Henry had, at some point before leaving England, become staunch Quakers. Soon after joining their brother in Plymouth, they found themselves uncomfortable with the religious persecution there. Arthur moved to Marshfield, ten miles to the north, where his house became a headquarters for Quakers and his relationship with the authorities remained difficult for the remainder of his life. There he "entertayned the forraigne Quakers who were goeing too & frow ... producing great desturbance." He was repeatedly fined and jailed for holding Quaker services, or Meetings, in his house, and for "resisting the constable of Marshfield in the execution of his office and abusing him in words by threatening speeches."

Henry, the youngest Howland brother, also an intractable Quaker, was repeatedly brought before the court and fined, but eventually he decided to move farther from Plymouth's gaze and influence. In November 1652, Henry Howland, along with Ralph Russell from Pontypool, Monmouthshire, who had worked as an ironsmith in the Plymouth settlements of Taunton and Raynham, were among a group of settlers of various religious groups—Quakers, Baptists, and Puritans who hoped for more tolerance for all Christian persuasions—who purchased from the Wampanoag Indian sachem Massasoit and his son, Wamsutta, a 219-square-mile tract of land in the extreme south of Plymouth Colony, close to Rhode Island—southern Massachusetts today. This parcel stretched inland on both sides of the Cusenagg River (as the Indians called it), where it met the coast of Buzzards Bay—named for the bustard cranes that roosted on its shores. This is a gentle coast, protected from the open sea by Cape Cod to the east and the pretty Elizabeth Islands to the south. The winters along this shoreline are the mildest in New England, and in the summers it is "fanned by breezes salt and cool."

The land was gently sloped. In its dense woods were trees of a size to produce wide boards, in varieties handy for every kind of construction: cedar, white birch, oak, elm, maple, and pine. There was open grassland for grazing, and barrens covered in season with blueberries and cranberries, elderberries and wild strawberries. There were grapes on vines, and natural orchards of apple trees, pears, cherries, quinces, and trees of hickory nuts, hazelnuts, acorns, and chestnuts. Wild rice was found in the lowland marshes, which were home to geese, swans, and ducks. Clams, quahogs, and mussels clustered in the tidal river mouth and in the offshore shallows, lobsters and crabs skittered below the ledges, and the ocean waters, already famed for their abundance of cod, also teemed with sea bass, mackerel, and bluefish.

The purchasers paid Massasoit and Wamsutta "thirty yards of cloth, eight moose skins, fifteen axes, fifteen hoes, fifteen pairs of breeches, eight blankets, two kettles, one cloth, £22 in wampum, eight pairs of stockings, eight pairs of shoes, one iron pot, and ten shillings in another commodotie." Both sides were pleased. (Only twenty-six years before, Peter Minuit, a leading official of the Dutch West India Company, bought the far smaller, twenty-three-square-mile Manhattan from local Indians for a similar pile of cloth, metal, goods, and trinkets worth sixty guilders.)

Twelve years later, in 1664, this large and bountiful area of woods, meadow, wetland, river, and shore was incorporated as the township of Dartmouth. It was named after the port town in Devonshire, England, which occupies a similarly favorable site at the sheltered mouth of the deepwater river the Dart. Like that river, the Acushnet—as the purchasers called and transcribed the Indian "Cusenagg"—proved sweetly accommodating of the development of seagoing affairs. It ran straight inland between sheltering arms of good land, wide and deep enough for the maneuvering of large ships.

The settlers of this New World Dartmouth built small houses, farmed, and developed peaceful relations with the local Indians. But elsewhere in Plymouth, the Indian chief Metacom, or "King Philip," was selling every available scrap of the mainland under his control to Plymouth settlers in an effort to raise cash to buy firearms with which to drive those same purchasers off that land and kill them. When an

Indian favorite of Governor Josiah Winslow, who was feeding Winslow information about Philip's plans, was murdered by Philip's men, the murderers were quickly caught and hanged, and, in June 1675, war erupted.

As Philip and the Pokanokets launched attacks with the aid of the Narragansetts, other tribes, long bristling under the inevitable breakdown of relations between whites and Indians, took the opportunity to attack settlers in their own neighborhoods of Swansea, Middleborough, Taunton, Rehoboth, and other towns. Unlike most Puritans, who lived in townships, the early settlers of Dartmouth had shown their preference for independence by dispersing themselves over a wide swath of country, separated by streams, rivers, and woods. This scattering of farms and homesteads had the added advantage that it didn't appear to conform to the sort of recognizable community structure to which the General Court at Plymouth would have insisted on sending a minister of their own Puritan persuasion. But it was too open to allow for any cohesive defense. Early in July 1675, a renegade sachem named Totoson and a group of Wampanoags ran through the woods and meadows of Dartmouth, burning nearly thirty houses and killing many people, "skinning them all over alive . . . cutting off their hands and feet. . . . Any woman they took alive they defiled, afterward putting her to death." Families were too far apart to group together and fight off attackers. They could only try to defend their homes, and those who weren't killed escaped to the soldier-enforced garrisons on the Apponagansett and Acushnet rivers.

Henry Howland's forty-year-old son, Zoeth Howland, was killed in an Indian raid. But by the following year the English had prevailed, and the Indian rebellion had been efficiently put down. Most of Philip's allies had deserted him, and his wife and son had been taken prisoner (according to one account, they were transported as slaves to Spain).

On August 12, 1676, fleeing white and Indian pursuers, King Philip was shot through the heart by a Pocasset Indian named Alderman, using an elderly musket.

It was years before Dartmouth recovered. As a result of the war, the Plymouth General Court ruled that all future settlements be built with homes located close together for mutual protection, and slowly Dartmouth was rebuilt as a small village along the river.

One of its first communal buildings, erected in 1699, was a "meeting house for the people of God in Scorn Called Quakers."

Five

The Killing Floes

As the *Monticello* and thirty-nine other whaleships gathered, push-ing at the melting ice still blocking the Bering Strait in June 1871, they began killing walruses. Vast herds of the brown, wrinkled, elephantine creatures lay on the floes in full view of the whale-ships, grunting, bellowing, or asleep in the sun, as the ice drifted slowly northward on the current with the advancing fleet. When the wind was in the right quarter, their strong smell carried for miles across the clean ice to the whalers.

The walruses were part of the same ecosystem that brought the plankton and the whales to these rich arctic waters. Their diet of clams and other shellfish lay in the silt beneath the floes in the shallow, mineral-rich waters of the continental shelf between Alaska and Siberia. More localized in their habitat than the pelagic, migrating whales, the walrus herds spent the winters at the southern edge of the pack ice in the Bering Sea and moved north on the melting floes through the Bering Strait into the Chukchi Sea during the spring—exactly in tandem with the whaleships. Although they had long been hunted by the Eskimos, this predation had been so small that when the whalers first encountered them in the 1840s, the walruses showed no fear of the men or their ships, but approached them out of curiosity. And in those early years of arctic whaling, faced with an abundance of their primary prey, the whalers had left the walruses unmolested. But in just four years, between 1848 and 1852, whalers killed a third of all the arctic bowhead whales they would catch between 1848 and 1914; by 1869, two-thirds of that overall catch had been taken. In August 1859, at the end of a dismal arctic season during which they had caught not a single whale on either side of the Bering Strait, the men of the New Bedford whaleship *Cleone* began killing walruses. The ubiquitous animals who lay around the ships on the ice "cakes" had previously been considered unworthy of the whalemen's efforts. But the *Cleone*'s crew found that a single mature bull yielded around twenty gallons of oil (about two-thirds of a barrel), and from that moment on, the view from the deck of a whaleship in the Bering Strait was changed forever.

Walrusing increasingly became a factor in the profitability of whaling, whose primary resource had been in decline for decades. As demand grew, walrus oil proved at first almost as valuable as whale oil; but eventually, as refining techniques improved and walrus oil proved easier to refine than whale oil, its price rose even higher than whale oil. Compared with rowing after a whale in a small boat, followed by a dangerous struggle at sea or amid the ice floes, walrusing was irresistibly convenient: a man could walk up to a walrus as it lay on the ice or the shore and plunge a lance into the desired spot at the back of its head. While making slow progress early in the season toward the whaling grounds farther north, a ship's crew could kill 500 walruses, netting 300 barrels of oil, perhaps half the seasonal catch for an arctic whaling ship at this time.

The surge in this preseason hors d'oeuvre of killing was sudden and devastating as walruses were reassessed by whalers as a prized commodity: from just three walruses killed in 1855, the number rose to 35,663 during the 1876 season. At that point the walrus population collapsed. Less than half that number, 13,294 walruses, were killed by whalers the following year, and the numbers would drop into the hundreds less than ten years later.

Both the whale and the walrus had long been a staple food of the Eskimos. Before the 1850s, whales had been plentiful along the arctic coasts, easily caught by the natives—in small numbers that had no effect on the size of whale populations or on the whales' awareness of these predators. But since the appearance of the American whaling fleets, they had become scarce, and much warier when found, and the Eskimos had shifted their dependence to the walrus, not only for food but for clothing, boots, tools, and many items of daily use in their culture. Now, with the same terrible efficiency and consequences they had brought to whaling, the New Englanders were decimating literally an ocean of walrus herds, and by 1871 the natives along the Alaskan and Siberian shores were facing starvation.

It was an act of supreme generosity by the Eskimos to feed the crew of the *Japan*. "I felt that I had been taking the bread out of their mouths," Captain Barker told his listeners. Later he wrote to the New Bedford *Republican Standard* newspaper: "Yet although they knew that the whaleships are doing this, still they were ready to share all they had with us. The wholesale butchery of the walrus pursued by nearly all the ships during the early part of each season will surely end in the extermination of this race of natives who rely upon these animals alone for their winter's supply of food."

Barker returned from his winter in the Arctic a changed man. He declared that neither he nor anyone aboard a ship he commanded would ever kill another walrus. He urged the other captains to give it up, though he knew what he was asking of them.

> I have conversed with many intelligent ship masters upon this subject since I have seen it in its true light, and *all* have expressed their honest conviction that it was wrong, cruel, heartless, and the sure death of this inoffensive race [the Eskimos], that they would be only too glad to abandon the thing at once, if their employers would justify them. . . . To abandon an enterprise that in one season alone yielded 10,000 bbls. oil, for the sake of the Esquimaux who have found an advocate in one that has passed a few months with them, may seem preposterous and meet with derision and contempt, but let those who deride it see the misery entailed throughout the country by this unjust wrong, with death knocking at the door, while hunger was staring through the window, as I have during my travels, and I feel quite sure a business that can last not longer than two or three years more, will be condemned by every prompting of humanity that ever actuated the heart of a Christian.

The following year, another whaling captain, who signed his letter simply "A Shipmaster," published a similar appeal in the New Bedford *Republican Standard*, but he was realistic about the response to this inconvenient truth: "I have seen most of the captains lately arrived home, and they all tell the same story—that the natives are or will starve if the business is not stopped. Some say, 'I never will take another walrus,' but several others I have talked with say they won't take walrus if others will not, which means just this, 'I shall take all I can.' But it wants the condemnation of the shipowners and agents here in New Bedford, for I think their ships can be better and more profitably employed in whaling."

But New Bedford's shipowners and whaling merchants—the Howlands and their peers who read these entreaties—remained unmoved by such appeals. Walrus catches in 1871 were still rising, along with their significance in terms of profit. The dire predictions for the welfare of native peoples on the far side of the world meant nothing to them. What would happen was in the future, and it was going to happen to someone else. This was the way of the world—scientists from mid-century onward could now understand such apparent calamities through the wonderful new lens of Darwinism that put a fatalistic spin on misery and famine, and pious Quakers could, if they wished to, see in it the unfathomable hand of God. He had placed the walrus on the ice floes alongside their ships as surely as He had filled the seas with whales. Such explanations absolved them of moral responsibility.

By 1871, the crystalline surface of the ice stretching across the Bering Strait had become the dark, slippery floor of a sixty-mile-wide abattoir. For the Eskimos, this harvest was too great and wanton to profit from its leftovers. Years of natural stocks of this food source were butchered in a few months, most of it going to waste. Settlements along the strait were able to make some use of the meat of carcasses stripped of their blubber by the whalemen, but elsewhere the scarcity was pronounced: whalemen had seen natives on the ice thirty and forty miles from land trying to capture a single walrus.

"This cold winter," the "Shipmaster" had written, "I have no doubt, there is mourning in many an Arctic home as the little ones cry for something to eat and the parents have nothing to give, for the walrus are killed or driven far away."

Most of the whalemen agreed, sharing the fulsome expression of sentiments common to even the staidest newspaper writing of the day. But they had barrels to fill, and money to earn, that would be filled and earned by others if they did not, so they went "walrusing" as usual.

In 1871, most walruses were still killed by "iron"—harpoon and lance—or club. This method had the disadvantage of startling the entire herd on a floe when one of its members was attacked. The others would begin to slip off the ice into water, but the whalers still caught great numbers of them while they swam, hauling them back onto the ice to be skinned.

Ships' logs recorded the daily tallies. Aboard the *John Wells*: June 23: "*At about 5 o'clock [p.m.] commenced walrusing.*" June 24: "*Fine weather walrusing all day & night got about 75 in number.*" June 25: "*A wild goose chase after walruses. we got 3 or 4.*" July 1: "*Light breeze from South'rd 5 boats [the* Wells's *five whaleboats] walrusing got about 30.*" July 2: "*Light breeze boats off about 30 miles from ship walrusing got about 50.*" July 3: "*Went off after walruses came in thick fog got 15 I believe.*" July 4: "*Light breeze boats off walrusing got about 40.*"

The count aboard the *Henry Taber*: June 25, 20 walruses; June 26, 40; June 27, 48; June 28, 14—before wind and rain sent the boats back to the ship that evening.

Aboard the nearby bark *Elizabeth Swift*, also of New Bedford: July 1, 41 walruses; July 3, 51; July 12, 41; July 13, 20; July 14, 41.

Captain Thomas Williams, of the *Monticello*, allowed his twelve-year-old son, Willie, to go walrusing in the first mate's boat. It was the boy's first view of a live walrus up close, and he never forgot what happened.

The first walrus struck promptly drove his tusks through the side of the boat, tearing out a piece of plank large enough to have sunk us in minutes if the crew had not been used to such experiences. The walrus was promptly dispatched by a thrust of the lance, the boat pulled to the ice, hauled out and a canvas patch tacked over the hole in about the time it takes to tell it. [Canvas and tacks were routinely carried aboard whaleboats on walrus hunts.] After enough walrus had been killed to make a boatload they were hauled on the ice, skinned, and the blubber packed in the boat, when we returned to the ship.

Willie spent long days in the boats and on the ice through late June and most of July, watching the *Monticello*'s crew go about their work. The scale of the slaughter, and its pragmatic purpose, quickly eliminated any sensitivity another boy of twelve, even of his era, might have felt for these creatures.

While an old walrus will weigh over 2000 pounds [older bulls may weigh up to 4,000 pounds], you are not properly impressed by their size even when they are in full view on the ice, because having no legs they are always apparently lying down. In the water their size is still more deceptive, as you only see their heads and a small part of their back. Their movements, too, are so clumsy, that it is extremely funny to see them on the approach of a boat get off the ice, the females fairly shoving their young overboard in their anxiety to get them out of danger, and all the bellowing and barking as though bedlam had broken loose. At times, the water around the boat was fairly alive with young and old walrus; but as no one else seemed alarmed I took it for granted that there was no danger, although at first my nerves got a few bad "jars," when upon hearing a terrific bellow at my back I would turn to find myself almost within arm's length of a rather vicious looking combination, of a round head, wicked black eyes and a pair of long drooping white ivory tusks, but I soon learned that he was the most frightened of the two and promptly escaped if possible, either by diving or swimming away from the boat. Now and then a female walrus separated from her young, or an old bull walrus slightly wounded, would make a rush for the boat, sometimes causing an accident to some member of the crew, although I do not recall any that were fatal. The boats, however, were frequently stove so much so that it usually took about a week after the walrusing period was over, to put them in proper repair.

In less than a month, the *Monticello*'s men killed over 500 walruses, netting 300 barrels of oil. This full-time occupation for the ship and its men coincided with the summer solstice and allowed for great productivity:

It was no uncommon occurrence to see thousands of walrus upon the ice within an area of easy vision, and as the sun never set during this period, the hours of work were only limited by the physical capacity of the men, and that was tried to its utmost.

But Willie was writing of the last year or so, when walrusing was a mere addendum to whaling, practiced with whaling's tools and methods. Within a very few years, the walrus harvest had become a main event in the Arctic, more dependable than whaling, and its efficiency was greatly boosted by the use of Sharps or Henry buffalo rifles. Captain Calvin Hooper described how the effectiveness of this was maximized by killing the first animal with a single shot to the temple:

At the first sound of the rifle they all raise their heads, and if one has been wounded and goes into the water the rest all follow; but if the shot has been effective, they soon drop their heads and go to sleep again. This is repeated a few times, until they become so accustomed to the firing that they take no notice of it. Then they are approached within a few feet and dispatched as fast as guns can be loaded and fired.

New Bedford captain Leander Owen, originally from Maine, was an expert at this. By himself, he once killed 250 walruses that lay on a single slab of ice. In one forty-eight-hour period in 1877, Owen shot 700 walruses.

Once the killing was finished, a boat's crew began the grisly job of butchering the walruses, stripping the carcasses of their blubber, and using axes to chop the tusks out of their jaws. Though considered inferior to elephant ivory because of their more granular core, walrus tusks were readily sold for shipment to ivory markets in New York, London, China, and Japan.

As the whales grew shyer and scarcer in the Arctic, more walruses were taken. John Bockstoce, the preeminent historian and authority on American whaling in the western Arctic, estimates that of about 150,000 walruses caught by the whalers in the years 1849–1914, 85 percent of these were killed during whaling's waning decade of the 1870s. "As appalling as the size of this catch was, the damage to the population was almost certainly greater," writes Bockstoce. "The total kill was probably more than twice the size of the catch. Mortally wounded animals often escaped from the whalemen and, at times, the warm blood flowing from the slaughter broke up the ice floes, resulting in the loss of part or all of a particular harvest."

This slaughter—far in excess of anything Captain Barker had seen or imagined during his hungry winter with the Eskimos—had devastating repercussions for his hosts. Though predictions of starvation for the natives had been made for some years, reports of a widespread tragedy were carried aboard ships sailing out of the Arctic after the winter of 1878–1879. "Fully one-third of the population south of

St Lawrence Bay perished the past Winter for want of food," Captain
Ebenezer Nye wrote to the New Bedford *Republican Standard*,

> and half the natives of St Lawrence Island died, one village of 200
> inhabitants all died excepting one man. Mothers took their starving
> children to the burying grounds, stripped the clothing from their
> little emaciated bodies, and then strangled them or let the intense
> cold end their misery. . . . The people have eaten their walrus skin
> houses and walrus skin boats; this old skin poisoned them and made
> them sick, and many died from that. They also ate about all of their
> dogs and there are but three boats and three dogs left at what was
> once the largest settlement of Plover Bay.

A wishful story spread among the natives left alive that a Russian
warship would come in the summer and destroy the whaleships for
killing the walruses, but no Russian ship came. The American whalers,
however, did what they could to provide aid to the native villages, feeding Eskimos who came aboard the ships and taking tons of their own
food supplies ashore, though this was too little and too late.

The U.S. Revenue Service cutter *Thomas Corwin* discovered the extent of the disaster at St. Lawrence Island, at the southern end of the
Bering Strait, where at least 1,000 of the island's population of 1,500
had starved to death.

By the 1890s, the walruses had gone the way of the whales, their
numbers shrunk to scarcity that finally made hunting them unprofit-
able, which was all that saved both species from total extinction.

IN LATE JULY OF 1871, with the fleet stretching from St. Lawrence Island
in the south to the north end of the Bering Strait, a strong northeasterly

wind began to blow across the Chukchi Sea. The ice that had blocked the strait was pushed south, through it, opening the passage to the north; and the ice that had clung to the Alaskan shore began to break up as the wind pushed it out into deeper water, creating the start of a channel of clear water between the ice and the land. This was what the fleet had been waiting for. The whalemen hoisted their boats aboard and beat toward the northeast, leaving the blood-soaked killing floes behind. Men were sent aloft to the crow's nests and began again to look for the whales, which would also follow the opening channels in the ice.

Six

The Nantucket Paradigm

One morning in the fall of 1659, before they were apprehended and hanged for not taking off their hats, William Robinson and Marmaduke Stevenson, along with Edward Wharton, took shelter from a rainstorm in the house of a farmer, Thomas Macy, in Salisbury, north of Boston. Macy himself had been caught in the storm and was soaked to the skin when he arrived home, moments before the Quakers knocked at his door. He found his wife sick in bed, so he was too busy to entertain his guests beyond allowing them to stay until the weather improved. He spoke few words with them, though he admitted later that because of their speech and "carriage" (hats on), he thought they might be Quakers. Macy was a Baptist, not a Quaker, but his notions of hospitality were as plain to him as the weather. His guests stayed about three-quarters of an hour, until the rainstorm passed, then thanked him and left.

Nevertheless, the Boston court took exception to this minimal act of hospitality and fined him five pounds. Macy was outraged, and his outrage made history.

"He could now live no longer in peace, and in the enjoyment of religious freedom [i.e., the freedom to extend Christian hospitality to anyone of his choice]," wrote his descendant, Nantucket historian Obed Macy.

> He chose therefore to remove his family to a place unsettled by the whites, to take up his abode among savages, where . . . religious zeal had not yet discovered a crime in hospitality. In the fall of 1659, he embarked in an open boat, with his family and such effects as he could conveniently take with him, and . . . proceeded along the shore to the westward. When they came to Boston bay, they crossed it, passed round Cape Cod . . . thence they crossed the sound and landed on Nantucket without accident.

This same journey today in a well-found yacht requires precise navigation to negotiate the extreme tidal currents and shifting sandbars that lie between Cape Cod and Nantucket. Macy was not ignorant of these dangers. This hazardous voyage, of several days' duration, risking wife and children in an obviously overloaded open boat in changeable fall weather through a stretch of the most disturbed waters off the New England coast, tells us everything about the vehemence of Thomas Macy's feelings. He was responding to the same charges and persecution that seven years earlier had driven Henry Howland and others to purchase the land that became the settlement of Dartmouth.

A year later, ten more families from Salisbury had joined the Macys on Nantucket. They purchased the island from Thomas Mayhew of Martha's Vineyard (who had bought it from a group of absentee English aristocrat speculators).

But when these bold, independent-minded people tried to scratch a living from this place, they were at a serious disadvantage compared with settlers on the mainland. The fishing in the tidal-ripped waters around the island was good, particularly of cod, but with little to augment it from ashore, it made a thin living for the early Nantucketers.

From the earliest days of English settlement along the east coast of America, whales had been found stranded ashore, primarily along New England's great stretches of beach on southern Long Island and Cape Cod. "Whaling" then was no more than scavenging; such flotsam was cut up and the blubber, long known to provide a useful oil, was boiled in large pots set up on the beach. But these windfalls were infrequent on Nantucket. Whales weren't pursued and "fished" until the day, a year or two after Macy and others had moved to the island, when a live whale, of a kind locally called a "scragg"—a gray whale—appeared in the settlement's harbor. It swam tantalizingly close, back and forth in the shallows off the town, for several days. A barbed spearhead was quickly fashioned by the local blacksmith, and a boatload of men eager to capture the whale set off with the spearhead and attacked and killed the whale. This appears to be the earliest account of a whale caught with a harpoon by the white settlers of America. The Nantucketers probably got the idea from watching the Indians, with whom they fished and were friendly, attempt the same thing.

Captain George Weymouth, exploring the New England coast and the waters around Nantucket and Dartmouth in 1605, observed of the natives: "One especial thing is their manner of killing the whale. . . . They go in company of their king in a multitude of their boats; and strike him with a bone made in fashion of a harping iron fastened to a rope, which they make great and strong of the bark of trees, which they veer out after him; then all their boats come about him as he riseth above water, with their arrows they shoot him to death." But, as

Weymouth indicates, "harping irons" were already well known. The Dutch had been whaling in open boats launched from the shore in Spitsbergen, far north of the Arctic Circle, since the late sixteenth century. A 1611 engraving of their techniques bears the description: "When the whale comes above the water, ye shallop rowes towards him and being within reach of him the harpoiner darts his harping iron at him out of both his hands and being fast they lance him to death." And the Basques were known to have hunted whales in the Bay of Biscay since the eighth century, using this same method, which remained unimprovable for a thousand years: despite all the Yankee ingenuity brought to the business, American whalers still threw harpoons with both hands from open boats until the invention and use of the harpoon gun in the second half of the nineteenth century.

It was the Nantucketers who revolutionized whaling at two signal moments that saw the business evolve from opportunistic beachcombing into a global industry. The first was their adaptation of the Indians' method of catching live whales from boats that encouraged them to hunt whales at sea rather than waiting for them to drift ashore. The immediate and subsequent success of this, and the infertility of their barren sandspit, led Nantucketers to put all their industry into the development of this "fishery." They hired more whalers from nearby Cape Cod to come to Nantucket, and coopers to make barrels, offering acreage and steady work for these outside contractors. From the start, Thomas Macy and the early settlers established good relations with Nantucket's local Indians, so these families became their partners in this early endeavor. Indian men joined the white men in their boats, and their wives were involved in the boiling of the blubber ashore. By the late seventeenth century, whaling was Nantucket's principal business, and almost every family on the island took part.

The type of whale initially hunted was a species whose characteristics, alive and dead, made it the most suitable—the "right" whale—to hunt: it was a slow swimmer, possessed thick blubber, and, most important, remained floating when killed, so that it was easily towed ashore. The right whale, as it came to be called, was found immediately offshore, its migratory path lying close to outlying Nantucket in the warm waters of the continental shelf between the tepid Gulf Stream and the American coast. Whales were often seen from shore, and Obed Macy records a comment passed down by generations of Nantucketers: "In the year 1690 . . . some persons were on a high hill . . . observing the whales spouting and sporting with each other, when one observed 'there,' pointing to the sea, 'is a green pasture where our children's grandchildren will go for bread.'"

Nantucket's whale fishery continued to prosper through the second half of the seventeenth century. Lookout posts—tall wooden posts with a sitting platform—were erected along the island's southern coast and manned, like modern lifeguard chairs; boats were launched when whales were sighted. But this was still whaling carried out from a shore base. About the year 1712, a whaler named Christopher Hussey and his crew of white settlers and Indians had set out after right whales, when a strong northerly wind sprang up and blew their boat out of sight of land, far out to sea—probably to the warm edge of the Gulf Stream. When the blow subsided, Hussey and his crew found themselves close to a pod of a very different sort of whale. These had enormous blunt-ended heads that appeared to comprise half the whale's body. Their jaw was nothing like the large baleen-filled scoop of the right whale, but was a long, narrow plank filled with teeth at the bottom of this head. At least one such whale had previously been found dead ashore in Nantucket, where it had aroused a frenzy of excitement. When cut open, its bulbous, bluff-bowed head was discovered to contain a reservoir of pure amber-colored oil that could be emptied out with ladles.

This was initially thought to be a reservoir of the whale's seminal fluid or sperm. It was quickly found to be far superior in quality to rendered blubber oil: it produced a cleaner-burning flame when lit—its primary use—but was also thought to have medicinal properties, both when swallowed and applied externally. For a time, Macy writes, this oil was esteemed to be worth its weight in silver. And many uses were found for those teeth, great ingots of a hard, fine ivory.

Hussey and his crew succeeded in killing one of these whales and towing it back to Nantucket, prompting the industry's second major evolution (in America), the second innovation by Nantucketers: the commencement of deep-sea whaling voyages, the duration and spoils of which were limited only by the size of the vessels. Larger ships were quickly built, capable of venturing far offshore and remaining at sea, cruising for whales, with stores to feed a crew for six or more weeks without returning to shore, capacious enough to be loaded with hogsheads full of cut-up whale meat and barrels filled with sperm oil.

Such ships were too slow and clumsy to follow and attack a whale at close quarters, so they also had to be large enough to carry small whaleboats—the size of Indian canoes—that could be lowered for the chase and the kill. Since these did not have to be especially seaworthy or comfortable for long periods, or carry much beyond the essential harpoons, lances, and rope, they could be lightly constructed for speed and maneuverability. Thus evolved the classic whaleboat: about twenty-eight feet long, double-ended for speedy reverses away from a whale's back and thrashing tail, oar-powered (though they also carried a collapsible mast and sail), rowed by five men and steered by the sixth, one of the ship's mates. These are the small cockleshells now seen only in whaling museums, and in paintings and illustrations, being tossed, pulled, or smashed to pieces by a whale.

As larger vessels made more voyages, more facilities to receive and process their cargoes were built ashore on Nantucket. New wharves for larger ships were constructed in the town's harbor; tryworks—sheds housing brick kilns and great iron cauldrons where the blubber was cut up and "tried-out" into oil—were erected near the wharves; warehouses to store barrels, coopering sheds, forges, shipbuilding yards, long rope-walk sheds, and soon candle factories and oil refineries were built. All quickly changed the appearance of what had been a sleepy settlement on Nantucket into a busy, and putrid-smelling, industrial town.

The business of the whale fishery became the primary occupation of almost everyone in Nantucket. Men were employed either aboard the ships or in the building of them and in the heavier manufacturing processes, while women, and many children, found work in the rope-walk and the candle factories, and in the importing and exporting busi-nesses that supported a growing town.

In 1715, three years after Christopher Hussey's epochal capture of a sperm whale, there were still only six vessels engaged in Nantucket's whale fishery, producing that year £1,100 for the island. But whale oil was becoming highly sought-after in America and England, and the industry's growth was explosive: by 1762, Nantucket had 78 ships at sea. The island's catch that year amounted to 9,440 barrels of oil—almost 300,000 gallons—from approximately 130 whales.

This, and the lesser efforts by whaleships sailing from New London and Sag Harbor, was enough to impact the numbers of whales found across a broad stretch of the Atlantic. By the mid–eighteenth century, both sperm and right whales were becoming notably scarce along the American coast. No longer were they seen cavorting in the coastal pas-tures. As Nantucketers sailed ever farther to find them, the direction of their search first arced back toward the Old World: north up Davis Strait to the arctic reaches of Baffin Bay, east to the Grand Banks and beyond, to the Western Islands (as the Azores, Madeira, and Cape

Verde groups were still known, even by Americans in a Eurocentric world). But whales (and the avoidance of French and Spanish privateers during a series of wars these two countries waged against England during the eighteenth century) led the voyaging whaleships inexorably in the direction of the geopolitical future: southeast, down the coast of Guinea, in West Africa, and then westward again, to "the Brazils," even as far south as the Falkland Islands, where Nantucket vessels were cruising by 1772. Then Cape Horn beckoned, beyond which lay a whole world of unknown whaling grounds to be explored in tandem with the irresistible westward roll of history.

Norsemen had sailed above the Arctic Circle in Scandinavia and Russia from the first millennium, but the Nantucket whalemen rediscovered arctic conditions for themselves, and they made their observations available to fellow whalers: *"The daylight goeth not out of the sky during the whole 24 hours."* On June 15, 1753, when the whaleship *Greyhound* lay in Davis Strait between Baffin Island and Greenland, her log recorded: *"At 10AM it grew thick of fog and we Brought to under a trisail & Foresail not daring to run we knew not whither among ye Ice or Fog. The weather is freezing cold; Nights short; Sea rowling and Tumbling. The Deep tedious; our cabbin a Delight; the fire pleasant, our allowance to every man on board his belly-full and more too if he wants. Alas, if it were not for hope the heart would fail."*

Nantucket's whalers lived routinely at sea for months at a time, as no one had before them. *"This morning I went out in my boat to the Carcass of a Dead Whale,"* wrote Francis Swain in the log of the *Speedwell* of Nantucket as it cruised in the South Atlantic on March 30, 1776. *"There was a great number of Albatrosses & I knocked down 52 of them with my lance Pole and haul'd them into the boat . . . they proved to be Excellent good Meat."*

These Nantucketers, "geographically situated as if on a mother ship anchored in the Atlantic," as historian Edouard Stackpole put it, were the world's first proficient oceanographers. In London, Benjamin Franklin's English friends asked him why their own ships were so much slower crossing the Atlantic than the Americans'. For an answer, Franklin wrote to his cousin, Nantucket whaling captain Timothy Folger, who told him about the phenomenon recorded by whalers of the warm river that flowed through the much colder Atlantic, from the Gulf of Mexico all the way to Europe. Franklin was the first to publish an article and a map of this "Gulf Stream."

THOUGH THOMAS MACY and most of the early settlers were not Quakers, Nantucket gradually became thoroughly Quakerized during the hundred years following their arrival. The community's origins and continued open-mindedness about matters of faith had encouraged a number of Quakers to relocate there, but there seems to have been no regular Meeting until Thomas Story, an early Quaker missionary from England, visited the island in 1704. He found willing believers—not yet Quakers—in Nathaniel Starbuck and, in particular, his wife, Mary. She was "a wise, discreet woman, well read in Scripture, and not attached unto any sect, but in great reputation throughout the island for her knowledge in matters of religion, and an oracle among them on that account, in so much that they would not do any thing without her advice and consent therein," wrote Story. With the Starbucks' help, he organized Quaker Meetings with islanders, including a large number of the local Indians, many of whom had already become pious Christians. Story left the island with a regular Meeting established at the Starbuck house, under the guidance of Mary, and "now her three sons and daughters, and sons' wives, are all in a hopeful way to the knowledge of truth, and liberty of the sons of God, with several other tender people at this time, in that small island." Story was later able to report that "the Lord did visit them, and gathered many there unto himself, and they became a large and living meeting in him."

Within sixty years of Story's visit, two of the island's three magistrates were Quakers, and most of the rest of the population were of the same persuasion. This religious solidarity had a profound impact on the island's primary commercial enterprise. Nantucket's genius in the business of whaling lay in the collective pursuit of a single engrossing occupation by its inhabitants, most of whom were connected by birth and an intimacy that stretched back over many generations, and now by religion. The business was conducted, Obed Macy wrote, as if by one family.

J. Hector St. John de Crèvecoeur, a French soldier who became a British subject, traveled through the colonies during the eighteenth century as a surveyor and salesman of cartographic instruments, and published a series of "letters" describing what he saw. He visited Nantucket just before the Revolution and was impressed by the degree to which the overarching ethic of Quakerism, with its "obedience to the laws . . . sobriety, meekness, neatness, love of order," and, most of all, its "fondness and appetite for commerce" affected the development of the people in tandem with their business on Nantucket:

At schools they learn to read and write a good hand, until they are twelve years old; they are then in general put apprentices to the cooper's trade, which is the second essential branch of business followed here; at fourteen they are sent to sea, where in their leisure hours their companions teach them the art of navigation, which they have an opportunity of practising on the spot. They learn the great and useful art of working a ship in all the different situations which the sea and wind so often require, and surely there cannot be a better or more useful school of that kind in the world. They then go gradually through every station of rowers, steersmen, and harpooners; thus they learn to attack, to pursue, to overtake, to cut, to dress their huge game; and after having performed several such voyages and perfected themselves in this business, they are fit either for the counting-house or the chase.

He also remarked a peculiar distraction that relieved the rigidly austere lifestyle of the island's Quakers:

A singular custom prevails here among the women, at which I was greatly surprised. . . . They have adopted these many years the Asiatic custom of taking a dose of opium every morning, and so deeply rooted is it that they would be at a loss how to live without this indulgence; they would rather be deprived of any necessary than forego their favorite luxury. This is much more prevailing among the women than the men, few of the latter having caught the contagion, though the sheriff, whom I may call the first person in the island, who is an eminent physician beside and whom I had the pleasure of being well acquainted with, has for many years submitted to this custom. He takes three grains of it every day after breakfast, without the effects of which, he often told me, he was not able to transact any business.[1]

1. This depiction of an island of dope fiends has been hotly contested on Nantucket, with claims that St. John de Crèvecoeur was a fabulist writing fiction, or that his sources were corrupt: "A lie. Without a shadow of foundation," wrote one island elder. Yet Nantucket historian and resident Nathaniel Philbrick, writing about Crèvecoeur in *The New England Quarterly*, notes: "The tendency of Nantucketers to close ranks against off-island . . . criticism is legendary. . . . And, more to the point, during recent sewer work in downtown Nantucket, many small glass opium bottles, part of the debris buried after the Great Fire of 1846, were unearthed. Although these remains are from a different era, they make one suspect that Crèvecoeur may not have been so misguided after all. Instead, he may well have probed more deeply into the island's secret self than most local residents considered acceptable." Opium was a readily available tonic in a town with efficient shipping connections to Europe, and its use was widespread in New Bedford a century later (see chapter 18).

. . .

THE FACT THAT THIS Quaker whaling cult floated on a sandy cloister out at sea undoubtedly helped establish, by the mid–eighteenth century, Nantucket's preeminence in the whaling business. But this handily situated platform was still small and required yet another sea voyage to transport its whale oil to any market. There were those who could already see the limits of such a location.

Such a man was Joseph Rotch. His father, William Rotch, born in Salisbury, England, in 1670, came to America around 1700 and became a prominent citizen in Provincetown. Joseph was born in 1704, and lived first in Braintree, then Falmouth. At some point he moved to Nantucket, where he married Love Macy, a descendant of Thomas Macy, and became a successful whaling merchant. Rotch was a Quaker, his sons were born on the island, and the Rotches became one of Nantucket's leading families. Yet perhaps because of a background more cosmopolitan than most of his neighbors', Joseph Rotch became restless on Nantucket. At the relatively advanced age of sixty-one, rich and secure by every measure of his time, he left Nantucket in 1765. Where he went indicates the scope of his ambition, and his appetite for renewal.

Seven

"Well Cut Up"

Forty ships pushed through the scree of heaving ice in July 1871, trying to outmaneuver each other up the narrow, shifting, seasonal waterway now opening between the pack ice and the Alaskan shore. At no point along its entire length from the Bering Strait to Point Barrow was this channel wider than the broadest reaches of Long Island Sound.

It resembled the end stage of a gold rush: too many miners jammed elbow to elbow, scrabbling over the remaining crumbs of a once fabulously rich vein. Yet still they came on, ignoring every sign of the vein's exhaustion, for there was nowhere else to go, and they knew nothing but mining.

This was the last profitable whaling ground on earth. The whalers had virtually exhausted the whale stocks of the Atlantic, Pacific, Indian, eastern Arctic, and Southern oceans. It had taken less than a hundred years.

* * *

IN AUGUST 1788, the British whaling ship *Emelia* sailed from London for what was then the most exploited known whaling ground in the world: the relatively shallow banks off the coast of Brazil. The tropical waters teeming with organic effluent from the Amazon and other rivers made a rich soup of nutrients and sea life, an ecosystem that drew great numbers of whales. This fabulous offshore repository of wealth had become known to seamen as "the Brazils" or simply "the banks." But the *Emelia*'s whalemen found few whales there, and those that remained had become wary of ships and men.

Already by the late eighteenth century, whale populations everywhere in the Atlantic had noticeably decreased. Even after the Revolution had destroyed or bottled up in port most American whaleships, those that still cruised the Brazil banks, mostly British ships, noticed a change.

The *Emelia* was owned by the premier English whaling merchants of the day, Samuel Enderby & Sons, who had long been engaged in business with merchants in Nantucket and had a strong connection with the island. A number of the sailors on British ships at the time were Nantucketers, the acknowledged world experts on whaling. Their island home had remained neutral throughout the Revolution, and Nantucket's whalemen found ready employment in the British fishery after the war. The *Emelia*'s captain, James Shields, and first mate, Archaelus Hammond, were both Nantucketers. Along the docks and in seamen's taverns in London before the voyage, they had met the captains of British merchant vessels sailing home across the South Pacific from China, and many of these had spoken of the great numbers of sperm whales they had seen in that ocean. So, late in 1788, off the disappointing coast of Brazil, Hammond—so the story goes—

persuaded Shields to sail the ship south and around Cape Horn into the Pacific.

This was no small decision aboard a ship fitted out to cruise the tropics. Cape Horn was already well known as a graveyard of ships and sailors, a place of consistently ferocious weather and abnormally large seas that could overwhelm the best-managed, best-equipped vessels. There was another route into the Pacific some miles north of Cape Horn, through the strait discovered by Magellan more than 250 years earlier, but few ships carried charts for the strait—or the waters around the Horn, for that matter. The only recommended tactic for getting from the Atlantic to the Pacific—if a ship wasn't going to sail east around the bottom of Africa and across most of the world—was to sail south, well offshore, before turning west somewhere below South America (there was no more precise instruction) and hope for the best.

The *Emelia* successfully rounded the Horn early in 1789—summer in the Southern Hemisphere—and sailed into an edenic new world where large ships were still relatively unknown and the whales cruising the vast ocean had never been hunted and knew nothing of men. In March, off the coast of Chile, sperm whales were sighted and boats were lowered to give chase. Mate Hammond's reached the pod first, and he became the first man (that is, of the history-writing American and European cultures) to harpoon a whale in the Pacific. The *Emelia* quickly filled all its barrels, turned south, and once again rounded Cape Horn. Heading north, in the middle of the Atlantic, she met the Nantucket ship *Hope*, owned by William Rotch. As the two ships passed within a few hundred feet of each other, Captain Thaddeus Swain aboard the *Hope* heard Shields on the *Emelia* shouting the information that he had come from "round Cape Horn with 150 tons sperm oil." Rotch, who in the aftermath of the Revolution was based temporarily in Dunkirk, France, and running a small fleet of his whaleships out of that port to supply the European market, soon sent four more of his ships to the Pacific by way of Cape Horn. Word spread fast. The first whaleships to head for the Pacific from American ports were the *Beaver*, from Nantucket, and the *Rebecca*, from New Bedford, both sailing in 1791. Both returned to port after seventeen months with their holds filled with sperm oil.

The so-called Golden Age of American whaling refers to the years between the 1820s and the 1850s, when the business, centered increasingly in New Bedford, reached its peak, but this boom truly dates from around 1790, for it was in fact powered by the discovery of the Pacific whaling grounds.

Yet such unrelenting success sowed the seeds of ruin. Sixty years after the *Emelia*'s discovery, well before the peak of the Golden Age, whaling captains were already looking back on what by then appeared to be the good old days. In 1853, a whaleship captain (he chose to write anonymously but was probably either Asa Tobey, captain of the *Lagoda*, or Charles Bonney of the *Metacom*, both ships and men from New Bedford) published a series of letters in the *Whalemen's Shipping List and Merchants' Transcript* charting the inevitable effect of the whalers' efficiency wherever they voyaged:

In the commencement of right whaling the Brazil Banks was the only place of note to which ships were sent. Then came Tristan, East Cape, Falkland Islands, and Patagonia. These places encompassed the entire South Atlantic. Full cargoes were sometimes obtained in an incredibly short space of time—whales were seen in great numbers . . . where they had been gambolling unmolested for hundreds of years. The harpoon and lance soon made awful havoc with many of them, and scattered the remainder over the ocean, and many I believe retreated further south—a few remain, as wild [i.e., wary] as the hunted deer. Can anyone believe that there will ever again exist the same numbers of whales? or that they multiply as fast as they are destroyed? . . .

After the Southern Ocean whales were well cut up, the ships penetrated the Indian and South Pacific Oceans, St. Pauls, Crozets, Desolation, New Holland, New Zealand, and Chili. I believe it is not more than twenty years since whaling began in either of these localities—but where now are the whales, at first found in great numbers? I think most whalemen will join in deciding that the better half have been killed, and cut up in horse pieces years ago. A part of the remainder have fled further south. A few yet remain, and most of them know a whale boat by sight or by sound. . . .

Then came great stories of large whales in large numbers in the North Pacific. The first voyages by their success created great excitement—the fleet there increased and was fitted out with extra care and skill, and in a few years our ships swept entirely across the broad Pacific, and along the Kamschatka shores. They moved round Japan, and into that sea and there whales were found more numerous than ever. The leviathans were driven from the bosom of that sea, their few scattered remnants running in terror whenever their enemy is near.

The pioneering captains of these whaleships, like the writer above, were master mariners and navigators, among the canniest and most skillful in human history. They came to know the sea and read the oceans with instincts that bordered on the extrasensory. Good navigators in any age (but especially before the widespread use of electronic navigation devices caused these senses to atrophy) necessarily acquired this skill: something inside them that grew to fill the gap between what was demonstrably known and what they desperately needed to know in crucial moments. Thus they became aware of the great ocean currents, discrete rivers running through the wider seas—the Gulf Stream, the Benguela off Africa, the Brazil and the Falkland, the Humboldt off Chile, the Kurio Shio and the Oya Shio off Japan, the Alaska, the Aleutian, the Kamchatka. They felt—in the spray on their faces and in the air around them—the temperature gradients where the edges of these currents, some cold, some warm, met the surrounding ocean; they saw the water change colors, and they observed closely the life in the water and the air that migrated along these highways. But all this they could only know by sailing blindly ahead, in many places without charts—often through dense fogs in high latitudes. Most whaling grounds were discovered by chance married to a seaman's intuition. As they were located, exploited, and depleted in sequence across the Pacific, ships sailed deeper into unknown and uncharted waters, looking for rich new pastures, hoping to stumble upon an epoch-making discovery like the *Emelia*'s.

One of the most curious, observant, independent-minded, and strong-willed of these pioneering whaling captains was Thomas Welcome Roys. Born on a farm in upstate New York, Roys shipped aboard a Sag Harbor whaler at age seventeen in 1833, and was a captain by the time he was twenty-five. Cruising off the Kamchatka peninsula of Russia in the North Pacific in the early 1840s, he noticed, and made careful note of, steady streams of migrating whales swimming to the north. In 1845, on his second voyage as a captain, the twenty-nine-year-old Roys was injured by a right whale off Kamchatka. The whale's thrashing tail destroyed the boat he was standing in and dumped him into the sea, breaking two of his ribs. After this accident, his ship, the *Josephine*, of Sag Harbor, New York, sailed to the Russian coastal town of Petropavlosk, where Roys remained to recuperate from his injury while his ship continued whaling with its first mate in command.

While he was ashore, Roys spoke with a Russian naval officer who had cruised north through the Bering Strait into the Arctic and seen unusual-looking whales there. Roys supposed these must be similar to the Greenland right whales that whalers had hunted in the high latitudes of the North Atlantic. No American or European whaleship had yet sailed north of the Bering Strait, and Roys began to think of the possibilities of a voyage there. He was so intrigued that before he left Petropavlosk, he purchased a hundred dollars' worth of Russian charts covering the waters north of the strait. Later, while still cruising in the *Josephine* on the right whale grounds off Kamchatka, Roys met and gammed with Captain Thomas Sodring of the Danish whaleship *Neptun*. Sodring told him of three strange-looking whales he had taken near Petropavlosk. He, too, had supposed at first they were right whales, until his crew began to cut them up: their blubber—evolved for colder arctic seas—proved to be extraordinarily thick, rendering enormous quantities of oil, and there was more "bone"—baleen—in their mouths than Sodring had ever seen in another whale.

After the *Josephine* returned to Sag Harbor, Roys was given command of another ship, the *Superior*. Having spent a significant sum on his northern charts, it's likely that he shared his thoughts about whaling in the Arctic with the *Superior*'s owners, Joseph Grinnell (of New Bedford) and Robert Minturn, of the whaling firm Grinnell, Minturn & Co. They considered arctic whaling too risky, and instructed him to sail not north but to the distant south, to cruise the remote but well-known wastes around Crozet and Desolation islands in the Southern Ocean, south of the Indian Ocean, almost halfway between South Africa and Antarctica. When he got there, Roys found these once plentiful grounds, where he had successfully hunted whales before, nearly fished out. He then sailed east (the only possibility for a whaleship east of Africa in the Southern Ocean, with its frequent and fast-moving westerly gales) until he arrived in Hobart, Tasmania. Begun as a penal colony in 1804, Hobart had developed into a major whaling port servicing the South Pacific whaling fleets by the time Roys arrived there early in 1848. It was probably in Hobart where a letter reached him with the news that his wife had died only a month after he had sailed from Sag Harbor the year before, shortly after the birth of their only son. This may have made him reckless, for he sent a letter to Grinnell and Minturn from Hobart telling them that he was sailing for the Bering Strait and seas north of there.

Months later, in late July, eight thousand miles north of Tasmania, at the extreme top of the Pacific, the *Superior* was nosing past the Dio-mede Islands into the Bering Strait. Aboard his ship, Roys had kept his intentions entirely to himself. His crew and officers had no idea he had sailed without permission, where he had brought them, or how far he was intending to go. They certainly knew they were in the far north— from the weather and glimpses of the coast; probably somewhere "on Kamchatka [grounds]," they supposed—but when they saw seven na-tive *umiak* canoes filled with more than 250 Eskimos paddling toward them from the low shore, they lost their composure. Eskimos in walrus-skin boats were not found at sea off the Kamchatka peninsula. At that moment, the *Superior* was becalmed, unable to move, unable to avoid the oncoming native flotilla, and Roys's men were terrified—he re-corded that his first mate broke down in tears. Roys himself didn't know if the natives, in such large numbers, outnumbering his crew by many times, had friendly or hostile intentions. Apart from harpoons, the only weapon aboard the *Superior* was "one Blunt & Sims revolver that would not go unless you threw it." But before the Eskimos got close enough for that, a breeze came across the water from the southwest. The men clapped on sail and the ship pulled slowly away—still to the north, and soon into an icy fog. Roys's crew remained so frightened that many of them "never expected to see home again."

When the fog cleared away a day later, whales were breaching the surface of the sea around the *Superior* in all directions, in numbers none of them had ever seen before. They appeared huge; the mates thought they were humpbacks, but Roys now believed he had found something new to commercial whaling: the polar whale the Russian naval officer and Captain Sodring had spoken of. The boats were lowered, although Roys's spooked whalemen "were not inclined to meddle with 'the new fangled monster' as they called him." Yet the will of the captain was rarely opposed, especially one as forceful as Roys. And despite their fears, the men were as keenly motivated as their captain: big fat whales meant money for all. The men did as they were told, got into the boats, and pulled off into the long arctic twilight.

It was midnight but still light when the boatsteerer in Roys's boat threw his first harpoon. It stuck fast and the whale sounded immediately. It swam along the bottom (only 25 fathoms, or 150 feet, deep here in the Bering Strait), towing Roys and his men in their boat for fifty minutes until Roys "began to think that I was fast to something that breathed water instead of air and might remain down a week if he liked." The mates were now convinced, by its size and lung capacity, that it was a humpback. Then the whale rose to the surface and was quickly and easily lanced and killed. Only when the whalemen began to "cut in" the whale alongside the ship were they finally persuaded they had caught something quite unusual. The baleen—the long, curved, keratinous fronds that hang in the whale's mouth like a dense curtain to filter out the plankton and shrimp from great mouthfuls of seawater— was twelve feet long, almost twice the size of right whale baleen; and the immensely thick blubber evolved for such cold seas produced

120 barrels (3,780 gallons) of oil, far more than the yield of most other whales.

Roys sailed the *Superior* and its unwilling crew another 250 miles north into the Arctic Ocean. They caught whales all the way, yet despite the sudden astonishing success of the voyage, in which every man would share, Roys's officers and crew remained spooked, "living in hourly expectation of some unforeseen calamity and almost beside themselves with fear," he remembered later. "I actually believe if they had any hope that open mutiny would have succeeded they would have tried it to get away from this sea."

Over the next month, Roys and his men caught eleven whales north of the Bering Strait, yielding 1,600 barrels of oil—several years' haul on a normal voyage—stopping only when the ship was full and could take no more. On August 27, the *Superior* turned south and sailed for Hawaii.

FROM HIS CONVERSATIONS with Russians in Petropavlosk, Roys would have known the likely intentions of the seven boatloads of Eskimos: they were hoping to trade. The exchange of iron, tobacco, and knives for the natives' seal, fox, and sea otter furs was already a well-established commerce. But the fears of his crew were not misplaced, and the hackles on the back of Roys's own neck would also have told him that the Eskimos were opportunistically prepared for any possibility, including taking over the whaleship by force—which, with his broken pistol and cowering crew, would have been a pushover if the ship hadn't conveniently sailed away.

The *Superior* was probably the first whaleship any of the Eskimos had seen, although it would have looked no different to them from the other square-rigged sailing ships whose appearance in arctic and subarctic waters was, just then, beginning to be not uncommon. Contact between Russian and European explorers, traders, and the native peoples of the Bering and Chukchi sea coasts was already more than a century old. Roys would have learned in Petropavlosk and elsewhere of Russia's longtime interest in the Arctic, begun in 1648, when a band of Cossacks, traders, and hunters looking for new plunder sailed out of the Kolyma River into the Arctic Ocean. Eighty years later, Czar Peter the Great appointed a Danish captain serving in the Russian navy, Vitus Bering, to lead an expedition from Kamchatka east to explore the North American coast. In 1728, Bering's two ships sailed north up the Siberian shore, through the strait that now bears his name, and then back again as far as Okhotsk. Many Russian expeditions followed, all bent on securing trade, fur, mining rights, and sovereignty on the coast of America, only fifty-nine miles from the easternmost tip of Asian Russia.

Roys would certainly have known of Captain James Cook's exploration of the Arctic seventy years earlier—Cook's surveys were the basis for many of the charts carried by American and British navigators throughout the Pacific. Cook was already famous, promoted to post-captain and a Fellow of the Royal Geographic Society, when he left England for the last time, on his third voyage, in 1776. Two years later, his ships *Resolution* and *Discovery* passed through Bering Strait and pushed as far north as 70' 41" N, the latitude of Wainwright Inlet, less than a hundred miles from Point Barrow, before being stopped by a "moveable mass of . . . heavy loose ice."

THE NEWS OF ROYS'S VOYAGE, radiating outward from Hawaii around the globe through the press, but most powerfully and quickly by word of mouth, was as electric and galvanizing to the whale fishery as the

Emelia's first voyage around Cape Horn. Roy's discovery of the western arctic grounds was the most important in the whole history of whaling. His men's fearful reaction to what they saw there was entirely reasonable: the Arctic was, by all seaman-like criteria, no place for an unwieldy wooden ship. Yet soon fleets would flock there in a feeding frenzy. Over the next fifty years, more than 2,700 whaling voyages were made to the icy wastes north of the Bering Strait. More than 150 whaleships were lost there. More than 20,000 bowhead whales, as Roys's big whale with the bow-shaped mouth full of baleen came to be called, were killed, hunted to near extinction.

In 1853, only five years after Roys's voyage, the anonymous whaling captain publishing his letters in the *Whalemen's Shipping List and Merchants' Transcript*, described what had happened since:

Then the great combined fleet moved northward towards the pole, and there the ships of almost all the whaling ports in the world are and have been for several seasons lending their united efforts to the destruction of the whale—capturing even the young. These polar whales were most easily captured, at first, but . . . his nature [has] been entirely changed by constant and untiring pursuit. He is no longer the slow and sluggish beast we at first found him. Particularly at the latter part of the season, they are very shy. I have often noticed, after one or two whales were struck in the morning, after the fog cleared, that the entire body of whales would be stirred up, so that it would be almost impossible to strike [another] one during the whole day. Within a space of from ten to twelve miles there would be from fifteen to thirty ships, all doing their best, but the greatest number were to be seen without any smoke [i.e., no tryworks burning, hence no whales caught]. On the 4th of September I counted fifty-eight ships, and only twelve of them were boiling. . . . I know that the whales have diminished since I was here two years ago, and that they are more difficult to strike. How can it be otherwise? Look at the immense fleet, stretching from Cape Thaddeus to the Straits! By day and by night the whale is chased and harassed—the fleet perpetually driving them, until they reach the highest navigable latitudes of the Arctic. The only rest they have is when the fogs are thick, and the wind high. There could not have been less than three thousand polar whales killed last season, yet the average of oil [for each ship in the fleet] is only about half as great as it was two years ago.

It is impossible now to read such a lamentation of the decline of nature in any but ecological terms. But the writer above, and the audience he was addressing, never thought about ecology. It would be a century before the work of Rachel Carson and others tipped the public consciousness into that direction. The shipmaster's last line reveals the true focus of his concern: "[These facts show that] it will not long be profitable to send ships to the Arctic."

Eight

The Newer Bedford

Dartmouth was still a quiet backwater of independent farmers, fishermen, and a few carpenters and blacksmiths, with no unifying central industry, when Joseph Rotch left Nantucket in 1765 with the intention of establishing a whaling port somewhere on the mainland. He had centered his search along the coast of Buzzards Bay, conveniently close to both Nantucket and Boston. The Acushnet River, running into the bay's north shore from far inland, was wide and deep enough to accommodate a squadron of large ships, but arms of land at the river's mouth formed a sheltered, landlocked harbor. There were long, straight stretches of river shoreline on which to build wharves and shipping facilities. Woods offering fine lengths of timber—completely absent in Nantucket—with which to build ships, houses, a port, and all its trimmings, lay in all directions.

Some whaling had been carried on here, though when Rotch arrived it was almost a hundred years behind Nantucket in its development.

Eighty whaleships sailed from Nantucket in 1756, while "several" set out from Dartmouth at about the same time. A rough map from this period shows only one structure on the western shore of the Acushnet, the site of present-day New Bedford. This was the "try house" belonging to one Joseph Russell, who was using the place as a base from which to send out whaleships, and to process their cargoes when these vessels returned home laden with hogsheads of blubber. His ancestor, John Russell, son of settler Ralph, had been the township's first representative at the General Court at Plymouth after Dartmouth's incorporation in 1664. Joseph Russell—the third of that name—had acquired a large parcel of land along the Acushnet's western bank. In 1760, he sold some of this land to John Loudon, a boat-caulker, who intended to set up his own boatyard; the next year, Benjamin Taber bought a site and erected a shed for boatbuilding and block-making; and house carpenter John Allen bought land nearby and built a house. In 1762, Elnathan Sampson, a blacksmith from Wareham, bought a site south of John Loudon's place.

Rotch first tried to buy land on the east bank of the Acushnet—the town of Fairhaven today—but here, too, lay an existing "try house and oyl shed" whose owner was unwilling to sell. Unable to secure the shore rights he wanted there, Rotch paddled across the river and bought up a large parcel from Joseph Russell. He soon employed the skills of his neighbors, and the names Loudon, Taber, Allen, Sampson, Russell, and Rotch became hallmarks in the whaling business that grew here.

Rotch's timing was pure kismet. He brought money and boldness to Dartmouth, but history made an alchemy with these. Whale products as illuminants and lubricants were relatively new and scarce at the beginning of the eighteenth century. Lighting and lubrication were still supplied by products that had served adequately for millennia. Sponge-like mosses soaked in animal fat placed in shells or stones were being used as lamps at least seventy thousand years ago. Palm, olive, and fish oils were used in lamps in China and Egypt long before Homeric times (though not generally in the Middle East or in Greece: torches are specified throughout the *Iliad* and the *Odyssey*). Tallow was the mother of all greases. Tubs of it were at hand throughout history, to swab every moving mechanism, from chariot wheels to guillotines. Easily made from the chopped-up, boiled-down, waxy white protective suet fat packed around the kidneys and loins of cattle, sheep, and horses, tallow had long been abundant. It worked well. It made soaps and candles. There was no need for anything else until, in the eighteenth century, everything changed—first, and most profoundly, in Britain.

By the mid–eighteenth century, Britain's colonies in Virginia and New England, as well as in India, the West Indies, and Australasia, were beginning to produce great quantities of raw material such as cotton, coffee, tea, sugar, spices, lumber, fur, and slaves. In return, the colonists and their growing towns and cities, and, by extension through trade, the colonies' natives—Indians, with their desire for metal and cloth—became an insatiable market for British and European manufactured goods. At home, Britain was discovering huge deposits of coal and iron ore beneath its ancient landscape. Throughout the eighteenth century, there was a merging of these and many other things. In 1709, the process that produced pig iron by smelting iron ore with coke and limestone in a blast furnace was perfected. Pig iron was the raw material for the great clanking wheels, the blocks, the levers, the pistons, and all the wheezing, racing machinery that was about to convert Britain from an agricultural to an industrial economy. The inventions of the fly shuttle, the spinning jenny, and the power loom transformed the discrete, homely, truly cottage industries of spinning and weaving into William Blake's dark satanic mills and factories that sprang up like brick toadstools all over England's pewter-gray, mineral-rich Midlands.

Threshing machines made large numbers of farmworkers redundant; parliamentary acts governing land enclosure forced people off the land and into growing cities, looking for work. They lived in wretched urban warrens that shocked contemporary observers who were bold enough to look through the doorways, and they bred like rabbits. Britain's population doubled in the eighteenth century. Light was needed in every hovel and home, shop and factory, and in the lamps of miners; and the gears and machinery of the Industrial Revolution would require millions of barrels of lubrication.

A lamp using a wick burning whale oil was found to be far superior to a flickering, smoky, tallow candle. Sperm oil proved even better, a brilliant, clear, nonsmoking illuminant. Lighthouses, once lit by braziers holding wood and coal fires, sprouted up everywhere once the technique of interlocking granite stones allowed them to be built on rocky outcrops at sea, and in the eighteenth century they were increasingly lit by sperm oil.

The new, faster-moving machines exposed the weakness of tallow: it lost its chemical stability when subjected to the heat and friction of high speeds. As machinery improved, better lubricants were sought and tried. The grease made from whale oil degraded at a much slower rate. Sperm oil, especially, retained its consistency and properties under conditions of extreme friction and temperature, and became highly valued as a lubricant of faster-running and increasingly fine and sophisticated machinery, from watches and clocks to high-speed textile machinery.

The impact of this scientific advance on the whale fishery in America was swift and far-reaching. Thomas Hutchinson, speaker of the Massachusetts House of Representatives in 1749, later (1771–1774) royal governor of the colony, wrote in his history of Massachusetts, first published in 1765: "The increase of the consumption of oil by lamps as well as by divers manufactures in Europe has been no small encouragement to our whale-fishery. The flourishing state of the island of Nantucket must be attributed to it. The . . . whale fishery, being the principal source of our returns to Great Britain, [is] therefore worthy not only of provincial but national attention."

The mid–eighteenth century was a period of rising fortunes in America, and spermaceti candles—brilliant, smokeless, but expensive— quickly became the preferred illuminant for those who could afford them. George Washington, who burned perhaps a dozen spermaceti candles a night at Mount Vernon, figured the cost to him at about £100 per year, a sizable lighting bill for those days. In 1761, the Reverend Edward Holyoke, president of Harvard, who appears to have been thrift-minded, computed that even if he burned the cheapest tallow candles, it was costing him £40 a year to light his house.

Lighting quickly became big business. The production of spermaceti candles became such a coveted industry that it gave rise to the first attempts at monopoly and price-fixing in America, by a cabal of merchants who sought to break Nantucket's control over the whaling industry. The manufacture of spermaceti candles, from the waxy "head-matter" found in the headcase of the sperm whale, was at first an industrial secret, pioneered by Benjamin Crabb, of Rehoboth, Rhode Island. In 1749, Crabb petitioned the Massachusetts General Court for, and was granted, the sole right to manufacture candles of "Sperma Caeti Oyle" in the colony. He didn't take up his grant in Massachusetts, however, but moved to Rhode Island, where he set up a candle-making operation for a Providence merchant, Obadiah Brown. Though Crabb and Brown tried to keep secret the details of their process, by 1760 there were perhaps a dozen spermaceti candle-making businesses in New England. Most of these were in Rhode Island. In 1761, in order to avoid cutthroat competition among themselves, and to discourage others, Brown and a group of eight other merchant firms formed the

United Company of Spermaceti Candlers. This "Spermaceti Trust," as it has been called, attempted to control the purchase (mostly from Nantucket) and distribution (among themselves, or for sale to London or Boston) of headmatter, and establish a minimum price for the sale of all spermaceti candles.

Three of the nine firms party to this agreement, and six of the twenty-six individuals representing them, were Jews who had come to America seeking, like the Puritans, freedom from religious persecution. They not only had found that freedom, but also had become among America's wealthiest and most successful merchants. The great leveler of the transatlantic passage, and the emphasis in America on what a man was capable of doing, rather than who he might claim to be, meant that rank in the colonies was determined almost solely by achievement rather than by any other baggage or perception of worth. The rising merchant class was, from the beginning, the aristocracy in America, and men like Aaron and Moses Lopez of Newport, Rhode Island, became its princes.

Brothers José and Duarte Lopez, ethnic Jews who maintained an outward devotion to Catholicism, had grown up in Portugal. As in many other times and places, assimilation was no protection. One of these "New Christians," as Jews who had converted to Catholicism during and after the Inquisition were called, the playwright António José da Silva, known as "O Judeo"—the Jew—was garroted and burned in public in Lisbon on October 19, 1739, because of his ethnic origin. By that time, José Lopez had already fled, first to England, then to America. Duarte joined him there in 1752, at the age of twenty-one, bringing with him from Portugal his wife and daughter. In America both men openly embraced Judaism for the first time in their lives, underwent circumcision, and formally adopted the names Moses (José) and Aaron (Duarte).

Though Moses first traveled to New York, he soon relocated in Newport. That town, famously blessed with an excellent natural harbor, had become one of colonial America's major commercial seaports by 1750, its waterfront lined with wharves and warehouses. Newport was home to a large group of "merchant grandees" and was an important market for slaves newly arrived from Guinea and other African coasts. Aaron Lopez joined his brother there.

Their timing was propitious. England's desire to see settlers in America encouraged even Jewish immigrants. In 1740, Parliament passed an act granting the right of naturalization to every foreign-born Protestant or Jew who resided in its American colonies for at least seven years. Jews were even exempted from the requirements of receiving Anglican Communion, and from taking an oath of allegiance "upon the true faith of a Christian." (The needs were not the same at home in England: when a similar—domestic—act was passed in 1753, granting naturalization to Jews residing there, so great was the public outcry that the "Jew Bill" was quickly repealed.) But the colonies were not without bigotry, particularly aimed at Jews. Moses Lopez was naturalized in New York in 1741, but when Aaron applied for naturalization in Rhode Island twenty years later (the same year he formed the Spermaceti Trust), he was refused. Rhode Island's legislators informed him that the intention of the parliamentary naturalization act had been to increase the number of inhabitants in the colonies, now deemed sufficient in number, and to propagate the Christian views with which the colony had been settled. Aaron Lopez's friend Ezra Stiles, later the president of Yale, commented at the time: "Providence seems to make everything to work for mortification to the Jews, and to prevent their incorporating into any nation; that thus they . . . continue a distinct people." A year later, after becoming temporarily resident in Swansea, Massachusetts, Aaron was naturalized in Massachusetts as a British subject.

Thirty years old in 1761, Aaron Lopez was a leading figure in the Spermaceti Trust, and one of America's most successful businessmen. His mercantile interests ranged far beyond candle-making. He was brokering and shipping pewter, indigo, sugar, tea, coffee, molasses, rum, chocolate, and soap. Many of these items he shipped to his premier "headmatter" suppliers in Nantucket, Joseph Rotch and his son, William, who sold these in their stores there. He also bought, imported, and traded slaves, and owned ships that carried them to America from Africa. Aaron Lopez's residence and business establishments on Newport's Thames Street were impressive. By the 1770s, he owned at least twenty sailing vessels, and had survived vicissitudes of business that had reduced many of his former partners. But the Spermaceti Trust did not last for more than a few years and was unable to break the de facto monopoly that Nantucket then enjoyed over all whaling-related enterprises. This was due as much to the intractable nature and determination of the Nantucket Quakers as to any other advantage they enjoyed—all of which stemmed in large part from that nature and determination. Henry Lloyd, one of Aaron Lopez's trust partners in Boston, advised him:

> I must caution you against being too nice [or] critical with the Nantucket men, for I can assure you that nothing can be done with them. . . . The only way is to make the best terms you can with them, whenever you have occasion to purchase; but tis in vain to attempt to tye them down to any measures they don't like.

The Nantucketers didn't like supremacy in another group. In 1770, William Rotch opened Nantucket's first spermaceti candle-making manufactory, at the head of Straight Wharf in the town harbor, and Rhode Island's momentary lock on the candle business was over. But in the Lopez brothers and their Jewish partners in the Spermaceti Trust—Jacob Rodriguez Rivera and the Hart brothers (Naphtali, Samuel, Abram, and Isaac)—the Quaker Rotches had discovered formidable rivals and dependable trading partners. They felt comfortable dealing with a clannish group held together by shared religious convictions and habits. They understood the desire for mercantile protectionism as had perhaps no other group since the Hanseatic League monopolized trade in northern Europe between the thirteenth and seventeenth centuries. In two centuries of Quaker dominance in the American whale fishery, the Jews of Newport were the only rivals the Quakers ever recognized as true peers.

Had he lived long enough, Aaron Lopez might have figured larger in the growth of the whaling industry, possibly in New Bedford after Joseph Rotch made his move there in 1765, or in the development of Newport—already a thriving international seaport when New Bedford was an isolated backwater—into a serious competitor. While Lopez and his family were visiting Providence in May 1782, the horse drawing him in a sulky (a light, two-wheeled carriage) veered too deeply into a pond, and the sulky began to sink. Lopez, aged fifty-one, who had never learned to swim, drowned in full view of his wife and children, who sat in another carriage on the nearby shore.

FOR ABOUT A CENTURY, from the 1750s to the 1850s, American whaling perfectly matched and complemented a rapidly changing world. The Industrial Revolution was greased by whale oil. It in turn drove the productivity and evolution of the whale fishery to its greatest heights. Joseph Rotch's relocation to Dartmouth came in tandem with this exponentially growing market for whale oil across the Atlantic—where most of the oil produced in America was then shipped.

Only four whaling vessels—owned by Joseph Russell, his brother Caleb, and a William Tallman—sailed to and from the try houses and "oyl" sheds on the Acushnet in 1765, the year Rotch arrived. Within ten years there were eighty ships, averaging eighty-one tons, operating out of Dartmouth, mostly from the west (New Bedford) bank of the Acushnet, and nearly all of them had been built there. Nantucket was still the industry leader, with 145 whaleships sailing from its harbor in 1775, but Dartmouth had become America's second-largest whaling port and was growing at a rate never seen in Nantucket. Boston, for all its merchants, money, ties to London, and long-established infrastructure, was a distant third—all these many Bostonian concerns were the discrete businesses of many, rather than, as in New Bedford and Nantucket, the single preoccupation of an entire population.

Most of the oil that landed in New England was shipped on to London. The early Nantucket whalers had sold their oil to Boston merchants, who simply transferred the barrels to their own ships and sailed them to England, at great profit. But, as with candle-making, the Nantucketers saw no need to hand the raw materials of a profitable business to someone else. In 1745, a Nantucket ship was sent to London in an attempt to bypass the Boston middlemen. The trip was doubly successful, for after the sale was made, the ship returned laden with British iron, hardware, hemp rope, sailcloth, and various other goods needed at home. American whaling merchants quickly built and began using their own "merchantmen" to take cargoes directly from the wharves in Nantucket and Dartmouth to London's dockyards, and to return, often by way of the West Indies, carrying sugar and molasses. Joseph Rotch's first large ship built on the shore of the future New Bedford was not a whaler but a merchantman, intended for this transatlantic trade. Her keel was laid under a grove of buttonwood trees beside the Acushnet, and he christened her *Dartmouth*.

This secondary trade further spurred the growth along Dartmouth's waterfront, which proceeded at a pace not seen before on American shores. Wharves, sheds, houses, and roads were quickly built along the Acushnet's west bank. Workmen from all over Massachusetts and their families arrived and settled. The area boomed with the raw ugliness of a gold-rush town. Local sawmills processed immense quantities of timber into lumber for ships and the unpainted houses that appeared up and down the river's west bank. The hill rising inland from the former lonely Russell tryworks—that now rises across the river from the Moby Dick Marina in Fairhaven, carrying traffic along I-195 between Cape Cod and Providence—and the woods on the Russell homestead were clear-cut, left stump-pocked, muddy, and scarred as tree trunks were dragged down to the river by teams of oxen. The noises of many businesses—the clanging of blacksmiths, the kerf-biting roar and scream of sawmills, the squeal of coach and wagon wheels, the jangle of harnesses, the pounding of mallets, and the thunk of adzes in the boatyards—carried up and down the river and rose into the nearby hills. Smoke hung everywhere in the air, except during the strong cold northwesterlies. A dark, sooty pall—an oily smog fed by chimneys, forges, shipyards, cooperages, sawmills, and brush fires burning in the surrounding fields—marked the town from far down Buzzards Bay. And as whaleships returned to the wharves every few days, their hogsheads of putrid cargo kept the fires burning nonstop in the riverside tryworks. Emissions of greasy particulate settled over the town like a glaze and gave it the permanent odor of burnt flesh and fat.

Rotch soon wanted to establish a name for the site of all this industry across the river from the original Dartmouth settlement. In deference to his friend Joseph Russell, whose name suggested a possible kinship with the English Duke of Bedford, whose family name was also Russell, Rotch called the place Bedford village. For the rest of his life, his fellow townsfolk flattered Joseph Russell with the honorific "the Duke." When the town came to incorporate itself in 1787, it was discovered that there was already a Bedford in Massachusetts, so it was renamed New Bedford.

BUT FIRST, Bedford village and its unparalleled industry were all but destroyed by revolution.

In June 1773, the Rotch ship *Dartmouth*, built under the buttonwood trees, sailed with a cargo of sperm oil to London. There, after unloading her barrels, she took aboard a cargo of tea chests for a return voyage. On the other side of the Atlantic, the *Dartmouth* tied up at Griffin's Wharf in Boston on November 29. Two other tea carriers, the *Beaver* and the *Eleanor*, arrived and berthed alongside her a few days later. But the unloading of the tea was held up for more than two weeks by Boston citizens, led by John Hancock and Samuel Adams, who opposed the threepence-per-pound tea tariff levied by the British government on shipments of tea from England, although this taxed tea was still cheaper than the Dutch tea then widely supplied to the colonial market by smugglers (New Haven merchant Benedict Arnold among them). It was the principle—taxation without representation—that angered the Bostonians and others. Francis Rotch, Joseph Rotch's son and a co-owner of the *Dartmouth*, made energetic, even heroic efforts, considering the prevailing mood in Boston, to find a solution between the Boston patriots and the patrician consignees of the cargoes—Joshua Winslow; Richard Clarke & Sons; Benjamin Faneuil, Jr.; and Thomas and Elisha Hutchinson, sons of Thomas Hutchinson, the royal governor of Massachusetts—to land the tea. But on the night of December 16, a group of militant patriots who had started calling themselves the

Sons of Liberty disguised themselves as Mohawk Indians and boarded the three ships, chopped up the tea chests, and threw the cargoes into the harbor water. It was a signal skirmish in the growing division not only between England and her prize colony, but also between neighbors and friends among the colonists, which was about to erupt into war.

Quakers were pacifists, and though most of Bedford's citizens were sympathetic to the American cause, few of them enlisted in the Continental Army. For more than three years after the war began, with the battles at Lexington and Concord in April 1775, Dartmouth and Bedford remained largely untroubled by fighting. But a number of privateering ships and their crews used Fairhaven as a base from which to attack the British navy, and their prizes had been sailed up the Acushnet River, until the area became notorious for anti-British shipping activity. The British would not make, or failed to make, a distinction between the two communities facing each other across the river. In dispatches to his superiors, British commander Sir Henry Clinton wrote that in early September 1778, he had directed a naval squadron "to Bedford, a noted rendezvous for privateers."

On September 4, two British frigates, at least one of them bearing forty guns, plus an eighteen-gun brig, and thirty-six smaller schooners and lighters carrying about 4,000 infantrymen, grenadiers, and some mounted troops, sailed from New London for the towns on the Acushnet River. There were fewer than 7,000 people living in the entire area of the original township of Dartmouth. A Continental Army artillery company of eighty men and four officers arrived a few days before the British, but apart from this token force it was thought that there were no more than "fifteen able-bodied men on this side of the river"—that is, men, other than Quakers, who were armed and prepared to fight in Bedford. On Saturday, September 5, the British arrived. Some of the troops were landed on Sconticut Neck, on the river's eastern, seaward-jutting arm, south of Fairhaven. The main body of the squadron, piloted by a royalist-sympathetic local Tory, sailed into Clark's Cove, inside Clark's Point, a few blocks from the center of Bedford village.

They were seen, of course. The weather was fine. And, with the neighborly intimacy of a civil war, news of the fleet's impending arrival had been circulating in Bedford and Fairhaven for more than two weeks. Since the middle of August, some villagers had been carrying merchandise and personal valuables into the fields and woods around town. William Russell, unable to carry his prized grandfather clock out of the house, removed its works and hid them in a stone wall in a field. Mrs. Taber left everything behind but a treasured warming pan. Mother Gerrish refused to flee with her neighbors until she had tidied her house. Others waited, too long, to see for themselves what would happen, as people often do, disbelieving until the end, when wars approach their doorsteps.

All day, troops and military stores were ferried ashore from the ships to the fields on Clark's Point and at the head of the bay below the town. At nightfall the troops marched from the fields through the streets to the waterfront.

"Tradition says," wrote New Bedford historian Leonard Ellis, "that the night was one of surpassing beauty, for the moon made it as light as day."

The British intention was to destroy the town's shipping business. Their first targets were the long ropewalk buildings and adjoining warehouses on the Rotch and Russell wharves; these were set afire in the beautiful moonlight, and more fires, whether set intentionally or not, soon spread and engulfed buildings along the entire riverfront and spread to the stores and houses in nearby streets rising uphill from the river. Twenty-six warehouses in Bedford and across the river in Fairhaven, containing such combustible stores as rum, sugar, molasses, coffee, tea, tobacco, cotton, medicines, sailcloth, cordage, shipping supplies, and gunpowder, were destroyed or blew up in the fire. Seventy ships of varying sizes were set afire and sunk in the river, where some of them remained hazards to navigation for many years.

Surprisingly few people were harmed. Miss Peace Akins, a relative of Joseph Russell's, was delayed as she tried to flee. "She had forgotten something (how like a woman!)," wrote Ellis in 1892. She was overtaken by the troops but was told she would not be harmed if she remained quiet. She stood to one side and watched the British army torch the town. But bloodlust was ignited in the fire and explosions, and three of Bedford's citizens, Abram Russell, Thomas Cook, and Diah Trafford, who may have attempted some resistance, were killed by the troops—Russell's head "being entirely cut to pieces," Cook's bowels ripped open by a bayonet, while Trafford, shot in the leg, would die the next day.

(One of the British officers in Bedford that night was Captain John André, a handsome but impoverished twenty-eight-year-old aristocrat. He was ambitious and looking for a faster route to a glorious military career than his current post as a bearer of dispatches seemed to offer. A year later, André was appointed to British intelligence in New York, where his natural talents led him into a spectacular scheme: he began a secret correspondence with General Benedict Arnold, hoping to lure America's most successful commander over to the British side. André was captured by American forces while helping Arnold cross British lines and was hanged as a spy on October 2, 1780.)

The destruction of Bedford by British forces was as complete as the routing and burning of Dartmouth during King Philip's War,

103 years earlier, but this time the scale of the wreckage of both property and the hopes that had been invested in it was far greater. Joseph Rotch, who had dreamed up Bedford's whaling industry and made a town for it, saw his home burned that night and, at the age of seventy-four, was so dispirited that he returned to Nantucket and remained there until his death, in 1784.

Nine

Neither Land nor Sea nor Air

After three seasons (1868–1870) of good whaling in excellent weather and forgiving ice conditions, the arctic whalers in 1871 were dismayed by the mass of the ice pack that was still, in midsummer, blocking their route north.

In July, the *Oriole*, a newly built New Bedford whaleship, struck floating ice south of the Bering Strait, off St. Lawrence Island. Little of the shock was transmitted through the heavily constructed vessel, and the collision was dismissed until a boatsteerer jumped down the forward hatch to look for a harpoon and landed waist-deep in icy water. Thomas Williams's *Monticello* and several other whaleships were cruising nearby, and Thomas (who had lost his own ship, the *Hibernia*, in exactly such circumstances less than a year earlier) was among the men who rowed over to the *Oriole* to offer assistance. With pumps going, the ship reached Plover Bay on the Siberian shore, where she was hove down onto her side on the beach with the hole above water. But the damage was found to be too great to be repaired in such a remote location, and the ship was declared a loss. Benjamin Dexter, captain of the *Emily Morgan*, bought the wreck, otherwise in good condition, for $1,350, and set his men to removing every piece of gear he could get out of her, to be kept or resold throughout the fleet. It was a stark reminder, if anyone needed it, of the danger and unpredictability of arctic conditions.

SOMETIME AROUND 330 B.C., a Greek merchant and explorer named Pytheas sailed from his home port, the Greek colony of Massalia (Marseille) on the southern coast of France, out of the Mediterranean, and headed north in search of distant trading ports. He sailed to Britain, where he observed the mining and processing of tin in Cornwall, and on up the Irish Sea, around the tip of Scotland. Then he wrote—though his own writings have been lost—that he sailed for six more days northward, to a place he called Thule, a name later appropriated by medieval geographers for their maps as "Ultima Thule," to mean a place beyond the borders of the known world. Pytheas had probably sailed to Norway, because it can easily take six days to cross the Norwegian Sea from Scotland in what must have been a heroically unsuitable boat, and he found barns there.

In Thule, he noticed, the sun disappeared only for an hour or two in the middle of the night. During his peregrinations around Thule, Pytheas found the sea "congealed" and encountered something he described as neither land nor sea nor air "but a mixture of these things"—as the Greek geographer Strabo, who was familiar with Pytheas's work, put it—"in which it is said that earth and water and all things are in suspension as if this something was a link between all these elements, on which one can neither walk nor sail." Pytheas was describing ice, almost certainly freshwater icebergs, drifting south from the fjord glaciers of Svalbard, Greenland, and Norway.

Off Alaska, Pytheas would have found different-looking, walkable ice. There are no glaciers slipping off the marshy tundra shores at the edge of the Alaska whaling grounds to release the wonderfully spired and castellated icebergs found in the eastern Arctic north of the Atlantic, or in the Antarctic. The pack ice surrounding the Yankee whaleships was made of frozen seawater, stuff the whalers, to a man, referred to as ice "cakes," because it was made of sheets that reminded them of pancakes. As Willie Williams wrote:

The pack ice is an enormous accumulation of cakes or floes of snow-covered sea frozen ice, of all shapes and sizes, but containing very few whose highest points are more than 10 feet above the sea level, and those have been formed by the crowding of one floe on top of another. There are very few level spots of any extent, the general effect being very rough. There are no icebergs as there are no glaciers in these northernmost parts of either America or Asia. The pack is not, therefore, in its individual parts imposing, grand or beautiful, but as a whole under all the varying conditions of an arctic sky, from brilliant sunshine to a leaden gloom, it is a magnificent spectacle; and when you stop to consider that it represents ages of accumulation and that there is beneath the surface nearly ten times more bulk than what you can see, you realize that there is something to be considered beside beautiful effects, that there is within it a power which cannot be expressed and can only be partially comprehended.

Though whaling fleets had been sailing into the ice for more than a century, the Arctic and most of the polar waste was still a vast unknown, barred by ice and the lack of technology to penetrate beyond its seasonally melting edge. Conditions at its farthest north, and whether there was land there or simply a frozen sea, could only be guessed at. It would still be more than twenty years before the first serious attempt was made to cross whatever was there to reach the North Pole. In 1893, the Norwegian Fridtjof Nansen sailed his purposely designed ship *Fram* from Christiania (now Oslo) to the Arctic Ocean north of Russia, where it was allowed to become frozen in the ice pack, from which position Nansen hoped the ship would drift with the pack across the Arctic Ocean, over the top of world, to within ski-trekking distance of the North Pole, and eventually reach the Atlantic. He didn't come close to the pole, but spent three years in the arctic ice pack. He found much of it a flat "ice-plain" of "cold violet-blue shadows, with lighter pink tints where a ridge here and there catches the last reflection of the vanished day."

But this desolate, occasionally beautiful, jumbled plain was a deadly threat to the whaleships and their crews. As Willie noted, most of the ice lay below the surface, where, in fog and snow, it could not be seen by men aboard the ships. For a wooden ship, however stoutly built, ice was no different from house-sized chunks of concrete or steel, the mass of even a small "cake" displacing far greater weight than that of any vessel, and, on contact, as unyielding as a granite breakwater. The Williams family had already seen their own ship sunk by ice, and again, at the outset of the 1871 season, witnessed the loss of the *Oriole* by a collision scarcely noticed by the men aboard her. Most whalemen, after one season in the Arctic, had seen or personally experienced the same thing. Ice cruised in constant company with the fleet, often yards from every ship's hull, an ever-present terror, implacable destroyer of ships, killer of men, the constant loom of misadventure; yet so also is the ocean, and the whalemen and their wives and children grew as used to it as to the sea and sky.

The *Japan*, a lucky ship until it smashed into Siberia, had already reached the Chukchi Sea, north of the Bering Strait, by late March, 1870. Conditions were markedly different for the fleet a year later. "The ice was still heavy and well to the south all across the ocean," wrote Willie Williams, as the fleet pushed north through the strait in July 1871, "and as the whaling the year before had been around Point Barrow, all the ships commenced to work to the northeast, in the clear water between the ice and the American shore."

Eskimos trading with the whalers that season advised them that the weather would not be favorable, that the ice would be slow to break up and early to return, and they urged the Americans to turn their ships around and sail south while they could. The whalers, some of whom had been sailing on these arctic "grounds" for twenty years, dismissed the natives' warnings. They knew from experience that easterly and north-easterly winds would eventually blow the ice away from the land, creating a channel between the land and the ice all the way to Point Barrow. The previous three years had seen steadily rising numbers of whales caught by whalers who had taken advantage of this seasonal waterway, who had sailed farther north each year, and remained there longer.

Whaling captains acquired firsthand most of their knowledge of the conditions they might encounter at sea and off distant coasts, the same way they learned navigation and ship-handling. This empirical education began when they first shipped aboard as green hands, and was added to over the course of many voyages. Competition was great and such information was jealously kept from foreign ships, but among friends and colleagues, and particularly among the captains of vessels owned by the same company, men shared this hard-won insider information. In time, such knowledge, spoken, written down in logbooks and letters, would inevitably become public and eventually be verified and gathered into "pilot" books, published by the United States Government Printing

Office in Washington. (While most seafaring nations—Britain, with a millennium of such nautical lore, being a preeminent example—have similar publications with their origins in the same sort of vernacular and empirical sources, it sometimes appears that less "salty" governments have copied, almost word for word, from the pilot books of other, better-informed sources.) The early editions of the *United States Coast Pilot* for Alaska, published in Washington, contained daunting descriptions of the ice and weather conditions faced by mariners navigating arctic coasts, much of it directly reflecting the experiences of nineteenth-century whaling captains, whose efforts comprised the earliest sustained attempts at arctic exploration and navigation:

> The bowhead whale keeps as far to the northward as he can find spouting holes, and to take him the whalers are obliged to keep as close to the pack [ice] as possible. . . . In Bering Sea [south of the strait] there is very little danger in entering the ice, as it is almost sure to open and offer a chance to escape before reaching the Arctic. With a knowledge of this fact, whalers sometimes enter the ice to the southward of the strait and endeavor to work through it if they have reason to believe, from the sudden disappearance of the whale, that there is clear water to the northward. In the Arctic, however [north of the Bering Strait], the pack is carefully avoided. . . . Point Barrow is approached with the greatest caution, as it is one of the most dangerous places in the Arctic. . . . By far the major portion of the vessels lost in the Arctic are wrecked in its vicinity.

Many early editions of the *United States Coast Pilot* for Alaska carried remarks by Captain M. A. Healy about the 1884 cruise of the revenue ship *Thomas Corwin* (the same vessel that had reported the extent of the 1879 famine in the Eskimo settlements). Like 1871, 1884 was an unusually severe season, and it confirmed for Captain Healy that "the experience of many years in the Arctic has demonstrated the fact that no rules whatever can be given as to the time of the breaking up [and the return] of the ice." Arctic pilot books note that "maximum fogginess occurs during the summer." Dense fog had been "almost constant" through the summer of 1884, and Willie Williams and all the logbook keepers aboard the other whaling ships recorded that it was nearly so during 1871. Healy wrote that "for weeks at a time it was impossible to take observations [i.e., to obtain a position by celestial navigation], dead reckoning was almost worthless, owing to the continual changes in force and direction of the currents." Then the navigator depended entirely on the lead line—a rope with a lead weight—to measure the depth of water beneath a ship, which would indicate shoaling and the approach of land. Fog distorted the views of whatever piece of shore might be glimpsed, "high bluffs often appearing like low beaches and small rocks looming to gigantic size," and the marshy tundra land was devoid of distinguishable landmarks. Among the best aids to navigation were the bird rookeries at King Island, the Diomedes, Cape Seppings, Cape Thompson, and Cape Lisburne. "The distance between these rookeries enables one to form a very accurate idea of the one he is approaching, while the cries of birds congregated at them answer the purpose of a fog signal."

Whalers also discovered that their compass—normally the navigator's most dependable and necessary tool—was often useless in the Arctic. The horizontal intensity of the earth's magnetic field becomes progressively weaker as a ship—or a compass—nears the North Pole, until the pole itself becomes an elusive abstraction. The magnetic north pole is actually hundreds of miles from the geographical pole and, the navigator discovers, is constantly on the move. "Measurements indicate that the north magnetic pole moves within an elongated area perhaps 100 miles in a generally north-south direction and somewhat less in an east-west direction," states the *American Practical Navigator*—a doorstopper volume generally referred to by sailors as "Bowditch," after its eighteenth-century originator, Nathaniel Bowditch—some edition of which was carried aboard many whaleships. This book's treatise on the capricious wanderings of the magnetic north pole could hardly enlighten a navigator: "Normally, it is at the southern end of its area of movement at local noon and at the northern extremity twelve hours later, but during a severe magnetic storm this motion is upset and becomes highly erratic. . . . There is some evidence to support the belief that several secondary poles exist." Location of the pole aside, the daily changes in its magnetic field could be as much and abrupt as ten degrees one way or another.

Some sailors even found their compasses affected by the wind in the Arctic, while acknowledging that this seemed impossible. Captain William H. Kelley of New Bedford reported this, guardedly, in a letter to the *Hawaiian Gazette* in 1874:

One of the perplexities of the navigator cruising in the Arctic Ocean is the singular effect northerly and southerly winds seem to have upon the mariner's compass. . . . Navigators have noticed that with a north or northeast wind they can tack in eight points, while with the wind south or southwest in from fourteen to sixteen points. All navigators know that for a square-rigged vessel to lie within four points of the wind [as the compass might have shown on a northerly tack] is an utter impossibility. . . . I have said this much to show the working of the compass in the Arctic Ocean during different winds, not that I admit that the wind has any effect whatever upon the compass.

For arctic mariners, wind shifts often precipitated a change of course, and, as slow as the ships were, magnetic anomalies in the Arctic left the compass needle far behind, and sluggish in catching up. "I have often seen the ship tack and the compass remain stationary," Willie Williams noted, "but by a vigorous shaking ... the compass needle would finally respond."

Into this featureless, disorienting environment sailed the fleet of heavy, tub-shaped, wind-powered whaleships. The *Corwin* was a coal-fired steamship, and Healy wrote that even at anchor, "moving steam had to be kept"—that is, the engines had to be kept running, in a state of readiness to haul anchor and steam to safety "to prevent being dragged ashore by fields of ice moving in the rapid and changing currents." The skill and difficulty of the negotiation of such constant obstacles entirely under sail can scarcely be appreciated by anyone who has not actually witnessed the maneuvering of a square-rigged ship from on board. Few modern sailors take the time to develop the skills, and the nerve, required to handle their highly efficient and maneuverable sailboats—to sail them in and out of a congested harbor or negotiate adverse piloting conditions—under sail alone, for when the wind drops or pipes up too much, they prefer, naturally, to push a button and start the diesel. Whaleships were to modern yachts what steamrollers are to race cars, yet their captains and crews sailed them like crack racing teams, through ice floes, up narrow inlets, turning them completely around inside their own length, and even sailing them backward when conditions warranted. They did this out of pragmatic necessity, but also with pride and pleasure. "The contest to be head ship was close and spirited," wrote Willie Williams of the fleet's race to the northern whale grounds, when ten or fifteen ships crowded the narrow and fickle waterway between land and ice:

> The right of way due to starboard tack was insisted upon fully as zealously, even to the limit of hair breadth escapes from actual collision, as ever seen in a cup race. Those old "square toes" with plenty of wind and a smooth sea, manned by crews every man of which by that time could qualify as an A.B. [i.e., able-bodied seaman], made a nautical picture rarely seen in even the great traveled highways of the ocean.

The suddenness and casualness of the loss of the *Oriole* were endemic to arctic navigation, where collisions with ice were an unavoidable, sometimes daily, occurrence. The single great advantage of having so many ships vying for the diminishing number of whales on the arctic grounds was the security they provided one another when cruising in close company. Never at any time during or after the collision did anyone aboard the *Oriole* fear for his life. The captains of nearby ships quickly came aboard to share their opinions of what might be done for the ship, no doubt enjoying refreshments laid on by the *Oriole*'s cook and steward, and to offer what they could of their own stores and men. And if a ship had to be abandoned, there was a floating village close at hand to take in its crew. In June 1858, the whaleship *Addison*, of New Bedford, struck ice off Cape Thaddeus in the Bering Sea. The *Addison*'s captain, Samuel Lawrence, had his wife, Mary, and seven-year-old daughter, Minnie, aboard. The whaling wives who accompanied their husbands were, manifestly, extraordinary women, particularly for their time, generally at least as brave as any man aboard, with an interest in the ship's business that was second to none. When the *Addison* was in trouble, Mary Chipman Lawrence was gratefully aware of the whaling community standing by, ready to help. From her diary, of June 17, 1858:

> *A sad accident happened to us this morning. In a thick snowstorm we hit a lone cake of ice. No one saw it, neither had any been seen during the morning. We were not aware that there was any within six miles, at least. The first thing I did was to get Minnie up and dress her. We were at breakfast, and I generally let Minnie sleep in the morning, as we breakfast early. I was very calm and composed while dressing her and was ready to collect my things preparatory to leaving the ship, as I expected we should be obliged to do. The ship was stoven some on her larboard bow, causing her to leak a little; but Samuel thinks when he can get up to the land into a bay where we can anchor to repair her a little, it will be perfectly safe to continue on whale ground for the season. Captains Freeman of the Tybee and Smith of the Fabius were on board during the day, and they considered that it was perfectly safe to do so. I believe I am truly thankful that it is no worse, and I shall retire to rest with a feeling of gratitude that the Addison is still my home. There are plenty of ships in sight, and I know that I should suffer for nothing; but for Samuel's sake especially am I thankful.*

The *Addison* was luckier than the *Oriole*. It was beached at Masinka Bay, a few miles north of Plover Bay, was repaired, and profitably saw out the end of the season.

The *Addison* did not go as far north, nor remain as long in the Arctic Ocean, as ships began to in later years. The increasing scarcity of whales would drive whalers to push the limits of whaling grounds, weather, and the balance between prudent seamanship and the tightening economic realities of whaling. In the arctic whaling seasons of 1868,

'69, and '70, ships probing farther north, and remaining there longer, did substantially better. The weather during these years was forgiving (the severe storm experienced by the *Japan* and the *Champion* in 1870 came in October, after most ships were south of the Bering Strait). Whales were taken in good numbers around Point Barrow well into September. The experience of the *Henry Taber* in 1870 was common: her crew didn't spot a whale for three months, until late August, and then caught seventeen during the following three weeks around Point Barrow. In 1871, every captain was determined to reach Point Barrow and stay there as long as possible. Captains whose long experience made them feel they were being foolhardy by cruising such waters at such late dates made some accommodation with their fears and discovered within themselves unimagined stoicism and skill, or else found themselves without a command. Less responsible crewmembers, whose eyes rested solely on their take of the profits, and who would not be blamed for the loss of or damage to a ship, could, and did, write to a ship's owners to complain if they felt their captain was being too timid.

So the fleet pushed north, negotiating conditions that in any other circumstances would have been considered unacceptable. But still they found they could not keep to the schedule of recent years, which had seen ships close to Point Barrow by early August. In August 1871 they were 150 miles south of there, facing apparently impenetrable pack ice, which was held against the land by a nearly steady wind from the north.

"*Wednesday [August] 2nd. Strong breeze from North'rd working to wind'rd foggy most of the time,*" wrote Nathaniel Ransom in the *John Wells*'s logbook, as the ship tacked again and again, pushing into strong headwinds, seeking any opening in the ice.

"*Thursday 3rd. Strong breeze from North'rd again. . . .*

"*Saturday 5th. Strong breeze from North'rd . . . found plenty of ice. . . .*"

But on August 6, the wind shifted to northeast, blowing off the land. The *Henry Taber*, at the front of the fleet, found a channel between the ice and the land off Blossom Shoals, and, working into this shifting opening, passed Icy Cape. Three days later, the *John Wells* followed her: *"Wednesday 9th. Fresh breeze from North'rd on wind forenoon pass icy Cape & blossom shoals found a very narrow passage through between land & ice afternoon a little more room to work ship made sail evening foggy came to anchor."*

The not unpleasant-sounding description "fresh breeze" used by these rugged whalers aboard heavy, slow-moving ships generally meant winds that were nearly gale-force. "Strong" winds would indicate a true gale. Understatement is a consistent factor in gauging reports of conditions faced by men aboard whaleships. Usually, the weather they faced was appalling.

The *Wells* found sixteen ships ahead of her, four of them "boiling"— giving off black clouds of greasy smoke as their tryworks melted blubber—a happy sight.

The next day, Thursday, August 10, after most of the ships had squeezed their way into the finger of water between the ice pack and the low dismal shore, Lewis Kennedy died aboard the *Henry Taber*. He was one of the crewmen of the *Japan* who had never recovered from his ordeal. Abram Briggs, the *Taber*'s logkeeper, recorded (in his characteristically tidy hand) this death in a neat, black-ink-bordered note in the logbook.

BLESSED ARE THEY THAT DIE IN THE LORD

IN MEMORY

Of Lewis Kennedy who departed this life Thursday August 10, 1871, at 12 [noon], he was a native of London, England, aged 24 years or thereabout he was one of the English Bark Japan crew that was wrecked In Oct last up here. We are now called upon to witness on this solemn occation, the last tribute & respect, paid to our fellow mariner & may we all bear It In mind that we have all got to go that way sooner or later. And from leaveing this World of Troubles & woe, he has entered Into a Heavenly mansion, where love & peace forever [reign]. The deceased died of the scurvy on the Lungs. Oh death where Is Thy sting. Oh grave where Is Thy victory.

A fleet of twenty ships, including the *Monticello* and the Howland brothers' *Concordia*, now crowded into the narrow channel that had opened between Icy Cape and Wainwright Inlet, thirty-five miles to the north. The wind fell light and settled into the northeast for a few days, and conditions at last seemed promising for the final push to Point Barrow, another sixty miles beyond Wainwright Inlet, where they all wanted to be, and where, they believed, lay the richest whaling grounds on earth.

But that spring an anomalous (compared with the patterns of the previous three years) stationary high-pressure system developed over Siberia. Through the spring and early summer, persistent cold winds—the northerlies noted by all the ships' logkeepers—blew across the Arctic Ocean, keeping the ice pack pinned to the coast of Alaska and preventing its normal melting and dispersal. The narrow channel that had opened up, as it had done in years past, would prove to be a temporary aberration that season. The ships had sailed into a trap.

Ten

The Profits of Asceticism

W ell, Hiram, I suppose thee is ready for work now," Caleb Well-worthy, a New Bedford Quaker and whaling merchant, says to his son in the 1890 novel *A Quaker Home*, by George Fox Tucker.

"Yes, I am ready if thee desires it," Hiram replies, "but I feel that I would like to remain in school a little longer."

"When a man chooses business as his occupation," his father tells him, "it is better for him not to remain too long in school."

It's June 1867, and fifteen-year-old Hiram has come home to New Bedford from the Friends' Boarding School in Providence, Rhode Island. He's supposed to begin work the next day in his father's countinghouse and offices on New Bedford's waterfront. Caleb outlines for the boy the shape of his apprenticeship:

To be a good businessman, Hiram, one must learn all the details. I want thee to keep at the books for several years, spending an hour or two on the wharf every afternoon when ships are fitting; and after that I want thee to devote thy attention exclusively to the mechanical parts of the business, and to the various details of purchases and sales. In eight or ten years thee ought to be able to fit a ship economically and well.

Young Hiram is appalled.

Eight or ten years! . . . Incessant labor and unbroken monotony, an uneventful home existence, no diversions to give variety to life . . . no society save that of Charity Jessop and her sober companions!

Tucker's novel is closely and avowedly autobiographical. Novelist George Fox Tucker (named by his rigorously faithful parents for the sect's founder) was born in 1852, the same year as Hiram, and also attended the Friends' Boarding School in Providence. His father, Charles R. Tucker, a contemporary of George Howland, Jr., and Matthew Howland, was an eminent and successful whaling merchant who "won, to an extent reached by few, the approbation and regard of his associates and of the community," notes a history of New Bedford. *A Quaker Home* details Hiram Wellworthy's resistance to following the career his father has planned for him; he wants instead to write novels and recoils at the aridity of business and the countinghouse, but eventually he compromises with his father and takes up the law. Author Tucker also served a brief apprenticeship in his father's business before turning to the law, and subsequently wrote novels. Strict Quakers, like the Tuckers, the Howlands, and the elite Quaker society that monopolized New Bedford's—and for a time the world's—oil business, did not read novels, let alone stand back and observe themselves or write memoirs of their lives. One may read in *Moby-Dick* and many seamen's memoirs of the procedure of chasing and harpooning whales and the whaler's life at sea, but Tucker's book provides one of the rare depictions of the hermetic world of Quaker home life, society, and the shorebound business of a Quaker whaling merchant. His characters speak and behave with artless inevitability (perhaps the believable flavor of the author's straitened early life), but the detailed specificity of Hiram's route to his father's office—"following Union Street to Front Street, I turned south and soon found myself at the office door . . . in the old brick building which stands at the head of Commercial Wharf"—reads true.

There was one large room, a portion of which to the right as one entered was partitioned off so as to form a private office or consulting room; and the large room itself was divided by a rail. The space on the side of this rail which was farthest from the door was called the inner office, and was occupied by father, the head bookkeeper, and Uncle Silas. I was now to join them. There were in the inclosure a safe; three high, long, old-fashioned desks, from which hung several pieces of cloth used as pen-wipers; a number of high stools, and one chair. The latter was for father's exclusive use. There were a few chairs outside the rail for those who came on business.

This is a description of the offices of Charles R. Tucker & Co., where the novelist sat and worked during his apprenticeship. It occupied the southeast corner of the large brick building on Commercial Wharf—the sort of building and harbor aspect that, in the grip of twentieth-century urban renewal, have revitalized old ports around the world. Many such can still be seen today farther west along I-195 in Fall River and Providence, and around Manhattan's South Street Seaport. But the building Tucker writes of was demolished, along with much of New Bedford's historic waterfront, in the early 1970s, more irreparably than the British fires of two hundred years earlier, to make way for the history-obliterating four-lane connector, Route 18, that now runs south from the interstate, along the Acushnet River, and effectively severs the waterfront from the town's historic district, which now gazes at a shoreline swathed in concrete. Of this busy world and time, there are photographs to show us what it looked like, but of the people and their tics and speech and prejudices, only George Fox Tucker's *A Quaker Home* remains as documentary evidence.

Caleb Wellworthy initially expects his son to do as he did: apprentice himself into the whaling business. This is what Charles R. Tucker expected of his son George, and what he himself had done in 1830, by entering the countinghouse of Quaker businessman Isaac Howland, Jr., then the most successful whaling merchant in New Bedford. Quakers didn't lavish money on their offices, and it may be presumed that the Howland offices of the early nineteenth century, situated in another brick building at the head of Howland's Wharf, four blocks north, resembled those of the fictional Caleb Wellworthy.

Isaac Howland, Jr. (the third of that name), was born in 1755. He was a tiny man, said to weigh between ninety and a hundred pounds—not the physique to make a career at sea, but "the fire of a strong determination burned in him," wrote historian and Howland genealogist William M. Emery. In later years, Isaac Jr. would say that he experienced great hardship and toil in accumulating his first thousand dollars. One of his reported early efforts was to buy the silk stockings worn by sailors arriving in New Bedford on trading vessels from the West Indies in the first years after the Revolution. Howland is said to have washed and ironed these stockings and sold them again for a good profit. This anecdote is probably more revealing of his inventiveness than of the route to that first thousand dollars, but it illustrates the wide embrace of Howland's enterprises before he concentrated on whaling.

New Bedford's whaling industry was slow to revive after the Revolution. The defeated British—London had been America's primary market for its oil—enacted laws against the importation of American oil. Joseph Rotch's son William attempted unsuccessfully to sell American oil to Europe from the port of Dunkirk. The Napoleonic Wars, between Britain and America's ally, France, resulted in the seizure of many American ships on the high seas—whalers and ships carrying whale oil were as visible and crucial to the economies of warring states as oil tankers and merchant ships were to Britain in World War II, and, like the transatlantic convoys in the 1940s, were sought-after targets. The resumption of open hostilities between America and Britain during the War of 1812 had a further dampening effect on every American port, but in particular on New Bedford, whose economy was almost entirely dependent on its shipping interests.

Before the Revolution, Isaac Howland, Jr., was involved in his father's merchant shipping enterprises. Even after this was ruined, he managed to keep his hand in shipping, and formed his own company, Isaac Howland, Jr., & Co. He was soon trading in anything that would turn a profit, while sending his ships to ports in neutral countries: to Göteborg, St. Petersburg, and Riga in the Baltic for Swedish and Russian iron, which was prized for harpoons and whaling lances, as well as to Europe and the West Indies. His store at the head of Howland's Wharf sold "fresh" Alexandria flour, corn, rye, beef, pork, cheese, tea, coffee, sugar, lumber, and Russian and "Swedes" iron.

Isaac's second cousin, Gideon Howland, Jr. (1770–1847), married Isaac's daughter Mehitable in 1798 and became a partner with his father-in-law in Isaac Howland, Jr., & Co. Gideon Jr.'s professional life up to the point of his marriage was a complementary contrast to that of Isaac Howland, Jr.: tall, with a commanding physique, he had spent years at sea, working his way up to the captaincy of a whaling vessel. After his marriage he retired from the sea and brought this practical side of seafaring to the business. It was after Gideon Jr. had joined the firm that Isaac Howland, Jr., & Co. became the dominant shipping concern in New Bedford.

The company was rigorous in sending to sea only well-equipped, seaworthy vessels, commanded by highly competent captains and crews—Gideon Jr.'s experience undoubtedly paid off here. The goods sold at the Howland company store were always first class, at prices that were fair. The dependability of every aspect of the Howland business became well known and trusted. This bred loyalty in customers and business associates. Yet these good practices, followed by other merchants in larger ports that never suffered the tribulations experienced in New Bedford, do not explain the ascent of Isaac Howland, Jr., and his company; nor do they explain the eventual world dominance of the whale fishery by New Bedford. "New Bedford is not nearer to the whales than New London or Portland," wrote Ralph Waldo Emerson, a frequent visitor to the town and, for six months in 1833, a preacher at the town's First Congregational Church.

At the root of the Howlands' and New Bedford's endeavors and singular successes lay the austere sensibility of Quaker doctrine.

From the inception of Quakerism, when its followers were persecuted by the established church and state, in both England and America, Quakers were, by avid choice and practice, outsiders to normal society, barred from government service, from civil and legal professions, and from universities; and their pacifism prohibited military service. Like the Jews of Eastern Europe, persecuted through millennia, what was left to them was trade, financial services, and medicine, and at these callings Quakers excelled. Through native ability, honesty, and energy, they became disproportionately more prosperous and influential than those who had been accorded every advantage offered by the society around them.

Quakers' honesty led them to pioneer uniform pricing, without discrimination or advantage, which won the confidence of the public market. In England and America they became leaders in textile, shipping, and pharmaceutical industries, in pottery- and clock-making and the manufacture of scientific instruments. Their reputation for honesty and prudent business practices and investment led to the establishment of Quaker-owned banking institutions such as Lloyds and Barclays. The Quaker Fry, Cadbury, and Rowntree families dominated the British chocolate industry for two centuries.

Thomas Chalkley (1675–1741), a Quaker sea captain, merchant, and minister, defined the Quaker rationale for financial gain through an industrious calling:

We have liberty from God, and his dear Son, lawfully, and for Accomodation's Sake, to work or seek for Food. . . . Our Saviour saith, Labour not for the Meat which perisheth, but for that which endureth forever. . . . By which we do not understand, that Christians must neglect their necessary Occasions and their outward Trades and Callings . . . else why did our Lord say to his Disciples: Children, have you any Meat? They answered, No; and he bid them cast their Nets into the Sea, and they drew to Land a Net full of great Fishes; and Fishing being their Trade, no doubt but they sold them, for it was not likely they could eat 'em all themselves. . . . The Farmer, the Tradesman, and the Merchant, do not understand by our Lord's Doctrine, that they must neglect their Calling, or grow idle in the Business, but must certainly work, and be industrious in their Callings.

In this spirit, Quakers believed that (a) by diligent pursuit of their calling, the Lord would bestow his blessing upon them in the form of material prosperity, and that this success was a sure sign of the Lord's approval; and (b) that there was no limit on the degree of prosperity desirable. More was better. Wealth indicated godliness.

The Quaker William Penn, onetime owner of an iron foundry in Kent, England, and the founder of Pennsylvania, had this economic advice for his children and followers:

There is no living upon the Principal, you must be diligent to preserve what you have, whether it be Acquisition or Inheritance; else it will consume. Frugality is a Virtue too, and not of little Use in Life, a better Way to be Rich, for it has less Toil and Temptation. . . . For this way of getting is more in your own Power and less subject to Hazard. . . . True Godliness doesn't turn Men out of the World, but enables them to live better in it.

Paralleling this frugality, Quakers practiced an almost Hindu asceticism, reflected in their personal behavior, speech, deportment, appearance, and concept of the world. They were most widely and easily distinguished by what they called "the plain language": their "thees" and "thous," which represented an expression of their belief in the equality of all people, from a time when "you" was the required address to superiors; and, of course, by the chronic refusal to doff the hat. Though no rigid laws were passed about dress, Quaker clothing was chosen for its plainness, warmth, decency, and suitability to the sex of the wearer. Any form of show or ostentation in apparel was discouraged to the point of de facto decree. Colors were generally of soft grays, dull drabs, sage greens, somber browns, and black. Costumes grew so uniform that by the late eighteenth century the regulation appearance for both sexes had effectively frozen into the style of the Quakers of Pennsylvania of one hundred years earlier: gowns, layers of petticoats, bonnets, and linens of uniform "drab"—a light, dull, neutral color—for women; frock coats, breeches, and vests for men. Those unremovable hats were wide-brimmed, gray, drab, or black. The attention paid to them and the insistence on wearing them may seem quaint or absurd today—as they often did two centuries ago to "the people of the world," as Quakers called everyone else—but to them, the hat betokened religious compliance as surely as the burka and chador have done in many Muslim cultures. For some, the width of a man's hat brim was an indication of the state of his soul. "After deep proving," wrote a Quaker in his diary, "I can but believe I have made some growth in grace the past year, and may without presumption add half an inch to the width of my hat brim." A woman in Nantucket who lived for years with her father-in-law only once saw him without his hat upon his head.

Jewelry was out of the question: Hiram Wellworthy's killjoy grandmother even admonished her daughter-in-law for wearing the spectacles that her husband had given her for her fiftieth birthday: "Deborah . . . the Discipline is decisive upon the matter . . . thee ought to know that gold-bowed spectacles are jewelry."

The interior and perceived worlds of the Quakers were equally severe. George Fox had disapproved of the names given to the days of the week, for these derived from the gods of pagan times—Tuesday from Zeus, Wednesday from Woden, Thursday from the thunder god Thor, Friday from the name of Woden's wife, Saturday from Saturn. Fox preferred enumerating the days of the week as they were described in the Book of Genesis: First Day (Sunday), Second Day, and so on. The same for the months, which Quakers called First, Second, etc.

Music was associated with worldliness and was therefore banned, both in worship and in the home. Similarly, dancing and dramatics. "The ears must be stopped to the sounds which ravished," young Hiram was told, "and the eyes must be turned away from the scenes which fascinated and inspired. . . . So opposed was grandmother to music that she believed it was wrong to even listen to the caroling of a bird." Literature for pleasure was pernicious; reading was restricted to the Bible and edifying tracts or useful technical information. Alcohol was forbidden.

Hiram's father, like many other Quaker parents, believed the young were to be educated only to the degree necessary to begin adult life; schooling beyond the early teens, which carried with it the dangers of inflammatory revelations, was discouraged. Beyond the essentials, and the acquired talents brought by various apprenticeships, it was felt that God could supply all the knowledge a person required, and even too much theological teaching was frowned upon, as the Lord's spirit could be tapped without the intermediary of a clergyman or his instruction.

This self-sufficiency, self-reliance, and rejection of worldly influences resulted in an asceticism rarely found elsewhere in the Western world. In *The Religion of India* (*Gesammelte Aufsätze zur Religionssoziologie*, volume 2, 1920), German sociologist Max Weber observed that there were many points of resemblance between the American Quakers of the nineteenth century and the Jains of India (500 B.C. onward). Weber noted that the life ethic of Hinduism had at one time effectively discouraged the development of bourgeois capitalism in India, despite a society with highly developed cultures of law, science, and government. Around 500 B.C., the Jains, a heretical Vedic sect, rejected the dominant Hindu views about religion and economics, and developed as a conspicuous exception. Jainism evolved as a reaction against the traditional view that Moksa, or Nirvana, the endgame liberation from the Hindu cycle of suffering, death, and rebirth could be achieved only by Brahmans, who had reached this highest echelon in the Hindu caste system through countless cycles of rebirth. Jainism, and later Buddhism, arose as a kind of "Nirvana Now" shortcut: a means of achieving salvation through one's efforts and behavior in the present life. Weber's comparison of the Jains and Quakers was further explored by Professor Balwant Nevaskar in *Capitalists Without Capitalism: The Jains of India and the Quakers of the West* (1971). Like the Quakers, Jains practiced a strictly ascetic lifestyle, abstinence from intoxicants, frugality, and detachment, inwardly and practically, from the world around them. Like the Quakers, who migrated to urban areas for the greater economic advantages afforded them there, the Jains congregated in cities (because their beliefs in the sanctity of all forms of life—including bugs—prohibited them from agricultural occupations). Both groups were pacifist. Because of their religious beliefs, the Jains, too, were barred from government and many professional occupations, and eventually took up trading and financial services. Any kind of deception was forbidden to Jains, and consequently they became trusted with money and in trade. As Jainism and the business acumen of the Jains developed, only the striving after, and undue attachment to, wealth for its own sake was forbidden—but not the acquisition of it. Jains became Rothschildian moneylenders, bankers, jewelers, cloth merchants, and industrialists who eventually controlled a large proportion of India's mercantile wealth. Quakers submitted themselves to the scrutiny of the elders at their Meeting Houses; the Jain equivalent was the *upasraya*, where the monks and nuns lived in segregated dwellings and counseled their lay congregants. In both places, conduct in daily life was reviewed and strictly determined by religious ethics.

Although subscribing to quite different theological beliefs, the Jains and the Quakers were almost identical in their clannish, thrifty, and hardworking lifestyle, and their dedication to a strict business ethic and absolute honesty in their business dealings with nonbelievers brought them to positions of superiority in the nonbelievers' capitalist world.

Among the whaling Quakers of New Bedford, the fruitful Howland family most perfectly represents the supremacy of this Quaker-merchant strain. Since Quaker Henry Howland, brother of the *Mayflower* John, had purchased, with others, the Dartmouth tract in 1652, six further generations of Howlands had branched and multiplied up and down both banks of the Acushnet. They farmed and fished, accruing solid gains on the land, in household goods, and in modest numbers of pounds, shillings, and pence. A few, like Isaac Howland, Jr.,'s father, took to the sea, but the coming of Nantucketer Joseph Rotch and his dreams of a whaling port on the Acushnet struck the watershed chord among numbers of Howlands, as well as others.

Isaac Howland, Jr.'s, greatest rival in the whale fishery was his distant cousin, George Howland (1781–1852), who established what was to become, through his sons, George Jr. and Matthew, the longest-running whaling business in New Bedford, and the last owned by Howlands—conducted too long, too late.

George Howland—Dartmouth founder Henry's great-great-great-great-grandson—was born on his father Matthew's farm in Acushnet, immediately north of New Bedford. As a boy, living and working amid pasture, rock, and livestock, he knew little or nothing of seafaring; his early education was restricted to the basics of reading and writing. Yet he was clearly ambitious for a larger life. At sixteen, he walked a few miles south and entered the waterfront countinghouse of William Rotch, Jr. (Joseph Rotch's grandson), and there he learned a whole world of improvement. William Rotch, Jr., had been born in Nantucket but moved, with his father, William Sr., to New Bedford after the Revolution—after Joseph Rotch had returned dispirited to Nantucket. George Howland did well in his employ, and within a few years he left Rotch & Co. to start his own business as an agent for whaling and merchant vessels. His offices were at the foot of North Street, close to the river. He soon built his own wharf—still marked "Geo Howland's Wharf" on an 1871 map of New Bedford. He had three children by his first wife, Elizabeth; two died, leaving only George Jr., born in October 1806, and Elizabeth herself died less than two months later. George married again in 1810, this time to his sixteen-year-old cousin, Susan Howland. He brought her home to a plain but substantial house he had just built (which still stands) at Seventh and Walnut streets on a hill above New Bedford's harbor. When they reached the house after the simple ceremony at the Friends Meeting House on Spring Street, a signal was made, and a brand-new whaleship, the *George and Susan*, slid from the ways at the builder's yard at the foot of Walnut Street and was launched in full (then unobstructed) view of the wedding party up the hill. The new Mrs. Howland observed the name of the ship, which had been kept secret from her, through a telescope. Though she was famously small, Susan Howland was evidently strong: she gave birth to fourteen children in that house, of whom six survived into adulthood.

Howland wasn't complacent about allowing his fortune to follow the whales. He foresaw that a substitute for whale oil would be found elsewhere and that New Bedford would not recover from the loss of its primary business. There was little sign of this until well after his death (in 1852), for the whale fishery was then still booming, ascending toward the financial peak it would reach in 1857, and New Bedford was fast becoming what many called a "city." But in the 1840s George Howland began energetically looking for an opportunity to diversify and invest outside New Bedford the enormous wealth he was accumulating. He was by then worth over half a million dollars, with a fleet of nine whaling ships, a wharf, a candle factory, and other businesses, all in New Bedford.

He believed land was the preferred and ultimate investment, so he traveled, looking for a suitable spot. He liked Haverford village, ten miles west of the center of Philadelphia: in 1848, he made a substantial gift to Quaker-run Haverford College. But the land didn't appear especially fertile, and Howland did not foresee the rise of suburban life. He liked New York City but found the real estate too expensive. Finally, Union Springs, in western New York state, seemed to George Howland destined to be a city of the future. It was on Cayuga Lake, halfway between Buffalo and the Hudson River, a link along the recently opened Erie Canal, which was carrying grain, cattle, stone, all the resources of the developing Midwest, across the expanse of New York. Howland saw the town as a new Chicago. He encouraged his children to settle there, built large houses for them, whole streets of stores and facilities. But he did not anticipate the coming of the railroads, which bypassed Union Springs and greatly undermined the commercial usefulness of the Erie Canal. Fifty years after his death, his assets in Union Springs were worth less than a tenth of his initial investment.

On his death, the bulk of what remained of George Howland's estate was inherited by his two sons, George Jr. and Matthew. Both were grown men at the time of their father's disastrous attempt at diversification; both had begun their working lives in their father's countinghouse and ran the business he had started. They absorbed this signal lesson of what follows when man fiddles with the Lord's most evident design—the Nantucket paradigm, pioneered by Quakers, which had been successfully transferred to New Bedford and faithfully transacted by their father and everyone they knew for more than a century, and which had made them all rich. George Jr. and Matthew would continue in the whale fishery far past its peak, in the face of every indication of natural exhaustion, and ride the industry's decline into ruin.

Eleven

The Ships and the Men

William Fish Williams's childhood homes, the ships *Florida*, *Hibernia*, and *Monticello*, were more alike than any three houses in a small suburban neighborhood. The distinguishing marks between these ships, and the ships of the 1871 arctic fleet, were fewer than those between a Buick and a Ford, discernible only by knowing observers.

Between the landing of the first sperm whale in 1712 and the outbreak of the Revolutionary War, the design of the American whaleship and the American whaleman's techniques evolved into the classic model that would remain essentially unchanged until the dissolution of the industry one hundred years later. Herman Melville, who shipped aboard the whaler *Acushnet* in 1841, might not have understood the workings of whaleships of the 1740s, but he would have been quite familiar with those of the 1770s. A whaler of the 1870s coming aboard a whaleship built a hundred years earlier in Nantucket or New Bedford would have found it smallish, but otherwise ordinary and serviceable. Once the design had been perfected, and with it the methods, they remained largely unimprovable. The whaleship *Maria*, built in Nantucket in 1781 by Joseph Rotch's son, William, was still working in 1866, well past the peak years of Yankee whaling. A few other venerable—and lucky—ships had similar careers: the *Rousseau*, owned by George Howland (he hated the "infidel Frenchman" name, but changing a ship's name has always been considered unlucky, so he purposely mispronounced it "Russ-o") and then passed on to his sons, George Jr. and Matthew, was built in 1801 and outlived two generations of her owners, to be broken up in 1893. Most famous of all is the *Charles W. Morgan*, "a ship on which Poseidon and gods of the sea must have looked with special favor, because not only did she survive for more than eight decades the countless hazards of the sea as an active whaleship, but also—and equally miraculous—she was saved at the end of her long career by men who had come to love her and saw in her, as the last of her kind, a need to preserve her for posterity."[1] The *Morgan*, built in 1841, twenty-five years before the Howlands' *Concordia*, is still afloat today at the Mystic Seaport Museum (in Mystic, Connecticut), a perfect time capsule of her time and purpose. These are extraordinary life spans for working *wooden* vessels, pointing not only to the duration of practical designs and techniques, but also to the economical habits of whaleship owners. Such ships paid for themselves many times over and made their owners rich.

They were as functional as spaceships. After Christopher Hussey and his crew had laboriously towed a single sperm whale back to Nantucket in 1712, prompting ships to voyage far out into "ye Deep," whalers evolved the technique of cutting up a whale at sea and storing the

1. Waldo C. Johnston, in *The Charles W. Morgan* by John Leavitt.

chopped-up blubber in hogsheads. Until mid-century, these vessels displaced between thirty and fifty tons and remained at sea until their hogsheads were full before sailing home, where the blubber was boiled and the oil extracted in tryworks ashore. But as they ranged across the more distant waters of the South Atlantic, on the far side of the tropics, the limited shelf life of blubber became apparent. It turned rancid fast, spoiling the oil, curtailing voyages and the opportunity to explore more distant whaling grounds.

The major innovation affecting the design and service of whaleships was the development of shipboard tryworks. These were essentially furnaces, solidly built of bricks, designed to burn tons of matter in giant iron pots for days at a time—not an item that suggested itself to shipboard use. Apart from the inherent difficulty of keeping such fires going aboard a ship at sea in all weathers, the weight of such a construction on the deck of what was already a top-heavy vessel posed serious stability problems.

A modern sailor who has some idea of the singular difficulty of simply staying put, holding on, managing the gear of even a small yacht in bad weather—of just making a cup of coffee in such circumstances—can appreciate the difficulties of employing men to cut up tons of meat and tend to burning fires aboard a large, heavy, complicated square-rigger, as the ship's entire deck and all its working gear become coated with a viscous, insoluble oil.

Small tryworks were first built on the decks of ships cruising the "southern fishery"—the waters of the Gulf Stream, the Western Islands, and across the tropics into the South Atlantic as far as the Brazil Banks—where blubber spoiled quickly. But these were ships of eighty to a hundred tons, and their tryworks were adequate only for small whales and small catches. The appearance in the late eighteenth century of shipboard tryworks big enough for the efficient processing of larger sperm whales, right whales, and arctic bowheads very quickly doubled the size of whaling vessels.

Aboard these bigger ships, men developed the rare abattoir skills of "cutting in" a whale at sea. For this, a large platform, called the cutting stage, was lowered on hinges until it extended horizontally far outboard of the ship's deck, above a captured whale that had been brought alongside the hull. Men stood precariously on the cutting stage, leaning against an improvised rail, wielding twenty-foot-long, razor-sharp cutting spades to "flense" the blubber off the whale below them, while the ship rolled and lurched in the ocean swell. The carcass was turned slowly by men on deck with lines hooked into the jaw, tail, and flippers, while long, thick strips of flensed blubber were cut, hooked, unpeeled like orange skin, and hoisted aloft with block-and-chain tackles. The water around the ship became viscous with blood—ten tons of it from a large sperm whale, handily enough to flatten breaking wavetops—and densely clustered with sharks. A Hitchcockian cloud of screeching seabirds filled the air around them, diving for scraps and offal. It was a scene that might have sprung from the imagination of Hieronymus Bosch, yet by the early nineteenth century it was being played out daily across the world's oceans.

With this leap in size, the paradigm changed once again. A bigger ship carried its own carpenter, blacksmith, cooper, and sailmaker to sea, along with a dedicated cook and steward; more whaleboats, now totaling five, were carried on stout wooden davits; barrels were carried packed with "shooks"—barrel staves—and iron hoops, so the cooper could make more barrels at sea as needed. These first true factory ships were big and self-sufficient enough to remain at sea indefinitely, and as crews ate their way through hundreds of barrels of food and otherwise reduced the gear in the hold, this cargo space was refilled by oil. Shipmasters were instructed not to return home until their vessels were full, even when oil could be off-loaded at convenient shipping depots such as the Azores or, increasingly, South American ports. The classic era of Yankee whaling—depicted by scratchings on whales' teeth, in paintings, and, most harrowingly and accurately, by Melville—had begun.

And "whalemen," these avid butcher-sailors, began to sign on for voyages they knew would last for years. Being men, they were vastly more unalike than their ships; but being whalemen, their woes were common to all of them.

IN JANUARY 1841, Herman Melville sat, as he makes Ishmael sit (*Moby-Dick*, chapter 7), in the chapel at the Seamen's Bethel, which still stands as it did then on Bethel Street, in New Bedford, prior to their departures aboard the *Acushnet* (Melville) and the *Pequod* (Ishmael). Naturally, both men were there at the same time of year: "It was cold as Iceland."

Both sailors, about to head off on a whaling voyage around the world, gazed balefully at the inscriptions on the cenotaphs screwed to the chapel walls beside them.

"Three of them ran something like the following," Ishmael tells us: "*SACRED To the Memory of JOHN TALBOT, Who, at the age of eighteen, was lost overboard, Near the Isle of Desolation, off Patagonia, November 1st, 1836 . . . ROBERT LONG, WILLIS ELLERY, NATHAN COLEMAN . . . Who were towed out of sight by a Whale, On the Off-shore Ground in the Pacific, December 31st, 1839 . . . CAPTAIN EZEKIEL HARDY, Who, in the bows of his boat was killed by a Sperm Whale on the coast of Japan, August 3rd, 1833. . . .*"

Dreaming up his big book down in "the insular city of the Manhattoes," Melville didn't want to travel all the way from New York to New Bedford to copy the exact inscriptions, so he made them up, adding "but I do not pretend to quote." Yet he caught exactly the flavor, the tragic untimeliness, and the exotic locations of so many whalemen's deaths.

Three examples on the walls of the bethel today read:

ERECTED

By the Officers and crew of the

Bark A.R. Tucker of New Bedford

To the memory of

CHARLES H. PETTY

of Westport, Mass.

who died Dec. 14th, 1863,

in the 18th year of his age.

His death occurred in nine hours

after being bitten by a shark,

while bathing near the ship,

He was buried by his shipmates

on the Island of DeLoss, near

the Coast of Africa.

. . . In memory of

WILLIAM C. KIRKWOOD

of Boston Mass. aged 25 y'rs,

who fell from aloft, off

Cape Horn, Feb 10, 1850.

and was drowned.

. . . to the memory of

NATHANIEL E. COLE

Boat steerer of Fall River Mass.

Aged 24 y'rs

EDWARD LAFFRAY

of Burlington Vt.

Aged 22 y'rs

FRANK KANACKA

Aged 19 y'rs.

all lost by the upsetting of their

Boat July 15, 1854.

In the Ochotsk Sea.

Whalers died far from home, in places most people had never heard of—though to New Bedforders in the mid–nineteenth century, the Sea of Okhotsk (in the western Arctic) was as familiar a name as Baghdad in our own time. Others—from the cenotaphs in the Seamen's Bethel—died in Calcutta, in Sumatra, and Wm. Googins, aged nineteen, was lost overboard in a nameless piece of ocean, but the place of his death was given a latitude and longitude—47.50 S, 173.20 W—and many in New Bedford would have known without looking at a map that this was in the remotest area of the South Pacific, on the New Zealand "grounds."

The whaleman's weekly newsletter, the *Whalemen's Shipping List and Merchants' Transcript*, of New Bedford, was filled with similar news: "carried out of sight by the whale . . . The ship cruised for two days for the missing boat, but could not find her"; "fell from the stern overboard and drowned"; "taken out of the boat by a foul line, and drowned." Or: "Charles W. Warner of Springfield, Mass. killed by a fall from the foreyard of the ship Mary & Susan, August 9, 1851." Such notices also routinely appeared in the Honolulu paper *The Friend*, published for whalemen and their families, who were increasingly spending time (many even took up residence) in what were then known as the Sandwich Islands.

These stark death notices were of enduring importance to the people of New Bedford and whaling communities everywhere. They were losing sons, husbands, and fathers as regularly as the losses in an endless war. If it didn't seem like war to them, but the normal attrition of life, it was only because these losses occurred throughout the whole of their lives, part of the daily news that arrived with the docking of every ship. But they memorialized their men and the details of their lonely deaths.

Fishermen still had the most dangerous jobs in America in 2005, with a fatality rate of 118.4 per 100,000 (nearly 30 times higher than the rate of the average worker). But today's fishermen are incalculably safer than the whalers of two hundred years ago. There were virtually no safety measures aboard whaleships. Half the men coming aboard at the start of a voyage were "green"—farmers' sons, poor city boys, and, in a few cases, romantic dreamers who had never sailed before. They learned their way up, down, and around the deadly maze of a square-rigged whaleship by following the man in front of them up the rigging and into a whaleboat. Their hesitations were answered with the bellowing of the mate, who could make his voice heard above the eldritch howling of a gale, and, in the more brutal ships, by the laying on of clubs, belaying pins, or any handy piece of rope improvised as a whip. It was always a savage initiation. *"John Prior . . . fell from the main top-galant cross trees . . . fracturing his jaw bone, and injuring him internally,"* wrote boatsteerer Dean C. Wright (see below), who witnessed this accident; *"he providentially fell upon a dog which was lying on deck, which no doubt saved his life."* Men fell in uncountable numbers from the masts, yardarms, and the cat's cradle of rigging that wheeled, arced, lurched across the sky, developing centrifugal forces that would terrify circus acrobats, and there was seldom a dog to cushion the blow.

The deck and interior of the ship itself offered only marginally better odds. "No man will be a sailor who has contrivance enough to get himself in jail," said Samuel Johnson, "for being in a ship is being in jail, with a chance of being drowned." Ships often sank at sea in bad weather, or ran aground on poorly charted coasts, or collided with ice. A whaleship was hijacked by convicts in the Galápagos, and whalemen were attacked by natives from the Equator to the Arctic. Melville's giant white sperm whale, Moby Dick, was based on the famous story (even then) of a great albino sperm whale, Mocha Dick, that repeatedly and intentionally rammed and eventually sank the whaleship *Essex* in 1820. Other whaleships were sunk, apparently purposely, by whales, while countless whaleboats were smashed by harpooned whales, intentionally and otherwise, and their crews were often dragged down to their deaths entangled in rope or simply drowned clinging to scraps of planking too thin to float a cat while waiting to be picked up—life preservers had yet to be thought of. All those Currier & Ives prints and magazine illustrations showing splintered boats and men being tossed rodeo-style into the air by a bucking sperm whale weren't exaggerating anything: it was as dangerous as it looked, or as one easily imagined it to be.

The inside of a whaleship was no place to find solace from the terrors without. Whaling artist and historian Clifford Ashley described the fo'c'sle of the whaleship *Sunbeam*, which he shipped aboard as a common seaman:

On a clutter of chests and dunnage the boatsteerers sprawled, drinking, wrangling, smoking. . . . The floor was littered with rubbish, the walls hung deep with clothing; squalid, congested, filthy; even the glamor of novelty could not disguise the wretchedness of the scene. The floor was wet and slippery, the air smoky and foul; often a bottle was dropped in passing, or an empty one smashed to the floor. Through it all was an undertone of water bubbling at the ports and a rustle of oilskins swinging to and fro like pendulums from their hooks on the bulkhead. Roaches scurried about the walls. A chimneyless whale-oil lamp guttered in the draft from the booby-hatch.

For whalers who survived the chase and the accidents, a long whaling voyage could be as grim as a prison sentence. An early-nineteenth-century whaler, Dean C. Wright, found that, as in jail,

in a whaleship may be found men of all classes, from the lowest to the very first circle in society. The whaling business is, in fact, a general receptacle for every kind of adventurer on the ocean. The ships very frequently go to sea with men in them who have been educated in the first institutions in the country, and been in extensive and respectable businesses on shore, but have been reduced in their circumstances by intemperance, or met with some misfortune and, in a fit of despondency, have entered on board for a whaling voyage, with no specific object in view but a vague idea of something which they do not understand is continually before them, and they are kept along in a kind of delusion untill the ship sails, and then, when the vast ocean separates them from their friends they arouse themselves to the recollections of what and where they are, and what and where they might have been. They find themselves on board of a Cape Horn whaleman, and unless they run into disgrace by leaving the ship, they have got to spend three or four years of the prime of their life in a business which they do not understand, and from which they will not recover any thing commensurate to the time spent.

Like many whalemen, Wright came to hate whaling. In his seaman's papers (official credentials, written by a ship's agent), issued at New

Bedford in 1835 for his first voyage, he gave Avon, New York, as his hometown, and his age as seventeen. Six years later, working his way up, he joined the whaleship *Benjamin Rush* as a boatsteerer or harpooner. By then he seemed unmoored between ambition and the status of his new job, as he wrote in his journal, on June 16, 1842:

A man who has been one voyage in the whaling business and then will ship again to do a boatsteerer's duty must be either mad or drunk, or else a fool or a saint. . . . For he is not respected at all, he has more work to do than all hands besides, and he has no privileges whatever but to bear the blame for every thing which may go wrong in the ship. If the Capt finds a smoothing plain dull he immediately says that a boatsteerer has been planing his Iron pole [harpoon] and dulled it. If there is two quarts of tobacco juice found spit on the deck . . . it is lain directly to the poor boatsteerer . . . [who needs] to be a sailor, a whaler, a mechanic, a saint, a bully, a man of no kind feeling whatever, and very little sense. He ought to be a man who can be spoken to in any tone of voice and called by an epithet, and still give a fawning, sycophantic answer; one who is built of steel and hung on spring steel, and cannot tire, and does not require any sleep or bodily rest of any kind; one who can content himself without any place which he can call his own, or where he is not liable to be crowded out. And he ought to be a man who can be an officer and still be a tar, one who can walk to leeward and not be offended at having any one spit in his face . . . who can show himself worthy of confidence in all cases and not have any placed in him, & be contented to be called a good man, and used like a dog—and do all this for the sake of advancement of which he is not at all sure, when it is done. A Boatsteerer is placed between two fires, being neither man nor officer, yet required to be both. He is beneath the officers and not above the men. He has to obey every body and be obeyed by nobody, give no ungentlemanly language to any person

*but take it from every person, look cross at none but be frowned upon
by all.*

So why the repeated embrace of such humiliation and hardship?
Why was he there? Why did young men from all over New England
walk to New Bedford and other whaling ports and sign on as crew to
seek a very uncertain, palpably dangerous fate that lay over the horizon?
It was not, on their first or even second voyage—a total of four to eight
years—for money. While some men became wealthy through whaling,
working their way up to captain, able to build a captain's house ashore,
perhaps even becoming a shipowner and retiring on the proceeds from
cargoes of oil and bone, the pay for the common seamen who "came up
through the hawsepipe" was not enticing.

"Well, Captain Bildad," asks Captain Peleg, when the two old Quaker
captains, part owners of the *Pequod*, squint at Ishmael as a prospective
crewmember. "What d'ye say, what lay shall we give this young man?"

"Thou knowest best," was the sepulchral reply, "the seven hundred
and seventy-seventh wouldn't be too much would it? . . ."

It was an exceedingly *long lay* that, indeed; and though from the
magnitude of the figure it might at first deceive a landsman, yet
the slightest consideration will show that though seven hundred and
seventy-seven is a pretty large number, yet, when you come to make
a *teenth* of it, you will then see, I say, that the seven hundred and
seventy-seventh part of a farthing is a good deal less than seven
hundred and seventy-seven gold doubloons; and so I thought at
the time.

Whalemen, from the captain down, worked for a "lay," a fractional
share of the ship's net profit from a voyage, after all the expenses had

been deducted. Though shipowners' agents, who hired crews, might easily have befuddled green hands with such fractions, as Melville lampoons, most offered standard lays for recruits and positions. For a common unskilled seaman in the early to middle nineteenth century (when data sets become abundant), this averaged between 1/180th and 1/200th of the net profit, which might ultimately net a sailor six to eight dollars per month. This was about 60 percent of a laborer's wages ashore. Out of this sum, a seaman's food and new issues of clothing would be deducted. A whaleman returning home from three years at sea might collect little more than $100 at the end of the voyage. Skilled seamen, stewards, cooks, carpenters, coopers, sailmakers, and captains did better. A captain received, on average, one-fifteenth, or a "15 lay," which worked out (between 1840 and 1866) to between $70 and $130 per month. But captains often received bonus payments over and above their lays, and even cooks made money on the sale of the ship's slush (its refuse of grease and fat), and this could often substantially improve their earnings.

A first voyage was a whaler's apprenticeship, and his low wage the price of entry into the profession, if he chose it. If he was young and not discouraged by his first voyage, a returning sailor might reasonably hope for advancement. More than half the crew aboard a ship might leave it—through death, dismissal, or desertion—before a voyage's end. Men handy with oars and a harpoon, and those gifted with good eyesight who regularly spotted the spouting of whales, moved up fast, becoming boatsteerers and mates, and their lays bettered dramatically: an 85 lay for a boatsteerer, 55 for a third mate, 40 for a second mate, a 25 share for a first mate. After several good voyages, a captaincy lay in the offing for solid—and lucky, always a factor at sea—men in their early thirties.

Discipline aboard a whaleship was paramount to the success of the voyage; the safety of the ship and of the lives of all aboard her depended on it. As soon as a ship left port, its crew was assembled and addressed on the subject by its captain. He told them that all orders must be executed at once and without questioning their necessity. Punishment for lapses in discipline was usually immediate and brutal. Men were routinely knocked down by an officer's, or a captain's, fists. The men who administered such treatment had to be skilled, confident, self-reliant fighters. "In all my experience on a whaleship I never saw the Captain or an officer hit a man with anything but his bare fist," remembered William Fish Williams.

> I do not doubt that belaying pins and handspikes were used on some ships to enforce discipline but it did not happen on any of the five ships on which I spent my days at sea.... The captains and officers that I knew intimately were men who did not need such aids and would have looked upon their use as an admission of weakness. The sailors rarely harbored a grudge against an officer for enforcing discipline with his fists but the use of a belaying pin was rarely forgotten and never forgiven.

In the often terrifying environment of a whaleship, the threat of immediate physical punishment was the only persuasive authority. "It was the deduction of the captains of that day from their experiences, that . . . authority must be asserted instantly and effectively. Experience had shown them also that nothing is more effective than physical force." Respect was equally demanded: "No sailor ever came aft with a pipe in his mouth; that is, not a second time. What happened the first time depended upon whether the officer of the deck decided it was simply ignorance or a dare. If the [former], he would be told by most officers not to let it happen again, but if the latter, he would be promptly and efficiently knocked down." Insubordination or defiance were best handled with equal promptness and efficiency. Williams later recalled his father's response to a large group of crewmen who were trying to desert the whaleship *Florence* in Guam:

> My father came on deck and met the crew on the port side amidships and asked them where they were going. One of the men spoke up and said they had gone as far as they intended to and they were leaving the damned old hooker before she dropped from under them, also, he advised my father to step aside if he did not want to get hurt. That was the end of the conversation, my father went into action and ploughed through the front ranks of the group with both arms working like pistons of an engine and men going down like tenpins. The men in the rear took one look and bolted for the forecastle. One man stumbled and fell just as my father was about to hit him but, instead of waiting for the man to get up, he grabbed him with one hand around an ankle and the other in the seat of his pants and hove him down the forecastle scuttle in the rear of the last of those endeavoring to get below.

It was the dominance of whaling in New England society that drew men to it for a hundred years from the late eighteenth to the late nineteenth centuries. Whaling became to New England, and to New Bedford especially, what the automobile industry would become to the Midwest and to Detroit—what gold was to San Francisco, and the building of the pipeline was to Alaska in the 1970s. As the whale-oil business geared up along the shores of the Acushnet, with expanding boatyards, ironworks, and candle factories, as more and more ships headed off to sea and returned home with stories of the South Pacific, "the Brazils," the "Japans," and the China Seas, people looked to it as a part of the natural order of things, and naturally became a part of it.

Men went whaling first before deciding that it wasn't for them and opening a grocery store, which almost immediately could prove more profitable by selling goods to the expanding populations of New Bedford and surrounding towns. There was a sizable preexisting population in and close to coastal Massachusetts, and many a boy who lacked a clear opportunity ashore went to sea with a sense of inevitability.

As with soldiers who have been home on furlough and then return to war, the theme of unhappily finding oneself at sea once more, after having been safely home with loved ones and friends, is repeated over and over in the journal writings of whalers—a griping common to all professional seamen down to the present time. The fact that they are away more than they are home is central to the alienation that professional seamen feel from society, and through which they are seen. Seamen have always been marginalized characters, true satellites orbiting society, connected to it mainly by a thick cord of longing. Seamen are absent for much of what other people would consider the crucial episodes of family life—births, birthdays, anniversaries, children's firsts, illnesses, and the bad times out of which a tempering strength and deeper love are forged. Many seamen never acquire the connection with their families and society that most of us carry around inside us, a connection that may be the most lasting measure of who we think we are.

Some whalers went to sea for one voyage—or less—and discovered that such an isolation was not for them, as it is not for most people, and subsequently took up trades and professions ashore. But others, who went back to sea again and again, and made a life of being away, found that this segregation suited them. And—no small consideration—it supplied years of steady work.

On board a ship, sailors, like men in prisons, knew precisely who and where they were in the scheme of things. They were the second or third mate, or the carpenter or cook or boatsteerer, or a plain seaman, and their lives ran—and were run for them—like clockwork. Their realest everyday world, the entirety of it, was what physically lay within the circumscribing horizon, a distance of about eight to ten miles from the observer's eye. There was no existential confusion aboard a whale-ship, and (unlike in prisons) no real disharmony among the crew—for that couldn't last. Men could dislike or hate one another, but they made peace with themselves and their demons within the confines of their cloistering enclosure, as hermetically sealed as a spaceship. Men grew a thick carapace of self-sufficiency and burrowed deep into themselves.

A whaleman departing from New Bedford in the nineteenth century was setting out on a voyage that often lasted three to four years. In all that time he might receive two or three letters from home, sent aboard other ships that might encounter his, or were "posted" by a sailor at designated places such as the barrel used by whalers as a mail drop on Floreana Island, in the Galápagos. By the time he saw them again, his loved ones might have sickened, died, married someone else, or lost the bloom of youth and grown fat. Much of the physical world he had known at home, too, changed and often passed away between trips home: buildings demolished and erected, political regimes come and gone, presidents assassinated, people and communities grown and realigned. But also the converse: while so much had happened to sailors in the meantime, it could seem unbelievable, as if in a dream, that home could be so little changed. They came back as if to Earth from years on a penal colony on the moon. These sailors, with seasons piling up into years in which to nurse their longings and anxieties, wrote much and fulsomely of what they felt.

The dilemma of longing for those at home yet needing to leave them—and stay away for years on end, for the purpose of earning a living—is perfectly caught in New Bedford captain Samuel T. Braley's journal entry for the last day of 1849:

On the first of January last I was off the Island of Ceylon looking for whales, and soon after was obliged to leave for home, having tryed in vain to get more provision in order to lengthen my voyage and I started with a heavy heart expecting to meet nothing but cold looks from my owners [the 1,800 barrels of sperm oil he was bringing home pleased the owners] and to find her whome I had long cherrished as the Idol of my heart numbered with the dead; not having heard a word from her during the whole time of my long stay. . . . [The] long looked for, though dreded moment at lengt arrived we cast our anchor in the harbour of New Bed-ford, and although it was mid-night I hastened on shore, determined to know the worst as soon as possible. . . . I found my way to a livery stable and after much ado I got the hostler up and . . . he harnesed me a horse. . . . It was a fine summers morning and I enjoyed the ride very much every-thing was quiet, and as I past objects that were familiar to me, I thought how little they had changed in the course of three years and a half. At lengt . . . I reached the dwelling of that being most dear to me on earth I drove up to the gate, quietly hitched my horse, and went to the doar how my heart beet but as I knocked, and knocked again before I awoke any one of the household, at last I heard a moove within and a voice . . . which I knew to belong to the Father of my wife . . . I entered and seated myself without serrimony while he went to get a light and to call Marry [sic] Ann. . . . then he came back with a light, and sat down to have a yarn, but what he said I know not for my eyes were fixed on her chair . . . and my thoughts were with her that I heard in another room; how I wished that he would go but he seamed not to notice my uneasiness and sat still, for how long I know not but it seamed to me an age and I was on the point of asking for Mary Ann a second time, whin he took the hint and started, then my heart jumped up in my throat and I could hardly breath but the long looked for moment came at last and she entered the room and [c]losed the door, I flew to her caught her in my arms, I ga[z]ed into her face and insted of finding the raviges of the iron hand of disease I beheld the smile of health and youthfull beauty which excelled any thing I had ever seen in that face before, and above all it was lit up with the blush of maiden modisty that would hardly permit her to wellcom her wanderer back; but oh that kiss! from those sweet lips that were pressed in fondness to mine; it went to my fingersends, and told me in plainest turms how much I was beloved by that little heart that I felt flutter so plainly shall I ever forget it? yes, when I forget to breath It was the happiest moment of my life. . . .

But the end came as must allways be with human happiness. . . . I am now farely started on a long and tedious voyage and whin I look forward upon it my heart sinks to think of the tryals that mist be contended with and obstickles that must be overcome . . . and if I am spared to meet her again nothing shall part us but the fear of starving so has passed the year, how the next one will pass is unknown but at all events I shall not see my wife, nor the next, nor the next but I hope the time will come that I shall again be happy.

Captain Braley went back to sea because it was the only way of life many men knew, the only industry that offered the possibility of steady work.

The modern seaman's homecoming may not be so freighted with emotion: arriving home by car or cab, carrying a duffel bag, glancing at the yard, the scattered toys, it appears almost as mundane as a daily return from the office; modern professional seamen have blunted loneliness and isolation down to a very tolerable inconvenience, managed with cell phones, conjugal visits aboard, and regular trips home. But these periodic visits between lengthy absences have the same effect on these seamen and their families as they did 150 years ago. Being away from home is surely the reason many modern sailors' marriages continue to work. They can stay away and gaze at their loved ones in picture frames in their cabins, and leave the exhausting work of raising a family to their wives and the children's coaches and schoolteachers. When they do go home their guest appearance seldom lasts long enough to upset the status quo there; soon they'll be gone, and everyone knows when, and they hang on, waiting for them to go. Families become used to the long absences, and the spells at home, and the continuity of his schedule, on which the seaman, his wife, and his children come to depend as routine. But he is still away for at least eight months a year, a familiar stranger in his own home. Like the absent whaler, his most constant reality is his ship. It's the only place where he really belongs.

The absences endured by whalers and their families now seem otherworldly. Whalers led lives resembling nothing so much as science fiction. Contained in a small, world-girdling capsule, they matter-of-factly went where few if any had gone before them, and they remained away for years at a time. One whaling captain calculated that at an average rate of four miles per hour while at sea over a period of forty-one years, he had sailed more than 1,191,000 miles, and during all that time had spent four years and eight months at home.

And there was the otherworldly nature of the work itself. Only in the literature of myth, the Homeric monsters of Scylla and Charybdis, tales of the Hydra, the Kraken, and in movies like *Godzilla*, can a comparison be found for the physical scale of man to monster, for the whalers' puny, archaic, pitchfork weaponry, and for the fear men felt when they got the full measure of what they were up against: "Don't ye look ahead an' get gallied, 'r I'll knock ye stiff wi' the' tiller," the mate tells Frank Bullen, an English whaler who sailed aboard the New Bedford whaleship *Cachalot*. The men who rowed the dainty whaleboats right up to the broad backs of cruising whales were forbidden to look over their shoulders at what they were approaching for fear the sight would "gally" (frighten) them. They sat pulling with their backs to the bow and the whale ahead, instructed to keep their head and eyes facing straight aft. Only the experience-tempered mate steering the boat and the harpooner readying his "iron" could see what was coming.

Of the many memoirs written by common sailors, some published more than a century ago, and others that continue to be found in old attics, Bullen's *The Cruise of the Cachalot*, despite the dime-novel clichés, is perhaps the most authentic and detailed description by a whaleman of what exactly that work entailed.

Silently we lay, rocking lazily upon the gentle swell, no other word being spoken by anyone. At last Louis, the harpooner, gently breathed "blo-o-o-w;" and there, sure enough, not half a mile away on the lee beam, was a bushy cloud of steam apparently rising from the sea. . . .

"Stand up, Louey," the mate murmured softly. I only just stopped myself in time from turning my head to see why the order was given. Suddenly there was a bump, at the same moment the mate yelled, "Give't to him, Louey, give't to him!" and to me, "Haul that main sheet naow, why don't ye?" [Most whaleboats carried collapsible sailing rigs.] I hauled it flat aft, and the boat shot up into the wind, rubbing sides as she did with what to my troubled sight seemed an enormous mass of black india-rubber floating. As we crawled up into the wind, the whale went into convulsions befitting his size and energy. He raised a gigantic tail on high, threshing the water from side to side until the surrounding sea was white with froth. I felt in an agony lest we should be crushed under one of those fearful strokes. . . .

By the time the oars were handled, and the mate had exchanged places with the harpooner, our friend the enemy had "sounded," that is, he had gone below for a change of scene, marvelling no doubt what strange thing had befallen him .. . .

[While line was paid out as the whale pulled the boat] I had ample leisure for observing the little game that was being played about a quarter of a mile away. Mr Cruce, the second mate, had got a whale and was doing his best to kill it; but he was severely handicapped by his crew . . . for two of them . . . had gone quite "batchy" with fright, requiring a not too gentle application of the tiller to their heads in order to keep them quiet. . . . [Mr. Cruce's] energy in lancing that whale was something to admire and remember. Hatless, his shirt tail out of the waist of his trousers streaming behind him like a banner, he lunged and thrust at the whale alongside of him, as if possessed of a destroying devil, while his half articulate yells of rage and blasphemy were audible even to us.

Suddenly our boat fell backward from her "slantindicular" position with a jerk, and the mate immediately shouted, "Haul line, there!" . . . After what seemed a terribly long chase, we found his speed slackening, and we redoubled our efforts. Now we were close upon him . . . abreast of his laboring flukes; now the mate hurls his quivering lance with such hearty goodwill that every inch of its slender shaft disappears within the huge body. "Lay off! Off with her, Louey!" screamed the mate; and she gave a wide sheer away from the whale, not a second too soon. Up flew that awful tail, descending with a crash upon the water not two feet from us. "Out oars! Pull, two! starn, three!" shouted the mate; and we obeyed as our foe turned to fight. . . .

The whale's great length made it no easy job for him to turn, while our boat, with two oars a-side, and the great leverage at the stern supplied by the nineteen-foot steering oar, circled, backed, and darted ahead like a living thing. . . . When the leviathan settled, we gave a wide berth to his probable place of ascent; when he rushed at us, we dodged him; when he paused, if only momentarily, in we flew, and got home a fearful thrust of the deadly lance.

All fear was forgotten now—I panted, thirsted for his life. Once, indeed, in a sort of frenzy, when for an instant we lay side by side with him, I drew my sheath-knife, and plunged it repeatedly into the blubber, as if I were assisting in his destruction. Suddenly the mate gave a howl: "Starn all—starn all! oh, starn!" and the oars bent like canes as we obeyed. There was an upheaval of the sea just ahead; then slowly, majestically, the vast body of our foe rose into the air. Up, up it went, while my heart stood still, until the whole of that immense creature hung on high, apparently motionless, and then fell—a hundred tons of solid flesh—back into the sea. . . .

Blinded by the flying spray, baling for the very life to free the boat from the water with which she was nearly full, it was some minutes before I was able to decide whether we were still uninjured or not. Then I saw, at a little distance, the whale lying quietly. As I looked he spouted, and the vapour was red with his blood. "Starn all!" again cried our chief [whose] practiced eye had detected the coming climax of our efforts, the dying agony or "flurry" of the great mammal. Turning upon his side, he began to move in a circular direction, slowly at first, then faster and faster, until he was rushing round at tremendous speed, his great head raised quite out of the water at times, clashing his enormous jaws. Torrents of blood poured from his spout-hole, accompanied by hoarse bellowings, as of some gigantic bull, but really caused by the labouring breath trying to pass through the clogged air passages. . . . In a few minutes he subsided slowly in death, his mighty body reclined on one side, the fin uppermost waving limply as he rolled to the swell, while the small waves broke gently over the carcass.

Bullen called this "Abner's whale," because it had been sighted by a Vermonter named Abner Cushing. After a long spell without a catch, the captain had promised twenty pounds of tobacco, instead of the usual ten, to the man who first spotted the next whale taken and brought successfully to the ship. (Most whalemen were addicted chewers of tobacco; "plugs" and cut cubes of black Navy brand tobacco made good trading currency aboard ship and ashore, and were used as poker chips by sailors.) Abner had been the man aloft on lookout when he saw the spouts of this large sperm whale. "He brought his bounty forrard, and shared it out as far as it would go with the greatest delight and good nature possible."

Only a few weeks earlier Abner had been disciplined for the theft of a few potatoes:

By means of two small pieces of fishing line he was suspended by his thumbs in the weather rigging, in such a manner that when the ship was upright his toes touched the deck, but when she rolled his whole weight hung from his thumbs. This of itself one would have thought sufficient torture for almost any offence, but in addition to it he received two dozen lashes with an improvised cat-o'nine-tails, laid on by the brawny arm of one of the harpooners.

Bullen was sailing in the 1890s, far past whaling's peak years, yet conditions aboard whaleships even then were unchanged from a hundred years earlier.

To understand that the sailors who did this work were not prisoners or galley slaves, or involuntary victims nabbed by press gangs, but employees who did it routinely, generally cheerfully, often (for those who didn't jump ship, like Melville) for years at a time, is to know that such men, like their ships, were peculiar adaptations of their time, and they will not be seen again.

Twelve

Old Lights and New

W hile George Jr. and Matthew Howland, and George Tucker and his autobiographical creation Hiram Wellworthy, dutifully attended the Friends Academy, and the Friends boarding school in Providence, and trod the hidebound path prescribed for them by their parents and their social milieu, they did so in the calm center of a storm of change. While these young men were growing up, New Bedford was becoming one of the more cosmopolitan spots on earth; ships arrived daily with news and people from the farthest reaches of the world. Beneath the gaze of the great houses of the whaling merchants rising on the hill above the harbor, whole shanty neighborhoods of foreigners and heathens sprang up along the tidy Acushnet shores. The impact on the staid and settled town created by its Quaker patriarchs, and their circumscribed world order, and eventually the patriarchs themselves, was steady and unstoppable.

Around 1819, an old Nantucket whaleship named *The Ark* was

sailed to New Bedford to be broken up at Rotch's Wharf (the massive oak and ash framing timbers and pine and cedar planking from many whaleships were recycled into house structures and furniture). From the wreckage, the ship's sternboard, with "*The Ark*" carved into it, was saved and mounted as decoration on another old whaler, the *Camillus*, which sat in the mud at the foot of High Street. Its rig had been removed, a house built upon the deck, with a portico walkway running entirely around the hull. For several years it was used as a houseboat by sailors and their families in reduced circumstances. "But [it] soon came to a baser use," wrote New Bedford historian Leonard Ellis, "and finally was a brothel of the worst character. Its existence was a moral offence to the community, and its removal was earnestly desired by good citizens."

The whale fishery, less active than the merchant shipping business at the end of the eighteenth century, had been slow to recover from the Revolution. In 1806 and 1807, only a single whaleship returned to port in each year with a cargo of oil. Gradually this improved: thirteen whaleships and their cargoes sailed into New Bedford in 1810. But ongoing hostilities between England and her former colony, embargoes on American oil, and the War of 1812 (1812–1815) took their toll, until in 1814, again, only a single whaleship sailed up Buzzards Bay into the Acushnet River. But after 1815, mercantile relationships between America and Britain began to be reestablished, and business picked up again. Two ships returned to New Bedford in 1815, seven in 1816, twenty-eight by 1820. Forty-six ships sailed into the port in 1830, with cargoes valued at $3,487,949, and by then the whale fishery had become the economic base of the town.

New Bedford's population doubled between 1820 and 1830, but few of these newcomers were Quakers. Men and their families from all over New England walked and rode to New Bedford to service the whale fishery that was growing both in size and fame, and many more men arrived by sea. New Bedford society changed swiftly, from a staid, inward-looking religious community made up almost entirely of the descendants of white English settlers, into an informal world's fair of all the people and cultures connected by the world's oceans.

For every whaleship on the waterfront—the town had fifteen wharves by 1823, and there were perhaps thirty to forty vessels in port at any time through the 1820s—there were thirty seamen gathering for a voyage to the far side of the world, or arriving home from one. Brutal men, coarsened beyond normal limits, at the beginning and end of a virtual prison term.

In addition to Queequeg the cannibal—who has been out trying to sell a shrunken head—with whom Ishmael shares his bed, Melville fills the Spouter Inn with such a rabble:

> They were nearly all whalemen; chief mates, and second mates, and third mates, and sea carpenters, and sea coopers, and sea black-smiths, and harpooneers, and ship keepers; a brown and brawny company, with bosky beards; an unshorn, shaggy set, all wearing monkey jackets for morning gowns.

And in the streets:

> In New Bedford, actual cannibals stand chatting at . . . corners; savages outright; many of whom yet carry on their bones unholy flesh . . . Feegeeans, Tongatabooans, Erromanggoans, Pannangians, and Brighggians, and, besides the wild specimens of the whaling craft which unheeded reel about the streets . . . there weekly arrive in this town scores of green Vermonters and New Hampshire men, all athirst for gain and glory in the fishery.

All these—and Lascars, Malays, Frenchmen, Britons, Scandinavians, Germans, Dutchmen, Spaniards, freed slaves and blacks from other countries, "kanakas" from the Hawaiian Islands, Maoris from New Zealand, and great numbers of Portuguese seamen from the Azores and Cape Verde Islands—filled New Bedford. They lived in warrens along the waterfront, across the river in Fairhaven, at the fringes of the towns and their societies, but with their own community increasing faster than any other group in town. They were not ascetic businessmen, but lonely, frequently drunken adventurers who arrived in New Bedford with ravening appetites, and their presence inevitably overwhelmed the genteel nature of the town.

In August 1826, *The Ark* (the former *Camillus*) became the focus of the civic outrage. One evening a mob of good citizens gathered on the waterfront to attack it. Its inhabitants and patrons, having learned in advance of the attack, had readied stones and bottles of scalding water. As the mob approached, stones flew in both directions. Then a ship's gun was brought down the street and positioned to fire on the hulk. Great show was made of ramming a "ball" and cartridge into the gun's muzzle, until the defenders lost their nerve, surrendered, and disembarked. The gun was later found to be loaded with mud. The attackers then scaled the hull on hooks and ladders and *The Ark* was torn apart with axes and crowbars and burned. Fifty citizens were later subpoenaed for rioting but were acquitted.

A second *Ark* was soon established aboard the hull of the former whaler *Indian Chief.* The town's inexorable rise in worldliness is reflected in the observation by the *New Bedford Mercury* that "Ark the second transcend[ed] as a den of abominations anything that tradition has to relate of Ark the first." "It was occupied by the worst classes and was the abode of debauchery and evil doing," wrote Ellis, who believed that the habitués of the second *Ark* also caused trouble ashore. "Citizens were in daily fear, not only of their property but of their lives." In the spring of 1929, the Elm Street Methodist Episcopal Church was set on fire, supposedly by the desperate characters from *The Ark*.

On August 29, 1829, the town's good citizens again took action. On that evening, 200 men gathered in the town hall to discuss plans. A number of Quaker elders, including Gideon Howland, Jr., son-in-law of Isaac Howland, Jr., came to the meeting to try to dissuade the crowd from violence. Local lawyer Timothy G. Coffin (who pops up anecdotally at moments of civil unrest during this period in numerous histories of New Bedford), also appeared at the town hall that evening to read aloud the laws against rioting. No attention was given to these pacifist pleas. At nine p.m., a group of rioters descended to the waterfront and began wrecking the second *Ark*. Lawyer Coffin followed them with a lantern and pleaded again for restraint, but his lantern was blown out and he was bodily lifted and passed over the crowd's head to the rear of the mob. *The Ark* was set on fire, and the fire spread to the shore, where it burned several houses. The *New Bedford Mercury* deplored the riot, but observed: "As with other maritime places, there is a degraded class of population brought within our borders."

NEW BEDFORD'S wealthy Quaker merchant families made up only about 10 percent of its population in the mid-1820s, less by the end of the decade. The greater number of upstanding (though less pacifist, *Ark*-burning) citizens were aligned with the town's Episcopal, Baptist, and Unitarian churches. These were the tradespeople who had come to service the whaling and shipping businesses: the blacksmiths, shipbuilders, coopers, sailmakers, ropemakers, candle-factory workers, and their families. And along the waterfront ebbed and flowed an initially transient but increasingly resident and growing community of sailors, dockers, "alongshoremen," and foreigners, mostly Azoreans and Cape Verdeans, until the part of town they lived in came to be called Fayal, after the port from which many Azoreans had sailed aboard New Bedford whaleships.

The town's leaders—solid, sober, religious, above all wealthy, men—naturally arose from the Quaker whaling merchant elite, which had been the dominant group for more than a hundred years. They first built their houses near the waterfront, on the onetime farmland bought by their Rotch and Howland ancestors from Joseph Russell. But as the waterfront developed and the warehouses arose and thousands of barrels of whale oil with their attendant stench accumulated on the busy wharves, and the noise and traffic and inhabitation of workingmen swelled around them, the Quakers moved uphill, six and eight blocks inland, where they created a leafy suburb and built real mansions with carriage houses and large gardens whose perfumed trees and flowers offset the fishy miasma that lay along the river's shore. But they could not escape the worldly influence that rose uphill with them and inevitably became part of their lives. The Quakers' expressed desire to live in a cloistered community apart from "the world's people" was thwarted by the success of their business interests, and finally made impossible by the very nature of whaling, which forced upon them a global outlook:

The Balaena—Capt. Gardner—4 1/2 months from Wahoo [Oahu] with 2100 bbls. sperm oil arrived this morning. . . . The Leonidas—Capt. Potter—from the coast of Japan, arrived this evening full of sperm oil. . . . The brig Minerva Captain Wood—from the coast of Africa full of sperm oil also arrived this evening. . . .

The ship George and Susan, [Captain] Upham, arrived from the coast of Japan with 2000 bbls sperm and 200 of whale oil.

These are extracts from the 1823–1824 diary of Joseph R. Anthony, a dark, handsome, twenty-six-year-old Quaker who was then working in the Rotch countinghouse (where George Howland had learned the business). He was a cousin of Cornelius Grinnell, who in turn was related by marriage to Gideon Howland, Jr., Isaac Howland, Jr.'s, cousin—so went the degrees of relatedness among the Quakers of New Bedford. Joseph Anthony had married Catharine, one of five daughters of Gilbert Russell, great-grandson of Joseph Russell. The Russell girls were extremely petite, weighing between eighty-eight and ninety-four pounds, and said to be the most beautiful in New Bedford. Anthony was already well-to-do; he was working at Rotch & Co. to learn the business. On almost every day of the year he recorded in his diary—always his first entry of the day—the arrivals and departures of whaling ships, as well as the merchant vessels that sailed routinely between New Bedford and New York and Europe. Until the advent of transatlantic telegraphy in 1866, no information traveled faster than by ship, and Anthony and the other businessmen of New Bedford learned as early as anyone in America the news of the world: "Accounts from Europe rec'd this evening state that the Holy Alliance had broken up, and that there were good reasons to believe that France would soon declare war with Spain." (His intelligence was correct. Four months later: "News received this morning of the Declaration of War by France against Spain, and that hostilities had commenced.") By the 1820s, Joseph Anthony and the other Quakers of New Bedford had become, through their interests in foreign markets, highly sensitized to world affairs and were among the most well-informed people on the planet. Although the old school—the fictional Wellworthys, and George

Howland and his family—studiously shunned the tastes and amuse-
ments of Boston, New York, and London, not to mention Pernambuco
and Trieste (from which Anthony received letters written by his best
friend, Moses Grinnell, who was traveling for the family firm), there
were many, like Anthony, who embraced foreign trends. He ordered
clothing and fruit trees from England; he bought casks of wine from
Lisbon and Madeira, and decanted them into bottles in his cellar. He
traveled often to New York, dining with wealthy friends there; he
frequented—almost obsessively—the theater on Broadway, and had
business dealings with John Jacob Astor.

At home in New Bedford, Anthony's lifestyle was anything but ascetic. On most days he lunched and dined out with friends or entertained at home. He ate oysters and stall-fed pigeons and partridge pies,
roast beef, lobster, and spareribs from his own pigs. He liked to drink,
and frequently confided the results to his diary: *"For my own part I was
pretty well cut."* And the next morning: *"Felt shocking bad all the morning
from last night's frolic."*

There was little public entertainment in New Bedford, but Anthony
was ready for whatever turned up:

> *A company of black theatrical actors arrived in town. They intend per-
> forming a few nights. Much sport is anticipated. Went to a party this
> evening at Francis Rotch's. . . .*
>
> *[Several days later:] After tea Warren and myself went to the African
> theatre at Cole's Tavern. The play was "Pizarro." It was real sport for
> a time and quite a burlesque of the stage. One of the fair damsels gave us
> two good songs. We left at nine and went back to Father's and had a
> little supper. . . .*
>
> *[And a week later:] The Selectmen have forbidden the African Corps*

performing any more of their theatricals, and have threatened them with
a prosecution.

As a young man, Anthony maintained a large home and servants: *"Dec 6th. Devoted the day to piling up wood at home and overseeing Howard [a servant] saw. Found the old adage true that the eyes of the master are worth more than his hands."* In later years, he built his own mansion, filling an entire block between Orchard and Cottage streets, west of County Street, amid the other nobs on the hill above the harbor.

Yet for all his sport and worldliness, Anthony was a regular attendee of the Quaker Meeting, often spending, as many did, an entire Sunday listening to the sermons of local and visiting Quaker preachers. He was certainly devout in his way, but he found his ideas increasingly at variance with the Meeting's elders. So did others. Their problem, according to New Bedford historian Daniel Ricketson, a near contemporary of Joseph Anthony's, was "too great intimacy with the people of the world . . . bringing in the spirit of the world and its attachments and associations . . . [resulting in a] liberality of sentiment." Ricketson noted the sudden arrival of these attachments and liberalities:

Then came a great change in our quiet hamlet—fashionable costumes and parties became the vogue with music and dancing. . . . One of our leading merchants who had been strict in the use of "plain language" and dress, after a winter spent in Boston, returned home with a fashionable blue coat and gilt buttons, and used frequently in his conversation with his friends the then fashionable exclamation of surprise "Good God, sir!" dropping altogether his Quaker phraseology and habits.

Among these renegade members were Joseph Anthony's diminutive but fashion-conscious sisters-in-law, local beauties Mary and Susan Russell, who shared his taste for worldly amusement. The Meeting's elders formally disapproved of the girls' comportment. Anthony recorded:

> *The overseers of the meeting entered a regular complaint . . . against Mary and Susan for not conforming to the Discipline in all the important points of Dress, Address, attending disorderly meetings (viz. the marriage of Jeremiah Winslow and mine) and frequenting places of public amusements. . . . The girls have got their feelings a good deal excited and will probably resign their membership.*

This censure by the local Society of Friends of two of its members for trivial-seeming matters was emblematic of a larger rupture then occurring in New Bedford's Quaker community, and elsewhere. Asceticism is more easily practiced poor. While the Quaker dress code had struggled under the austerity of "the Discipline," good money was being spent on the best imported somber-hued woolens, finest thread-count drab lawns and linens, and technically illicit gold-framed spectacles. A nineteenth-century op-ed writer who wrote under the pseudonym "Old Cribton" observed that "the Friends had . . . long been laying by money from the sheer want of opportunities of getting rid of it"; but Joseph Anthony and his generation were fast discovering and enjoying those opportunities. Many Quakers took much of this in stride, while others, the old school, reacted to such modernity with waspish admonishments.

These disagreements were most sharply and acrimoniously drawn first in the Massachusetts town of Lynn, which was suffering the effects of its own economic good fortune. From colonial times (until the late nineteenth century) Lynn was a center for tannery and shoe-making industries; the town had provided most of the boots worn by Americans during the Revolution, and after the War of 1812 its Quaker merchants were flush with cash.

In response to criticism by the elders, the "New Lights," as the younger, worldlier Quakers came to be called, began to question the severity of the old hard-line doctrines. They claimed they represented no change from the pure Quakerism of George Fox, who had advocated a personal "inner light" relationship with God, without the need for interpretation or the intervention of others. The "Old Lights" objected to any opposition toward their guardianship of the traditional lifestyle and tenets appropriate for the Society of Friends.

In Lynn, Mary Newhall, a woman in her thirties, and an ideological descendant of Anne Hutchinson, emerged as the preeminent New Light preacher. She was said to have "a fatal facility of entering into mystical speculations and . . . great powers of language to express her thoughts." Lynn's old-guard Old Lights at first urged her to stop her preaching, but she refused. Her gift—evidenced by the response it provoked on both sides—was from God, she said, and she "could not decline to exercise it upon the command of men." So she was ordered to stop. Emotions ran high at the Lynn Meeting. A New Light proponent, Benjamin Shaw, a cordwainer, appropriated one of the raised seats in the ministers' gallery to harangue the elders. He was ordered to come down but refused. A physical scuffle ensued; Shaw held on to his seat, which broke before he was pulled away. Another New Light, Caleb Alley, raised his hands "in a fighting attitude" toward the men dragging Shaw out; Alley's father, John, then tried to rush the ministers' gallery and began screaming when the Old Lights tried to stop him; meanwhile, Jonathan Buffum, a housepainter known for his "ungovernable temper," reached the high seats and began yelling: "You that profess to be Quakers, Christians, have shown forth by your conduct the fruit of your hell-born principles this day. You thirst for our blood, you want to feed upon us; this I call spiritual cannibalism!" On the following First Day (Sunday), John Alley came to the Meeting wearing a sword. He was restrained, his belt cut, and the sword removed. That afternoon he came to the Meeting again, and then he, Buffum, and Shaw occupied the gallery seats. They were hauled out, into a crowd of two hundred that had gathered to see the expected show. Cries of "Mob! Mob!" rose from around the Meeting House, until a deputy sheriff appeared and took the New Lights prisoner. They were sent to trial in Ipswich, where the court heard that Benjamin Shaw had also disrupted a recent Meeting at Seabrook, New Hampshire, by climbing into the building's beams and acrobatically swinging into the gallery of high seats. At the Ipswich trial he was found not guilty by reason of insanity. After the trial, the Lynn Meeting disowned Mary Newhall and thirty of her New Light followers.

Mary Newhall began to appear and preach in the New Bedford Meeting. Joseph Anthony listened and approved: *"Mary Newell [sic] preached an excellent sermon at the afternoon meeting."* A week later:

> *M. Newell gave us another sermon to my great satisfaction and I hope to that of many others. . . . About one third of the assembly kept their seats to show they were not in unity with her—no opposition, however, otherwise than not rising at her prayer was manifested by the Old Lights.*

Mary Newhall had tea with Anthony and others at his father's house the following day. And a day later, a Tuesday, Mary Newhall preached at New Bedford's First Congregational Church. Anthony attended, and so did many other Quakers.

There were no swords or scuffling at the New Bedford Meeting, but feelings there grew passionate enough for genteel demonstrations:

At meeting this morning as Eliza Rotch [New Light] was passing up the aisle to take her seat on the high seat, Debby Otis [OL] moved her seat to block up the passage. Eliza stopped and stood in the aisle for 10 or 15 minutes, then took another seat. . . . Phebe Johnson [NL] came in after Eliza, took the high seat by passing Debby. After sitting some time she arose and denounced a woe upon those who interposed the work of the Lord, and cut poor Debby up very handsomely. . . . In the afternoon [meeting] Phebe and Debby had a good deal of spatting.

When several Old Light elders were assigned to pay a home visit to Mary and Susan Russell, to give them a good talking-to, the girls refused to see them and, in April 1823, submitted their resignation to the New Bedford Meeting. While affirming their belief in the fundamental principles of the Society, they wrote that the "deviations from the Discipline" with which they had been charged "have long been considered by the Society, not very important in their nature; and not such, we believe, as friends have deemed necessary to lay before their meetings." And in view of "the conduct of some of the overseers towards us; the spirit in which the report was carried forward; its reception in the meeting; and above all, the present situation of the meeting; we think it most proper to relinquish our right of membership."

The zealous admonishment by New Bedford's Quaker elders of two pretty girls for their deviations from the dress code didn't rock the community, but it presaged a profounder disagreement. A year later, the Society split deeply when the Old Lights charged Elizabeth Rodman and Mary Rotch with supporting the heresy of Mary Newhall, and threatened to remove their status as elders. Both women were unimpeachable pillars of the Quaker community, members of the town's oldest and wealthiest merchant families. In March 1824, over widespread protest, the Old Light faction disbarred the two women from the eldership. The action was widely deplored by many members. Their indignation led a large number of them away from the Society into other churches, and created a schism from which New Bedford's Quaker Society never recovered.

Joseph Anthony turned to the Unitarian church:

> *The house was completely filled and the services were very interesting and impressive. Great liberality of sentiment was advanced; no particular creed was required. . . . I was very much pleased with the services, and have concluded to take a pew with Mr Smith, believing that the moral lectures and instruction which I shall receive from Mr. Dewey [minister] will be of more advantage to me than to attend the [Friends] meeting, the proceedings of which have been of late so counter to my ideas.*

George Howland remained deeply entrenched with the Old Lights. In that straitlaced, unyielding environment he raised his sons, George Jr. (born 1806) and Matthew (1814)—younger than Joseph Anthony (1797) by a decade and more, yet living in a world whose values and prejudices had been formed a century earlier. Like their father (and Hiram Wellworthy's father, Caleb), the boys accepted that world without question. The fact that such wealth had been created by conforming to those values and prejudices, and that the boys were the recipients of such unequivocal approbation of their Creator; the fact that Saybrook, New London, Mystic, Edgartown, and Sag Harbor (none of them Quaker towns) all competed in the whale fishery and none came close to New Bedford's dominance (Nantucket being the only near rival), only confirmed the correctness of the Quakerism of their fathers, and of their fathers' fathers.

While Anthony looked ahead, embraced change, and profited by it—a Darwinian outlook, though he wouldn't have known it as such—George Jr. and Matthew Howland went to the Friends Academy, and the Friends boarding school in Providence, and finally into their father's countinghouse, remaining studiously blinkered to the racier trends circulating at home and abroad, cleaving to the strictest tenets of their church, and maintaining an absolute belief that all that existed—including the business model worked out by their fathers, with the help of the Lord—had been set unalterably in place by Him and was surely smiled upon by Him and should not be tampered with. The Dodo principle.

Thirteen

Frequent Visitors

Through early August of 1871, the wind remained light and the weather fair along the Alaskan shore. The fleet of whaleships continued navigating their way through the channel that lay between the low, sandy coast and the ice pack five miles offshore. This was the accepted tactic, seeking the leads through the ice that would continue to open—it was believed—as the prevailing northeasterlies pushed the floes farther and farther out into the Chukchi Sea as the summer progressed, eventually leaving open water all the way to Point Barrow. As shipmasters pushed their vessels along the traceries of open water, with men aloft shouting down what they could see ahead, the mates and the boat crews routinely continued to set out in the small whaleboats to chase whales. Many were sighted and caught, for the whales, too, found themselves largely confined to the waterway, and greasy smoke from the tryworks rose into the cold air over the fleet.

But on Friday, August 11, 1871, the day after the young Englishman

Lewis Kennedy, of the wrecked *Japan*, died aboard the *Henry Taber*, there was a change of wind. It now rose strongly from the northwest, a direction perpendicular to the northeasterly trend of the coastline and ninety degrees off the desired, supposedly prevailing slant, and the ice pack drifted quickly toward the land. The larger, deeper floes grounded on the offshore shoals and sandbars, forcing the ships to scuttle into their lees, squeezing into a channel that was suddenly reduced from five miles wide to a mile or less, with a bottom that was unfamiliar, lumpy with unmarked shallows, often no deeper than a ship's keel. There was no escape from this narrowing strip of water, for the wind also compacted the smaller "cakes" of ice, closing off the open leads that had threaded through the dispersed floes. The New Bedford whaler *Seneca*, farthest to the north, found itself stuck fast in the ice while carrying full sail. Many whaleboats and their crews suddenly found miles of ice between them and their ships. Some boats were temporarily abandoned, others were dragged by their crews across the ice back to the channel and their ships.

On August 13, the wind dropped to light airs, though still from the northwest. At eight a.m., the *Seneca* once more found ice closing around her. The crew sank blubber hooks on the end of long lines into the ice and tried to haul the ship into clear water, but even carrying full sail, the *Seneca* was soon frozen in place again.

The next day the light wind moved back into the northeast. The ice loosened around the *Seneca*, and by noon she sailed into clear water and anchored in six fathoms—thirty-six feet—of water. From her deck, twenty ships could be seen stretching away to the south, all anchored or moored to ice cakes. Near the *Seneca* was the encouraging sight of the *Elizabeth Swift* with two bowhead whales tied alongside her hull, ready to be cut in. These two whales had been caught the day before, but ice moving on a fast-flowing northeast tide had come between the

Swift and her boats, which had then spent a long day towing the whales back to the ship against the tide.

Still the crews aboard the ships continued whaling, often dragging the whaleboats hundreds of yards across the ice. Whales were caught and pulled alongside the ice floes as they would have been fastened alongside a ship's hull, the blubber and "bone" cut off as best as conditions would allow. With the great number of ships in the area, many whaleboats chased after the same whale, some "mating" with other ships' boats, sharing or dividing the spoils according to the whalemen's etiquette governing who had spotted the whale first and who had helped. Many harpooned whales escaped to seaward beneath the ice, pulling the boats behind them until they fetched up against the floes and their crews had to cut away the lines leading down under the ice.

The wind continued light, though encouragingly, from the northeast, sometimes bringing dense fog, while the ice continued to pack along the shallows just beyond the narrowing waterway. By August 17, there were thirty-three whaleships pinned inside the floes along the coast, still seventy miles or so south of Point Barrow. Men continued whaling, every one of them believing the wind must soon blow more strongly from the east or northeast and push the ice out to sea. Some ships sent men in their whaleboats miles to the north to look for whales with supplies for camping out on the shore or the ice for days. Few had any success. On Tuesday, August 22, three of the *Elizabeth Swift*'s boats set out for the Seahorse Islands, beyond Point Belcher. They found the waterway completely blocked by a wide swath of ice running from the offshore pack all the way to land. The men hauled their boats across the beach into the unfrozen lagoon inside Point Franklin and rowed northeast into the wind and short chop on the water, but once beyond the tip of Point Franklin, they were stopped again by ice. They returned to the *Swift* the next day.

Exactly one year earlier, in August 1870, the *Elizabeth Swift*, the *Seneca*, the Howlands' *Concordia*, the *Hibernia* (with Thomas Williams and family aboard), the *Japan* (with Captain Barker and his crew aboard), and at least thirty other whaleships had all been sailing off this same stretch of coast, tacking north in strong northeasterly winds, often blowing at gale force. There had been *"quite a quantity of ice about,"* according to the *Swift*'s logbook, but the strong—*"vary ruged"*—winds blowing off the land had kept the sea channel open all the way to Point Barrow and beyond, and all these ships had chased and caught great numbers of whales, unimpeded by ice. Since the coastline here trended in a northeast-southwest direction, it might be supposed that the north-easterly winds of 1870 would merely have pushed the ice in a south-westerly direction, paralleling the shore. But the earth's spin creates a deviation, the Coriolis effect, making sea ice move at an angle of thirty degrees to the right of, or clockwise to, the wind direction in the North-ern Hemisphere. Thus, the northeasterlies of 1870 had actually pushed the ice west, to seaward, opening the channel between the pack ice and the land.

That August of 1870, ships had remained in the vicinity of Point Barrow, steadily catching whales until late in September. For most of that time the wind had continued blowing strongly from the northeast, what the whalers took to be the prevailing conditions that they were now, in August 1871, expecting to return at any time. These were "fa-vorable" conditions that, a year ago, had kept all these ships, and the unlucky *Japan*, whaling far north of the Bering Strait until they were overtaken by the great storm of October 4–10.

As LIGHT WINDS BLEW through the middle of August and the ships lay pinned inside the ice, Eskimos, of the Iñupiaq tribes, appeared on the low shore. They were drawn by the spectacle of so many ships held captive and the opportunity to trade.

Captain James Cook and his men had met and traded for fur with Eskimos in the Bering Strait; later, after Cook's death in Hawaii in 1779, his crew sold the sea otter furs they obtained here to Chinese buyers in Macao for fabulous prices. In 1826, the British explorer and surveyor Captain Frederick Beechey managed to sail his ship *Blossom* a few miles beyond Cook's farthest northerly point before being stopped by ice, but members of his crew reached Point Barrow in the ship's boat, the first Europeans to do so. By the time Captain Thomas Roys pushed the *Superior* and her reluctant crew north of the Bering Strait in 1848, not only trade but Russian Orthodox missionary activities were well established south of the strait. But apart from the rare exploratory expeditions of Cook, Beechey, and the Hudson's Bay Company agent Thomas Simpson, who reached Point Barrow with a small party in 1837, the Iñupiaq Eskimos of the northwestern coast of Alaska, north of the Bering Strait, remained in virtual isolation from Russians, Americans, and Europeans.

The native coastal peoples[1] from the Bering Strait to Point Barrow had long been accomplished whalers. Organized whaling, as opposed to windfall beachcombing, had been practiced intermittently by the inhabitants along the northwest coast for more than three thousand years. In a landscape of treeless, permafrost tundra, the coastal Eskimos had evolved a mystically close relationship with the sea, the ice, and the sea mammals who, like themselves, inhabited essentially the same forbidding environment. Their world and spiritual views were defined by the sea and its animal realm, and the social and spiritual culture of the

---

1. Anthropologist Ernest S. Burch, Jr., uses the term "nations," the translation he prefers to "tribes," for the Iñupiaq word *nunaqatigiich* (regional groups).

coastal Iñupiaq was rooted in the whale hunt. While natives inhabiting Alaska's interior drew from a wide range of fauna to supply their needs—caribou, wolves, bear, mountain sheep, foxes, wolverines, waterfowl, and fish—the whale and the walrus provided almost everything to coastal peoples, and they concentrated their efforts on the hunting of these mammals. The arrival of the spring dawn, coming later every day, and the opening of the ice leads that soon followed, marked the start of the whaling season. *Umiaks*, the open fifteen-to-twenty-foot-long whaling boats fashioned from driftwood and bone, and covered with skins, were repaired and rebuilt; the long-evolved, beautifully intricate native harpoons, with wooden shafts, ivory sockets, toggle points, finger rests, gut lashings, and leather ropes were refashioned or made from scratch. Lookouts were posted along the shore. These activities were carried out by the whalers, always male, aided by their wives and children, effectively involving the entire community. The head whaler, the *umialik*, a man of great experience, skill, and, consequently, wealth, sought out and enlisted his crews by gift-giving and wife-exchanging. The social alliances of whaling crews—several to each community—were virtually tribes within tribes, involving tremendous prestige and importance. Tribal shamans (generally schizoid, compulsive, and/or hysteric individuals, according to social anthropologist Ernest S. Burch, Jr., an authority on the Iñupiaq Eskimos) sang songs, blessed the whaling crews and their preparations, and read auguries for success.

In March, camps, including wives and children, were set up on the ice. When a whale was sighted, a crew of seven to ten men ran their *umiak* into the ice "lead"—the watery opening in the ice where the whale swam—and paddled after it. As many harpoon points as possible were driven into a whale; the shafts would come free while the buried toggle points were attached to long lines tied to inflated sealskin floats, which dragged behind the whale as it fled from the initial attack, tiring it and preventing it from sounding for long. (This is exactly the same method used by Native Americans along the East Coast of the United States, as described by Captain George Weymouth in 1605.) The boat would again approach the exhausted whale, and the harpooner would lance the creature repeatedly in vital spots until it was dead. When the whale was brought ashore, or to the ice camp, it was greeted by the wife of the *umialik*, dressed in ceremonial clothing, who offered it a drink of fresh water and words of greeting and thanks. The whale's meat was highly prized and dispersed among the whaleboat's crew and their families and the whole community. Much of it was stored in ice cellars in the permafrost. Walrus was also hunted, though more easily. Walrus meat was less prized—it was given to the community's dogs. Late in the summer, at the end of the hunting season, the whaling communities set out for established trading centers, where they met caribou hunters from the interior and bartered whale and walrus oil for caribou skins. As the winters closed in, the men hunted seal, and inside their houses the whole community repaired and built new weapons, lines, nets, and clothing.

The Eskimos' communion with their environment was, like that of the whale and the walrus, a complete adaptation. It was mutually beneficial in the classic Darwinian mode: the hunters would more often catch the weaker, slower, older animals, leaving food sources and procreation to the fittest whales. They might have continued in this way indefinitely, as they had done for thousands of years, if the whalers in their wooden ships hadn't appeared in 1848, and subsequently in greater and greater numbers, destroying the natural balance of their world and invading their dreams with a host of destructive foreign passions, chief among them alcohol and tobacco. The Eskimos found themselves as poorly adapted as the walrus to meet this abrupt change.

"The natives were frequent visitors, but with very few and rare ex-

ceptions, they were to me extremely repulsive in looks and habits," recalled Willie Williams many years later. As a forty-three-year-old man,
he naturally remembered most clearly what he had noticed up close as
a twelve-year-old boy:

> They have a disgusting fad of making a hole through the cheek near
> the corner of the mouth, in which they place polished pieces of ivory
> or stone, and sometimes, empty brass cartridge shells. Then they
> gradually enlarge the opening by increasing the size of the orna-
> ment, until not infrequently it tears through into the corner of the
> mouth. You can imagine the appearance and the results, especially
> when they are chewing tobacco, by such an addition to an already
> liberal allowance for a mouth.

Willie remained curiously ignorant of the Eskimos, of the realities
of their life and culture, and of the incredible industriousness necessary
to fashion a life in the Arctic. He evidently still believed in 1902, when
he gave an address to the Brooks Club of New Bedford, what he had
been told about the natives he had met as a boy:

> They are confirmed beggars and not above taking things without
> your knowledge and consent. They are shiftless to the point of often
> failing, through no lack of opportunity, but from sheer laziness, to
> provide sufficient food for their winter consumption, entailing much
> suffering and often loss of life by starvation. They early took the first
> two degrees in civilization by learning to use tobacco and rum.

But he was partly correct: they had indeed acquired these vices. They
came to trade furs and clothing for rum and tobacco. Some exchanges
were made, mostly by boat crews meeting Eskimos on the ice or ashore.

Captains were leery of allowing natives aboard. There had been a few unpleasant incidents between Eskimos and whalemen, and these were always well reported. "Attack on a Whaler by the Natives" ran the headline of an article in the *Whalemen's Shipping List and Merchants' Transcript* of March 17, 1863. In June of that year, off Cape Bering, on the western (i.e., the Siberian) side of the strait, the whaleship *Reindeer* was approached by three "canoes with Indians on board." They had just visited another nearby whaleship and appeared to be "intoxicated." They wanted to trade for tobacco, and although this was produced, the Eskimos became belligerent and drew their knives, which were "two feet long and very heavy." The whalers grabbed their own knives, belaying pins, hand spikes, and crowbars, and a short battle took place on the *Reindeer*'s deck. At the end of it, a number of men were cut, none badly, and the Eskimos were thrown into their boats and paddled away.

Through the 1860s there were growing reports of incidents between whalers and drunken or aggressive Eskimos on the Alaskan coast. More were to come throughout the 1870s and 1880s, as Americans sailed to the Alaskan coast in greater numbers, and the plight, and attitudes, of the native peoples inevitably changed, usually for the worse as the formerly holistic nature of their culture became contaminated by the influence of the whalers. Willie's early prejudice was compounded by such reports, which were at variance with the kindness shown to Captain Barker of the *Japan*, and the experiences of many others, but it was an attitude shared by many whalemen, who saw only the negative aspects of the collision of their own and native cultures.

NOW, IN AUGUST OF 1871, the Eskimos again told the whalemen that conditions would not improve and urged them to turn their ships around and get away to the south the moment they were free. The whalers ignored them. Indeed, after weeks of light northeasterlies, the ice pack was beginning to loosen, and whales were visible. On Tuesday, August 28, the *Elizabeth Swift* was able to make sail and head to the north. Her crew saw *"quite a quantity of whales. Struck 24. Saved one."* The remaining twenty-three harpooned whales managed to dive under the ice and escape, dragging hundreds of fathoms of rope.

The other whaleships followed, always pushing their blunt bows north into the ice they were sure would soon break up and float away.

Fourteen

Paradigm Shift

The Howlands, Joseph Anthony, and their cousins and friends were fortunate sons of New Bedford society. Other young men their age, of considerably lowlier station, flocked to the town in the 1840s and 1850s, looking for a berth aboard a whaleship. The fine captains' houses lining the streets above the harbor were proof of the rewards and social improvement a young man with grit and luck might hope for.

Rowland Rogers, of Mattapoisett, was one of these young men. He sailed aboard a whaleship for three years, working for a 147th lay, which netted him, at the end of the voyage, $95.20, or a little under $32 per year. He decided whaling wasn't the life for him, but saw an opportunity ashore in catering to the growing number of whalemen and sailors setting up homes in the area. He moved his family to Fairhaven and opened a grocery store.

His son, Henry Huttleston Rogers, worked in the store after school, delivering newspapers and groceries by wagon, but the boy had an outsize measure of his father's ambition for business. Whether because of his father's unfruitful experience or the stench of whale oil that permeated Fairhaven, and New Bedford across the river, Henry wasn't interested in whaling. He was drawn to more modern ventures. When he left school in 1856, a tall, handsome, sixteen-year-old, he went to work as a brakeman on the new Fairhaven Branch Railroad. By the age of twenty-one he had saved about $300. He pooled his savings with those of a friend, Charles P. Ellis. With $600 between them, they managed to borrow another $600 and set out for Pennsylvania with the idea of getting into the exciting new "rock oil" business.

Two years earlier, in August 1859, petroleum oil had been extracted from the ground in Pennsylvania, the result of efforts led by a visionary entrepreneur, George Bissell. After graduating from Dartmouth College, Bissell spent ten years teaching and working as a journalist in the South before moving north again. While visiting his alma mater, he was shown a bottle of distilled rock oil, drawn from oil springs on a farm in Pennsylvania, and used as a patent medicine for cholera morbus, liver ailments, bronchitis, consumption—classic "snake oil," the variously packaged folk remedy for any number of complaints and agues. Such oil, in its crude form, had long been known in northwestern Pennsylvania, noted by trappers and explorers along the Allegheny River, and by the Indians of the area, who believed it had curative powers. The Dartmouth laboratory professor holding the bottle told Bissell that the stuff was flammable. Then, or sometime soon afterward, Bissell—an exhausted, dispirited academic—experienced the first of his two eureka moments that have become part of the recorded history of the petroleum industry: he decided rock oil might have commercial possibilities as an illuminating oil. Other oils had appeared to rival whale oil and smoky tallow candles: camphene, which was unstable and often blew up, and kerosene, or "coal oil," made from coal, were used in lamps that had been specially developed for them, but none of these had been produced in cheap abundance.

Bissell quickly formed the Pennsylvania Rock-Oil Company and leased the farmland where the oil he'd been shown had come from. He sent a sample of this oil to Benjamin Silliman, Jr., a distinguished professor of chemistry at Yale, to be analyzed for its potential properties. Silliman reported that the oil could easily and inexpensively be made into a high-quality illuminant. "Gentlemen," he wrote Bissell and his partners, ". . . your Company have in their possession a raw material from which, by simple and not expensive processes, they may manufacture very valuable products."

Encouraged, Bissell now turned to the process of obtaining the oil in quantities. So far, the only methods of collecting it had been skimming the surfaces of oily creeks and wringing the water out of oil-soaked rags. This had adequately provided the quantities demanded by the patent-medicine market, with its small glass bottles, but Bissell's dreams called for much more. His second recorded flash of illumination occurred as he stopped one day in the shade beneath a drugstore awning on Broadway, in Manhattan, looked into the window, and saw a bottle of Kier's rock oil, or petroleum, "celebrated for its wonderful curative powers. A natural Remedy; Produced from a well in Allegheny Co., Pa., four hundred feet below the earth's surface." The bottle's label showed a picture of a well-drilling derrick.

He would drill into the earth to obtain oil in commercial quantities, Bissell decided.

Bissell's investors, with varying degrees of faith, came and went. He eventually launched a new company, Seneca Oil, and looked for someone who would travel to the leased farmland in Pennsylvania and set up a drilling operation. One of Seneca's investors, a banker named James Townsend, was living in the Tontine Hotel in New Haven, where he began talking with a colorful thirty-eight-year-old out-of-work railroad conductor named Edwin L. Drake. Townsend hired Drake for the job and sent him south to Pennsylvania with bank drafts and letters of introduction describing the bearer as "Colonel E. L. Drake." Drake held no such military rank, but the title lent him a stature that was to help launch his wild scheme in the backwoods valleys along the Allegheny.

On the company's leased farmland beside Oil Creek, two miles from the run-down lumber town of Titusville, Drake spent more than a year setting up a steam engine that would drive a drilling rig. He hired a driller, William ("Uncle Billy") Smith, and Smith's two sons, who had worked on artesian salt-drilling rigs. As time passed with no results, most of Seneca's investors bailed, leaving Townsend to pay the mounting bills out of his own pocket. Eventually even he despaired and wrote to Drake to close up the operation. Drake had not yet received that letter when he arrived at the well on August 29, 1859, and found Uncle Billy and his boys filling pots, barrels, and washtubs with dark, viscous oil that was rising from their borehole, which by then reached sixty-nine feet into the ground. Drake attached a common water pump to the hole and began pumping up oil.

Bissell's intuition about the possibilities of petroleum oil was not original. He is the man history has remembered for his role in getting Edwin Drake to Pennsylvania, but many were already well aware of the potentials of rock oil. Within days of Drake's "discovery," speculators poured into Titusville and the surrounding area, buying up farmland at prices that doubled and tripled overnight. Bissell, too, arrived and spent hundreds of thousands of dollars, buying and leasing more farmland. The swampy land up and down Oil Creek turned into a vast tract of mud with the sudden traffic of people, lumber, and wagons. Derricks were erected, wells were drilled in every creek off the

Allegheny, and oil obligingly flowed: two, three, four thousand barrels a day, right away, and more bubbling up.

There was the immediate problem of what to do with it. There were not enough whiskey barrels, molasses barrels, casks, or milk cans in Pennsylvania—or, soon, in America—in which to store it all. Reservoirs were dug in the muddy earth, lined with logs and planks, wooden tanks built, though all these soon proved inadequate. Barrels—as suited to petroleum as whale oil—when they could be provided and filled, had to be transported to the nearest rail depots in Erie and Union City. "Teamsters equipped for this service seemed to fall from the sky," wrote Ida Tarbell in her groundbreaking *History of the Standard Oil Company*. Boys and men from surrounding farms dropped their tools and plows and headed to the nearest oil derrick with their horses and wagons. They were paid three and four dollars a barrel for hauling wagonloads of oil five or ten miles. But it was hard work: the roads, such as they were, deteriorated immediately to muddy canals across fields and through forests. Caravans of a hundred and more wagon teams were held up by broken wheels and deep mud holes and fallen and dying horses.

Roughly built flatboats were loaded with oil barrels and sent down Oil Creek—"a more uncertain stream never ran in a bed"—colliding with others, running aground, their wreckage piling up on the banks, the oil running freely down to the Allegheny and the Ohio.

The teamsters were eventually put out of business by pipelines. Almost from the beginning, pipes were laid, aided by gravity and pumps, but there were many early problems: they proved too weak, they burst or clogged; collection centers moved, leaving pipes heading nowhere. "Then suddenly the man for the need appeared, Samuel Van Syckel," Tarbell recounted. Van Syckel had seen much of his own and others' profits eaten up by the teamsters. He laid a two-inch pipe, with three relays, that carried eighty barrels of oil an hour from the wells to the railroad. "The day that the Van Syckel pipe-line began to run oil a revolution began in the business," Tarbell observed. "After the Drake well it is the most important event in the history of the Oil Regions."

The teamsters clearly saw the threat to their livelihood and dug up parts of Van Syckel's buried pipe, until armed guards were stationed along its length. They burned storage tanks, threatened well-drillers and owners whose oil was carried by pipe. But the pipeline had arrived, as surely as the oil, and the teamsters were finished—though the cutting and destruction of pipelines has remained an enduring form of sabotage.

Other advances were quickly made: wood-lined holes in the ground holding from 200 to 1,000 barrels were replaced by iron tanks holding up to 30,000 barrels; pipelines led directly from wells to storage centers and rail depots.

In the frenzied early days, oil buyers raced one another on horseback from wells to storage containers and rail depots, bargaining with producers and transporters. As rail lines were quickly laid between the Oil Regions and cities like Cleveland and Erie, the trains themselves, crowded with brokers, agents, speculators, and drillers, all of them smoking cigars and spilling whiskey, became de facto oil exchanges, the clattering wheels underfoot ratcheting up the hurtling momentum of epic enterprise.

By 1865, at least $100 million in capital had been sunk into the muddy, torn-up country between Titusville and Oil City; $350 million was spent in the region during the industry's first decade.

Alongside the production of oil arose the frantic, equally tumultuous industry of refining it—initially into kerosene, oil's first primary use. The process was easily and cheaply done, and a year after Drake struck oil, there were at least fifteen refineries up and down Oil Creek. Others sprang up all along the railroad lines between there and Pittsburgh,

Erie, and Cleveland. With its established rail connections and a location at the industrial center of the Great Lakes, Cleveland would become the country's leading refinery center by 1869. A young Cleveland accountant, John D. Rockefeller, was a month past his twentieth birthday when Drake struck oil. He had grown up on farms in New York and Ohio. Early in his life a number of empirically acquired lessons about the making of money made strong impressions on him. One of these he liked to relate for its clarity:

> Among the early experiences that were helpful to me . . . was one in working a few days for a neighbor in digging potatoes—a very enterprising, thrifty farmer, who could dig a great many potatoes. I was a boy of perhaps thirteen or fourteen years of age, and it kept me very busy from morning until night. It was a ten-hour day. And as I was saving these little sums I soon learned that I could get as much interest for fifty dollars loaned at seven per cent—the legal rate in the state of New York at that time for a year—as I could by digging potatoes for 100 days. The impression was gaining ground with me that it was a good thing to let the money be my slave and not make myself a slave to money.

At seventeen, Rockefeller was earning twenty-five dollars per month as a bookkeeper. He was always "saving a little money to put away." At nineteen, with his modest savings, he established a produce-trading business on the Cleveland docks with a thirty-one-year-old Englishman, Maurice B. Clark. They reportedly made $450,000 in their first year. In 1862, Rockefeller and Clark opened their first oil refinery in Cleveland. By 1865, it was the largest of Cleveland's thirty refineries, and that year Rockefeller bought Clark out for $72,500. He began buying other oil refineries, expanding and consolidating his business. In

1870, Rockefeller established the refining company of Standard Oil of Ohio, which, through the omnivorous incorporation of every competitor in its path, was largely successful in monopolizing the oil production and refinery industries in America, until that monopoly was broken by the Supreme Court in its historic antitrust case of 1911.

In 1861, young "Hen" Rogers of Fairhaven and his friend Charles Ellis opened their own refinery near Oil City. They named it the Wamsutta Oil Refinery after the Indian whose name and mark appeared on the deed recording the purchase of the territory of Dartmouth. They cleared $30,000 in profits in their first year of production. In Oil City they met a fellow Massachusetts man, Charles Pratt, who had worked for a company in Boston specializing in whale oil–based paints and other products. Pratt was quick to see the advantages of petroleum over whale oil and opened his own petroleum oil refinery in Brooklyn, New York. Pratt contracted with Rogers and Ellis to supply him with their entire product (for him to distribute) at a fixed price. When the cost of oil rose and Wamsutta couldn't meet its obligations, Wamsutta failed, heavily in debt to Pratt. Ellis returned to Fairhaven, but Rogers traveled to Brooklyn and told Pratt he would take responsibility for the debt and repay him. Pratt was so impressed that he hired Rogers. By 1867, Rogers was a partner in Charles Pratt and Company. When Standard Oil of Ohio had the company in its sights, Pratt and Rogers at first fought Rockefeller, but then capitulated, and Charles Pratt and Company was absorbed into the expanding maw of Standard Oil. Rogers eventually became a vice president of Standard Oil and, with investments in gas, steel, copper, coal, and railroads, one of the richest men in America. He acquired a reputation for ruthlessness in business, and the nickname "Hell-hound Rogers," and he is often cited as the quintessential "robber baron." But, like many of them, he was also a generous philanthropist, and donated millions of dollars for buildings and public works in Fairhaven.

PRODUCTION OF PENNSYLVANIA OIL rapidly increased on a scale beyond Bissell's, or any other oilman's, dreams: from 450,000 barrels in 1860 to more than 3 million barrels by 1862. The supply initially exceeded the demands of a market that was lagging well behind production: oil prices rose and fell mercurially, plummeting from ten dollars a barrel in January 1861 to ten cents by year's end. But on April 12 of that year, Confederate batteries began firing on the Union garrison stationed at Fort Sumter in Charleston Harbor, South Carolina, and war worked its industrial magic on the nascent oil business. Supplies of the cheap illuminant camphene, made from turpentine, which came from the South, were cut off, creating overnight a large and growing northern demand for kerosene made from Pennsylvania oil.

Abundant petroleum oil, and the resultant cheap kerosene, had a dramatic effect in the illuminant marketplace. In 1860, as the price of petroleum plummeted, whale oil was hovering around fourteen dollars per barrel. It was still the preferred illuminant for those who could afford it, and a superior lubricant, but the volume and the almost immediate availability of the output of the petroleum industry could not be ignored: a successful whaling voyage of three to four years might return three or four thousand barrels of oil; a single well in Pennsylvania could produce three thousand barrels of oil in a day. In its first six years, the petroleum industry produced more oil than all the whale oil brought home in the ninety years from 1816 to 1905.

· · ·

WHILE HENRY ROGERS, Charles Pratt, John D. Rockefeller, and count-less others recognized the sudden, gushing appearance of petroleum oil as an epic paradigm shift, George Jr. and Matthew Howland, and many other New Bedford merchants remained strangely oblivious to what was overtaking them. New Bedford remained cocooned in its history, complacent in the certainty of its holy mission and in the belief that things would go on as they had for more than a century. "Why not?" George Howland, Jr., had declaimed to his audience in 1864.

But coinciding with the sudden impact of the petroleum business, the Civil War proved a major disruption for the whale fishery. Seeking to put a stranglehold on the Confederacy's supplies, Gideon Welles, the secretary of the Union navy, sent agents to New Bedford and other whaling ports to purchase twenty-five old vessels, of at least 250 tons each, to be filled with blocks of granite, sailed south, and sunk in the harbor mouths of Savannah and Charleston, stoppering up the South's two most vital ports. For many whaling merchants, then burdened with aging vessels and a declining market, the appearance of Welles's agents, offering ten dollars per ton for their oldest, most decrepit ships, was a boon. Fourteen of the twenty-five ships were purchased in New Bedford; the rest were found in Nantucket, Martha's Vine-yard, New London, Mystic, and Sag Harbor. New England's ubiquitous fieldstone proved easier to obtain than quarried granite, and New Bed-ford's farmers reaped an unexpected harvest selling their stone walls to government agents at fifty cents a ton. The "stone fleet," as it came to be called, departed from New Bedford on November 20, 1861. The operation was supposed to be a clandestine war secret, but the town gave the fleet a send-off, with thousands cheering from the docks and a thirty-four-gun salute, with the result that the departure was reported the following day in *The New York Times*. Nevertheless, many of the Confederate forces in Savannah watching the fleet assemble outside the harbor believed it to be an invasion of warships, and, beating the stone fleet at its own game, sent a few of their own older ships out toward the fleet and sank them in the harbor channel. Many of the stone fleet's ships arrived, after their stormy passage south, leaking so badly that they sank or grounded in ineffectual positions outside the harbor or near the shore. The remainder of the fleet was directed to sail on to Charleston, where sixteen vessels were sunk in a checkerboard pattern across Charleston's main shipping channel. Secretary Welles was pleased with the result and ordered a second stone fleet organized and sailed south to Charleston, where it was also sunk in a checkerboard pattern in January 1862. The results did little to impede navigation into and out of Savannah and Charleston. Strong tidal currents racing between the Atlantic and the cities' inland rivers soon broke up the weakened wrecks, scattered and buried their stone cargoes in the silt and mud, or made new channels. But the action of the stone fleets—something that, had it been successful, might have proved ruinous to the commerce of the cities and their civilians for decades after the war—was widely seen as a barbaric war crime, something beyond the pale of the gentlemanly code of war as then conducted. It was denounced not only throughout the South but also in France and England, and excoriated by *The Times* of London, which observed: "People who would do an act like this would pluck the sun out of the heavens, to put their enemies in darkness, or dry up the rivers, that no grass might for ever grow."

The stone fleets may have been beneficial for shipowners, enabling them to sell off old vessels for good money, but the navy of the South had its own plans for disrupting the economy of the North, and the whale fishery lay directly in its sights. Confederate president Jefferson

Davis and secretary of the Confederate navy Stephen Mallory dispatched an agent, James Bulloch, to England to procure warships that would attack the Union's commercial shipping. Whaleships, as well as merchant vessels carrying oil from New Bedford to London—the oil tankers of the nineteenth century—were crucial to the Northern war machine. Britain was neutral during the Civil War, its subjects and businesses forbidden to aid either side. While Bulloch, an American, was allowed by law to commission the building and outfitting of ships in Britain, and even purchase arms there, he was careful to deal with different firms for every item, and keep his arms and ships separate, to minimize the possibility of his suppliers' being seen to be aiding the Confederate war effort. Even when his activities were discovered by Union spies and the British government was informed of his purpose, Bulloch was found to be operating within the strict letter of British law, and the government could not stop him. The Confederacy's loophole-enabled warship *Alabama*, a 210-foot steam-auxiliary-powered sailing ship, built by the Birkenhead Ironworks in Liverpool, was launched on July 29, 1862. It sailed immediately to the Azores, where Bulloch had already dispatched a ship loaded with arms and supplies. On September 5, off those whale-infested islands, the *Alabama* approached the Edgartown whaleship *Ocmulgee*. Flying the Stars and Stripes, the *Alabama* gave no alarm to the whalers, but as she hove up close alongside, the Union colors were lowered and the Confederate flag was raised. The whaleship's captain, Abraham Osborne, later deplored this subterfuge as a "disgraceful" ruse. Like all whaleships, the *Ocmulgee* was defenseless, barring the few personal firearms that might be carried by the captain or a mate. The *Alabama*'s captain, Raphael Semmes, ordered the ship's crew into their whaleboats, whereupon the *Ocmulgee* was burned. The whalemen were allowed to row themselves to a nearby island.

Whaleships proved the easiest of prey: they congregated in fleets on known whaling grounds and, like the *Ocmulgee*, could offer no defense. The *Alabama* captured and burned nine whaleships off the Azores during September. Over the next twenty-one months, she destroyed forty-six whaleships in the Atlantic, twenty-five of them from New Bedford. She was finally sunk off Cherbourg, France, by the USS *Kearsarge*, but Bulloch quickly purchased another British ship, the steam-auxiliary East India merchant ship *Sea King*. She was sailed to Madeira, where Bulloch had another supply vessel waiting to arm and outfit her. The *Sea King* was rechristened *Shenandoah*, and her new master was a luxuriantly mustachioed former U.S. Navy lieutenant from North Carolina, James I. Waddell. He was ordered to take his ship to "the far-distant Pacific," specifically to hunt down the Union's whaling fleet. Before the *Shenandoah* had left the South Atlantic, Waddell encountered and burned the New Bedford whaler *Edward* near the island of Tristan da Cunha. He sailed on to Melbourne, Australia, where the *Shenandoah* underwent repairs and loaded coal. It was early 1865 before she reached the Pacific. In the Caroline Islands, Waddell captured four whaleships, and with them their captains' detailed charts of the whaling grounds of the Pacific, the Okhotsk and Bering seas, and the Arctic Ocean—where he could sail directly and be assured of finding dozens of whaleships. In May, on the Kamchatka grounds, Waddell captured and burned the New Bedford ship *Abigail*. In June, his crew observed floating pieces of blubber in the Bering Sea and soon afterward encountered the ships *William Thompson* and *Euphrates*, both from New Bedford. Their crews were taken aboard the *Shenandoah* and the ships burned. The next day three more New Bedford whaleships, *Milo*, *Sophia Thornton*, and *Jireh Swift*, were captured—the last two after a chase through the ice floes. The captain of the *Swift* was

Thomas Williams; because of the war, his wife Eliza, son Willie, and daughter Mary were for once not with him but living ashore in San Francisco. At this point, Waddell had a full shipload of Union whaling crews as prisoners, so after burning the *Sophia Thornton* and the *Jireh Swift*, he ransomed the *Milo* to its captain for an IOU of $46,000, to be paid by the *Milo*'s owners to the Confederacy after the war, then loaded that whaleship with all the captured whalemen and set them free. The *Milo* sailed to San Francisco, where many of the whalemen promptly found berths aboard other whaleships.

Waddell had had no news of the war since leaving Australia until, late in June 1865, he found newspapers aboard a captured trading ship with reports of Lee's surrender at Appomattox and Lincoln's assassination. While this was disastrous news for the Confederacy, Waddell remained uncertain of the outcome of the war, so he continued to do what he could for the South. The *Shenandoah* steamed on through the Bering Sea, eventually capturing and burning another fifteen vessels, and sending a second ransomed ship full of prisoners back to San Francisco. Finally, anxious for further war news, Waddell sailed the *Shenandoah* south, where, in August, off the California coast, he sighted a British merchant ship, closed with it, and learned that the war was indeed over and that the South had lost. Realizing that his most recent captures and burnings had probably taken place after the war's end, Waddell continued sailing south, intent on avoiding capture. The *Shenandoah* rounded Cape Horn and, completing a circumnavigation of the world, reached England on November 5, 1865. The arrival was an embarrassment for the British government, which had allowed the ship to sail from there thirteen months earlier, and failed to stop it in Melbourne, by which time it had already sunk a whaleship and its mission was clear. According to *The Times* of London:

The reappearance of the Shenandoah in British waters is an untoward and unwelcome event. When we last heard of this notorious cruiser she was engaged in a pitiless raid upon American whalers in the North Pacific. . . . It is much to be regretted . . . that no federal man-of-war succeeded in capturing the Shenandoah before she cast herself, as it were, upon our mercy.

The American press urged that Waddell and his men either be tried in England for piracy or handed over to the U.S. government. The ship was turned over to the American consul in London, but Waddell and his men were set free. Waddell remained in England for ten years, until he was hired as captain on the mail packet running between Yokohama and San Francisco. He eventually settled in Annapolis and died there in 1886.

EVEN BEFORE EDWIN DRAKE HIT OIL, two of New Bedford's largest whaling merchants were getting out of the business, in favor of enterprises they believed held sounder prospects for the future.

Joseph Grinnell, born in 1788, was the heir to one of the town's largest and most successful whaling enterprises, formed by his father, Cornelius Grinnell, and his uncle, Gideon Howland, Jr. Joseph worked for them until he was twenty-two, when he moved to New York City and there, with another uncle, John Howland, started a trading and shipping business called Howland and Grinnell. They were very successful until the War of 1812, which again saw the destruction and confiscation by the British of American property and ships, including Howland and Grinnell's. John Howland returned to New Bedford, but Joseph, who could have gone home and worked for his father again, remained in New York. He was unusually independent-minded, and this fact would prove crucial to his later career, and to the future of New Bedford. With his cousin, the preposterously named Captain Preserved Fish, he started another shipping and mercantile business in New York, under the name Fish and Grinnell. Joseph's two younger brothers, Henry and Moses, later joined them. Captain Fish retired in 1825, and Robert Minturn, Henry Grinnell's brother-in-law, joined the firm, which then changed its name to Grinnell, Minturn & Co.—the firm that owned Thomas Roys's ship, the *Superior*.

In early middle age Joseph Grinnell returned to New Bedford, leaving his brothers and Minturn in charge of the business in New York City and Sag Harbor. As if to make up for leaving it in his youth, he then devoted himself to doing everything he could for his hometown. He became president of the Marine Bank, holding that position from its founding, in 1832, until he resigned, in 1878. He was president of the New Bedford and Taunton Railroad, and of the Boston and Providence Railroad. In 1843, he was elected to Congress to serve the unexpired term of the deceased New Bedford district congressman Barker Burnell (he was reelected for three additional terms).

While in Washington in 1847, Grinnell met with a group of businessmen who were interested in opening a cotton mill in Georgia, where the manufacture of cotton was extremely profitable at that time. Grinnell was intrigued by the plan, but the Mexican-American War had recently begun, in the wake of the annexation of Texas and the disputed territories, and the threat of hostilities reached deep into the American South. Grinnell proposed that the mill be built in New Bedford, where he was sure the investment would be safe, and where he knew a workforce was available. Whaling in New Bedford was then still approaching its zenith, already one of America's leading and most important industries, but Joseph Grinnell had a prescient notion that it might not always be so. He had been nearly ruined in whaling and shipping when young, and perhaps he had a better instinct than most for the vagaries of a business pinned to the imponderables of ships, the sea, and the already diminishing resource of whales.

Grinnell and his partners sought a subscription of $300,000 to capitalize the mill, and to build and outfit it with 15,000 spindles and 300 looms. It was to be called the Wamsutta Mill. Grinnell put up $10,000 of his own money, but despite great efforts, only $157,000 was raised. The whale fishery, then generating previously unimagined wealth and a dot-com-like frenzy of irrational exuberance, was sucking up every available investment dollar, and New Bedford was its Silicon Valley. "Everyone who had money to invest sought for opportunities to join with some favorite agent in the numerous vessels that were being added to the fleet," wrote historian Leonard Ellis. "The profits were large and very certain, and the entire prosperity of the place had grown out of it. This was the one great obstacle in the way of getting sufficient capital for the first mill."

Grinnell was bucking the trend. Finally he invested another $2,100 of his own money to bring the initial capitalization to $160,000. The mill was built of brick, at the north end of town, conveniently sited between the river and the New Bedford and Taunton Railroad line, both of which would be of use. Ten thousand spindles and 200 looms were installed. The first Wamsutta Mill began operation in the spring of 1849. As soon as its cotton products—shirtcloth, cambrics, muslins, cloths of all types and qualities—reached the market, they were successfully sold and created a demand for more. Coastal New Bedford was found to have natural advantages for the manufacture of cotton goods: there is a year-round dampness and softness to the air that is favorable for the handling of cotton yarns; winters along the Buzzards Bay shore are mild, and summers far cooler than those in Georgia, making comfortable working conditions for mill employees. According to Ellis: "From observations made from 1849 to 1874 the operatives in New Bedford enjoyed better health than those employed in interior towns, and consequently the amount of earnings was correspondingly increased."

So successful was the first Wamsutta Mill that a second was built alongside it and began operation in the fall of 1854. A third mill was built in 1860–1861, a fourth in 1870, a fifth in 1875, and a sixth in 1882. By then the Wamsutta mills employed 2,200 people, housing them in "comfortable" tenements with five to seven rooms in each unit at rents of $5.25 to $7.50 per month. Joseph Grinnell remained president of the Wamsutta Mills Corporation until his death in 1885. With uncanny foresight, he got out of the whaling business at its height and put his money in what seemed in the beginning a very dubious venture.

EDWARD MOTT ROBINSON was "from away." Born in Philadelphia, in 1800, to a prominent Quaker family, he began his business career manufacturing cotton with his brother in Rhode Island. But Robinson was an ambitious man and moved to New Bedford around 1833 to get into the oil business. His shrewdest move was his marriage, within a year of his arrival in New Bedford, to one of Isaac Howland, Jr.'s, two granddaughters, Abby. Two weeks after the wedding, Isaac Howland, Jr., died, leaving Robinson, with one other partner, in charge of the largest whaling fleet—eventually more than thirty ships—and fortune in New Bedford. Robinson was described as "forceful, energetic, pushing and far-sighted in business," and "not personally popular." He was a physically imposing man. Nelson Cole Haley, a harpooner aboard the whaleship *Charles W. Morgan* when it was owned by Robinson, later remembered him vividly, from when he signed his shipping papers in

Robinson's office in 1849: "I found him to be a tall man (six feet at least) with keen black eyes and a hawkbill nose, with a very dark complexion. I then saw why he was nicknamed 'Black Hawk.'"

Along with the industry's improving conditions, Robinson's intelligence and business sense were responsible for the continued growth of Isaac Howland, Jr., Company through the boon decades of the first half of the nineteenth century. Yet at the industry's peak, in the 1850s, he, like Joseph Grinnell, saw and acted upon early signs of whaling's decline. Before Drake's oil well, before the outbreak of the Civil War, and during the years of growing whaling harvests in the Arctic, Robinson began transferring his fortune and assets out of whaling and New Bedford. When his wife, Abby, died in 1860, he wound up Isaac Howland, Jr., & Company completely, selling off its ships and wharves, and his personal property, and moved to New York, done with whaling. (On Edward Mott Robinson's death in June 1865, his daughter and only child, Hetty Robinson, inherited his estate, worth over $5 million. Just two weeks after Robinson's death, Hetty's maiden aunt, Abby's sister, Sylvia Ann Howland, died, leaving Hetty another $2 million, making her the richest woman in the world. Later reviled as "the witch of Wall Street" for both her financial acuity and her infamous parsimony—she was unwilling to pay for a doctor until it was too late, and thus an infection in her son's leg resulted in a needless amputation—Hetty parlayed her $7 million into a personal fortune of $100 million by the time of her death in 1916.)

Neither Grinnell nor Robinson subscribed to the sense of divinely directed mission that kept many of New Bedford's Old Light Quakers, like George Howland and both his sons, unalterably wedded to the whale fishery. Grinnell and Robinson were Quakers by heritage, but they were businessmen first.

. . .

YET EVEN AS WHALE OIL became scarcer, and petroleum more abundant and cheaper, there emerged a new and surging ancillary market supplied by the whale fishery. Coinciding with the discovery of the arctic bowhead, richly endowed with an abundance of baleen of great length, came the demand for "whalebone," as baleen was termed. This had long been merely a by-product of oil-gathering; the densely fronded mouths of right whales had long been cast adrift after the blankets of blubber had been peeled off an animal. But from the mid–nineteenth century onward, an array of new products appeared that made ingenious use of this natural plastic: in addition to corsets and buggy whips and the hoops for increasingly fuller skirt fashions, baleen was used for umbrellas, parasols, neck stocks, canes, billiard-table cushions, pen-holders, paper folders and cutters, graining-combs for painters, fishing rods, bows, divining rods, boot shanks, shoehorns, brushes, mattresses, policemen's clubs, and a variety of medical instruments, including tongue-scrapers, probangs ("a slender, flexible rod with a sponge on one end used . . . for removing obstructions from the esophagus"), and applicators of iodine to the cervix for the treatment of tumors of the uterus. In 1848, the year Thomas Roys sailed into the Arctic, whalebone was worth twenty-five cents per pound. By 1863, it was worth more than $1.50 per pound. In that year, the ship *Onward*, owned by the Howland brothers' cousin Edward Howland, docked with a cargo of 62,100 pounds of "bone," fetching $95,000. Yet as the value of baleen continued to rise, the total catch was already dropping fast, from a high of 5,652,360 pounds landed in 1853, to only 488,750 pounds in 1863.

With the withdrawal, by the 1860s, of the businesses of Grinnell and Robinson and the rest of the fleet thinned out by the war, George Jr. and Matthew Howland found a greater portion of the whale fishery left to them. While others were diversifying, or abandoning the whaling business altogether, the Howland brothers' concentration of all their assets and focus on the single enterprise started by their father was paying more than ever. They were still making a lot of money "very fast lately in the whaling business," as R. G. Dun noted. They enjoyed numerous advantages over their remaining competitors: their firm was an old one, long established; their vessels, wharves, candle-making, and other interests had paid for themselves many times over. By sending a large number of ships to sea, they enjoyed the statistical unlikelihood of a significant loss of property—the loss of one ship would not be catastrophic to their business, and less costly than insuring their entire fleet. Matthew Howland, the mathematical-minded brother who kept to the countinghouse, calculated that in a ten-year period only 1.5 percent of New Bedford's entire fleet had been lost at sea. So, with insurance running at 10 percent (or more) of a ship's valuation, the brothers chose not to insure their ships, but rather to build another, the *Concordia*, and to send it, along with the rest of their fleet, to the Arctic.

Fifteen

"Our Dreadful Situation"

On August 29, 1871, the wind blowing over the arctic fleet, though still light, changed direction 180 degrees and swung into the southwest. Immediately, because of the Coriolis effect, the loosened pack ice began drifting east, shoreward again.

Early in the afternoon, both the *Monticello* and the *Elizabeth Swift*, dodging ice, ran aground. With a tidal range of only six inches in the vicinity of Point Barrow, the ships would not soon float off. The *Swift*, in fifteen feet of water, was stuck for nine hours before a large cake of ice pushed the stern of the ship free to a depth of twenty-four feet at ten in the evening.

Thomas Williams also managed to sail the *Monticello* into deeper water that afternoon, but while the *Swift* stayed anchored where she was, Williams—warier than ever of ice after the loss of the *Hibernia* the year before—now turned his ship around and started beating south-west against wind and tide in an attempt to get clear of both the ice and the shoals. "The sea room, however, was narrow," remembered Willie, "requiring short tacks and the taking of chances in the shoal water along the shore."

> We had only made a few miles to the south when one of those peculiar incidents happened which make sailors believe in luck, good and bad, only in this case it was bad. We were on the "in-shore tack" trying to make every inch possible, the order was given for tacking ship, all hands were on deck. . . . The ship was almost in the wind and coming [about] beautifully, another minute and she would be safe on the other tack. The calls of the leadsmen in the fore chains showed that we still had water under our keel, when of a sudden out of the gloom of the snow there loomed a floe of ice right under our weather bow. There was a bare possibility that the ship would swing enough to strike it on the other bow, in which event we were all right, but as the sailors said "luck was against us" she struck on her weather bow, hung "in irons" for a few moments, then slowly swung off and stopped; we were aground.

The sails were quickly furled and a boat lowered to carry an anchor out to windward and deeper water, to try to stop the ship dragging farther into the shallows. There was no physical sense of emergency: the night was quiet, the wind light, and the water in the lee of the ice was almost calm.

Willie remembered the next day, August 30, as "clear and fair," but Nathaniel Ransom, aboard the *John Wells*, anchored ten miles to the north, wrote in his ship's log: *"A thick snow storm all day."* It was probably on the following day, August 31, that the weather improved. *"Good weather,"* recorded Ransom on that day, and though there was *"lots of ice all around,"* Aaron Dean, the *Wells's* captain, still ordered two boats lowered to cruise for whales.

When the snowstorm cleared on August 31, the ships anchored near the *Monticello* now saw that she was stranded and sent boats full of men to help her. Their captains, always ready to drop everything to come to another's aid, sat in their sternsheets. To Willie, these other captains, all of whom he knew from many gams aboard his own and their ships, were heroes in the mold of his father. "The American whaling captain of that day was a plain, rather reticent, serious minded man utterly devoid of show or swagger. He held no commission and wore no uniform, but he could say with John Paul Jones, 'By God sir I am captain of this ship because I am the best man in her.'" Twelve years old, unmindful of the seriousness of the situation, Willie was only thrilled by the gathering of such men. "To me it was a gala day, the decks fairly swarmed with men, orders were executed with a snap and vigor that only a sailor can put into his work when he is pleased to." More anchors were rowed out and dropped in deeper water, their lines and chains hove up tight on the ship's windlass. The *Monticello's* bow was aground, her stern afloat, so barrels of oil were lifted out of her hold and rolled aft to redistribute weight. Finally she floated free and was towed out to where the other ships lay clustered together between the ice and the shallows, and there dropped her anchor. Though Williams was still determined to sail away as soon as possible, no escape yet revealed itself, so he waited, with the other ships.

The trapped fleet was now strung out along a curving fifty-mile-long sweep of the coast from a little south of Wainwright Inlet to Point Franklin in the north. While boats were still sent out to look for whales—there was little else to be done—some of the captains, like Thomas Williams, were no longer determined to reach Point Barrow, but hoped only to get their ships and crews safely away to the south. *"Oh how many of this ship's company will live to see the last day of next August?"* wrote the *Henry Taber*'s captain, Timothy Packard, with vivid foreboding on August 31.

ON FRIDAY, SEPTEMBER 1, the wind strengthened again until it was a "fresh breeze," still from the southwest. The current, though running strongly to the northeast beneath the wind, was in fact pushing directly onto the coast with the Coriolis effect, piling ice upon more ice. Captains sent men to the mastheads to look for leads to open water, but they saw only miles of jumbled, densely packed floes stretching away to seaward without a break, pressing toward the land, jammed up against the shoals, driving over them, forcing the ships ever closer to the beach.

Northernmost of the fleet on that day, the New Bedford ship *Roman* was anchored in the lee of the ice off Point Franklin. A studio photograph of her captain, Jared Jernegan, shows a Mount Rushmore visage of encircling beard, jutting, prognathic jaw, clean-shaven mouth clamped in a grim arc of implacable stubbornness; the large, deep-socketed, hooded eyes hold all the terrible, soul-etching memories of a lifetime at sea, every kind of maritime disaster, of whales, icebergs, and death. Though he is properly attired in frock coat, waistcoat, high collar, and tie, Jernegan's hairstyle is an arrangement of errant, flyaway quiffs, as if he had stepped directly out of a typhoon into the photographer's studio. No Civil War general's portrait showed a face sterner or more commanding. (*All* whaleship captains looked like this in photographs: manifestly stamped by weather and peril, hair barely restrained; perhaps it was a look they acquired by unspoken conformity to a desired type, the way twentieth-century American astronauts all looked like happy, corn-fed farm boys.)

The *Roman*'s boats had found a "stinker," a floating dead whale, probably one of the hundreds that had been harpooned farther south but had escaped beneath the ice. The whale was being towed alongside the ship and the crew were busy cutting it in, while the *Roman* lay tethered by "ice anchors" (probably large blubber hooks) to an acre or so of ice. Late in the morning of September 1, that slab of ice suddenly broke apart.

When I came on deck [Jernegan wrote] I saw the heavy drift ice had cracked the heavy point of ice that held our ship. I felt quite sure we was going to have trouble if this point of ice broke adrift. Shure enough, the whole of this broke adrift and swung around. I sung out, "Let go the lines to the ice anchors," but it was too late as the ship was drove astern, the rudder fetching up against the ice, carrying away all the pindles. Then the ship's stern was all stove in the heavy drift.

Ice worked right under the ship, raised the whole ship almost out on to the ice then her whole broad [starboard] side was stove in.

The *Roman* began to sink immediately. Jernegan ordered the three boats on the port side to be lowered onto the ice, while other crewmen jumped over the rail onto the ice to haul the boats clear as the heavy masts fell around them. Jernegan ran below to his cabin to save his two chronometers and a pistol, and with these in his hands he jumped down onto the ice. In what appeared to be the direst of circumstances, some of his crew began to panic, but Jernegan maintained order. He set his thirty-eight-man crew to dragging the three boats across the heaving floes, over pressure ridges, around gaping cracks that opened and closed, ready to crush the boats, toward open water.

Dangerously overloaded, with more than twice as many men in the boats as they were designed to carry, Jernegan and the *Roman*'s crew rowed twenty miles southwest, against wind and current, to where the nearest ships—the *Comet*, of Honolulu; the Howlands' *Concordia*; and the *Gay Head*, also of New Bedford—still floated free.

But at one a.m. the following morning, September 2, ice closed around the *Comet*, snapping her massive timbers between two large floes. She didn't sink right away; the ship was forced upward out of the water, as her crew jumped over the side onto the ice. The ship was slowly ground to pieces and the wreckage remained visible on the ice for days. Captain Packard, of the *Henry Taber*, and the captains of other ships anchored nearby, sent their boats to take off the *Comet*'s crew. Captain James Knowles of the *George Howland* purchased salvage rights to the ship's wreckage and whatever could be recovered of her stores and barrels of oil for $13—a reflection of how poor the *Comet*'s season had been, but perhaps there was a fitting or two aboard her that might have been worth a few dollars and the trouble to remove it.

The sight of the *Comet*'s toppled masts and wreckage strewn across the ice, and of the ignominious plunder of her cargo, was a grim specter of what now threatened every ship along the coast. With the coming and going of boats transferring the crewmen of both the *Roman* and the *Comet* to other ships, while others still rowed and sailed along the narrowing channel, looking for whales, news of what had happened traveled through the fleet within hours. It was dolefully recorded on the same day in logbooks of ships separated by many miles.

There was little change for the next five days. The wind remained light, from the south and southwest. Ships swung to their anchors in the current or moved as necessary to avoid ice—always, reluctantly, closer to the shore—while still sending boats off to look for whales.

On September 7, the second mate's boat of the *Emily Morgan* had the good luck to harpoon a whale. Moments later, that same second mate, Antonio Oliver, accidentally shot himself through the head with a bomb gun and was instantly killed. Many of the ships' logbooks noted this accident in identical words, leaving the impression of a boat rowing from ship to ship passing on this gruesome news.

On September 8, the wind strengthened. "Strong" and "fresh" were the words used in several logbooks, indicating gale force. It was still blowing from the southwest, and this stronger wind pushed ice grounded on the shoals farther into the waterway, forcing ships ever closer to the beach. Up and down the coast, this latest advance by the ice had an immediate effect on the fleet. The *Elizabeth Swift* was forced aground at three p.m.; her crew got her off four hours later. The bark *Awashonks* was crushed and sank. Although she was twenty miles to the south, the news of the *Awashonks*'s sinking reached the *Swift* at nearly telegraph speed.

With nothing to do but watch the advancing ice, go to the assistance of ships in trouble, and still send their men out whaling, the captains of most vessels were rowing to and fro, gamming with their colleagues, swapping news, and talking about what was to be done—but there was nothing to do except wait for a change of wind, and, finally, to decide what to do if it did not change. These captains were all champion stoics, well used to waiting out bad weather, but though they were courageous odds-players, they were not dreamers, hopers against unrealistic hope. They were men who recognized and seized the main chance when it came along, and now one was looming, one they all abhorred, but which looked increasingly necessary and urgent: abandonment of their ships. It might well be possible to continue dodging the encroaching ice for a few weeks more, but as September advanced, the weather would only grow colder, the ice thicker. If a route to the open sea couldn't be found soon, all the ships would be crushed, forcing their abandonment.

This, they knew, could be executed with a high degree of control and safety: each ship carried a minimum of five whaleboats, more than adequate as lifeboats capacious enough to carry her complement of men—and a number of women and children—and some provisions. Getting from ship to shore, at most half a mile away, would not be difficult. Once there, however, a severer trial would begin. The experiences of Captain Barker and the men of the *Japan*, related and discussed aboard every ship earlier that summer, had made this prospect vividly real. And the crew of the *Japan* had been a handful of men; here were more than 1,200 people aboard the trapped whaleships. The fleet carried food for no more than a season's cruise, and this season was almost over. The outcome for this large population ashore was plain: death by starvation and cold.

"Ice boun on wone side and land on the other," lamented Captain Valentine Lewis, of the *Thomas Dickason*, describing the whaling captain's worst definition of lying between a rock and a hard place. Lewis also usually sailed with his wife, Ethelinda, but this summer he had, like Jared Jernegan with his wife, left her safely ashore, in Honolulu. *"God have Mercy on this Whaling Fleet and deliver us from the cold and Icy shores."*

There was one possible alternative to this grimmest scenario: it was believed that a few ships had not been caught by the ice but still cruised in open water to the south. If the whaleboats, carrying 1,200 people, could reach these ships, they might all get away before the onset of winter. But the decision to abandon the fleet—while most of it still floated intact—had to be made soon, before any ships to the south, discouraged by the ice and unaware of the plight of those to the north, turned and sailed for home.

On September 9, a group of captains met and agreed they could wait no longer. They decided to try to lighten one of the smallest vessels in the fleet, the 270-ton *Kohola*, of Honolulu, by transferring its barrels of oil, water, and other provisions to another ship, hoping thus to reduce its draft sufficiently to allow it to sail through the shallow water inside the ice at the south of the waterway. Once free, it was to try to contact any vessels still cruising in the open sea beyond. The *Kohola* sailed only a few miles before grounding in six feet of water off Wainwright Inlet. Captains Thomas Williams and William Kelley (of the *Gay Head*) then tried to lighten the even smaller 149-ton *Victoria*, of San Francisco, but she, too, soon grounded on shoals inside the ice, unable to get clear.

On the morning of September 10, the open water in the channel around the ships was found to have frozen during the night to the thickness of an inch—a stark indicator, with the failure of the *Kohola* and the *Victoria* to get clear, of what lay ahead. "Off this ship," is what every man was thinking, and some of them voicing. Captains and crews throughout the fleet now began packing whaleboats with food, gear, and sails (to use as tents if necessary). Unsure if they would find any ships beyond the ice, they knew now that no one could help them but themselves. A number of whaleboats departed for the south right away, hoping to row or sail clear of the ice and contact what ships might still be cruising there.

From the *Elizabeth Swift*'s logbook:

MONDAY 11TH.

. . . No change in the ice. The ships are all makeing preperations for sending provisions south thinking they will have to leave their ships

soon. New ice made last night quite thick so that it was dificult to get a boat through it.

The *Emily Morgan*, of New Bedford, was another "lady ship." At four a.m. on September 12, Captain Benjamin Dexter left the *Morgan* with his wife, Almira, in a whaleboat, *"to take his wife to a place of safety in the south,"* recorded his first mate, William Earle. What that safe place could be, unless aboard a ship clear of the ice, no one knew. Dexter left first mate Earle aboard the *Emily Morgan* with instructions to *"act according to circumstances . . . if the other ships are to be abandoned to abandon ours at the same time."* Earle also recorded his doubts and the limit to what he would do:

For my part, I will not cross the Arctic Ocean in an open whale-boat laden with men and provisions in the latter part of the month of September and October. As far as Icy Cape, there is no danger, but beyond that, (if all ships' companies have to take to boats to Behring's Strait) the sea is dangerous at this season of the year. Out of the 1,400 men not 100 will survive. I will return from Icy Cape if ships cannot be found.

On September 11, Captain D. R. Frazer, of the *Florida*, who had earlier set out to the south in command of three whaleboats, found the whaleship *Lagoda* in clear water ten miles off Icy Cape. Until that day, the *Lagoda* and six other whaleships had also been locked in the ice and trying to sail free. On the eleventh, the ice broke up sufficiently to allow them to work their way out into open water. If they had not been frozen until then, or if Captain Frazer's boats had not encountered them that day, the seven ships would have sailed south. Boats from the *Lagoda* were dispatched to other ships, which lay within a few miles of each other off Icy Cape. All agreed to wait until the boats from the fleet, with their 1,200 passengers, reached them.

Captain James Dowden, of the *Progress*, not far from the *Lagoda*, gave Captain Frazer this message to take back to the other captains: "Tell them all I will wait for them as long as I have an anchor left or a spar to carry a sail."

Frazer returned to the fleet with this message the next day, September 12. On that day all the captains met aboard his ship, the *Florida*, where they signed the following statement:

Point Belcher, Arctic Ocean, Sept. 12, 1871

Know all men by these presents, that we, the undersigned, masters of whale-ships now lying at Point Belcher, after holding a meeting concerning our dreadful situation, have all come to the conclusion that our ships cannot be got out this year, and there being no harbor that we can get our vessels into, and not having provisions enough to feed our crews to exceed three months, and being in a barren country, where there is neither food nor fuel to be obtained, we feel ourselves under the painful necessity of abandoning our vessels, and trying to work our way south with our boats, and, if possible, get on board of ships that are south of the ice. We think it would not be prudent to leave a single soul to look after our vessels, as the first westerly gale will crowd the ice ashore, and either crush the ships or drive them high upon the beach. Three of the fleet have already been crushed, and two are now lying hove out, which have been crushed by the ice, and are leaking badly. We have now five wrecked crews distributed among us. We have barely room to swing at anchor between the pack of ice and the beach, and we are lying in three fathoms of water. Should we be cast upon the beach it would be at least eleven months before we could look for assistance, and in all probability nine out of ten would die of starvation or scurvy before the opening of spring.

Therefore, we have arrived at these conclusions [after] the return of our expedition under command of Capt. D. R. Frazer, of the Florida, he having with whale-boats worked to the southward as far as Blossom Shoals, and found that the ice pressed ashore the entire distance from our position to the shoals, leaving in several places only sufficient water for our boats to pass through, and this liable at any moment to be frozen over during the twenty-four hours, which would cut off our retreat, even by the boats, as Captain Frazer had to work through a considerable quantity of young ice during his expedition, which cut up his boats badly.

It was awkwardly written, in part because it was painstakingly specific, and rang with a defensive solidarity. To abandon a ship and its cargo, together worth perhaps $50,000, in some cases much more— particularly those ships still floating sound and unwrecked in the channel—was, for these upstanding men, who were always mindful of their responsibility to their ship's owners (and many of them were themselves part owners of their ships), a terrible act that would carry a long shadow down through the remainder of their careers. For a seaman, the loss of a ship is always tainted with shame, no matter what the circumstances; and it is always subject to speculation, by those who weren't there, of what else might have been done. To abandon a vessel that, like most of the fleet, still floated sound and in good condition, was almost unheard of. Few of these captains would have left their ships unless all of them had agreed upon the necessity to do so, and then formalized that agreement in what amounted to a shared oath swearing to the extremity of their situation. They knew that other men, at home or in other ships, would question their decision. They had to affirm, to one another and the world, that there was no alternative.

They did so: every captain, except those, like Benjamin Dexter, who had already set out with his wife in a whaleboat heading south, signed this letter. They agreed to abandon their ships on September 14. But by then many boats and ships' crews had already left.

The Abandonment of the Whaling Fleet, 1871. From *Harper's Weekly.*
(Courtesy New Bedford Whaling Museum)

Sixteen

Abandonment

The 1,219 men, women, and children of the fleet now faced an open-boat journey through the harshest of arctic conditions. The distance to Icy Cape and where the waiting ships lay, on Blossom Shoals just off the cape, was forty to sixty miles, depending on the positions of the abandoned ships.

It was fifty miles for the party from the *Monticello*, a grueling trip in an exposed open boat. With Eliza, Willie, his ten-year-old daughter Mary, and himself, all crammed into a whaleboat with gear, provisions, and five or six other men at the oars, Thomas Williams decided to make the trip over two nights and two days. Willie remembered it all well:

I doubt if I can adequately describe the leave-taking of our ship. It was depressing enough to me, and you know a boy can always see possibilities of something novel or interesting in most any change, but to my father and mother it must have been a sad parting, and I think what made it still more so was the fact that only a short distance from our bark lay the ship *Florida*, of which my father had been master eight years and on which three of his children had been born.[1] The usual abandonment of a ship is the result of some irreparable injury and is executed in great haste [e.g., Williams's previous command, the *Hibernia*]; but here we were leaving a ship that was absolutely sound, that had been our home for nearly ten months and had taken us safely through many a trying time.

The colors were set and everything below and on deck was left just as though we were intending to return the next day. All liquor was destroyed, so that the natives would not get to carousing and wantonly destroy the ship. . . . Our boat contained in addition to its regular crew, my mother, sister and me, and all our clothing, bedding and provisions, so that we were loaded nearly to the gunwales.

Willie's nineteen-year-old brother, Stancel, Thomas and Eliza's firstborn son, who was one of the *Monticello*'s officers on this voyage, was in another boat. (Their second son, Henry, had died of scarlet fever at the age of nine, in 1864.)

They left the *Monticello* on the afternoon of September 13 and rowed and sailed twenty miles to the stranded *Victoria*, where they spent the night as guests of its Captain Redfield, who was still aboard with some of his men. They started south again early the next morning, rowing and sailing along the channel between the ice and the land, where, despite strong winds, the water was still reasonably smooth. Williams landed the boat on the beach just as darkness was falling on the second night. Tents, fashioned from sails, were erected to shelter

---

1. Willie in 1859; Mary in 1861; and Flora, who was born in the Japan Sea in 1867 and died in 1869.

Eliza and the Williams children, together with several other captains' wives and children; great fires were built on the beach, and meals prepared. During the night it rained heavily and the wind increased.

In the morning, "a good fresh breeze" was blowing. The boats set out for the ships, which lay several miles outside the sheltering ice pack in the open ocean. "It was a hair raising experience," remembered Willie.

> My father had decided to go aboard the *Progress*. She was still at anchor and pitching into the heavy seas, that were then running in a way that would have made you wonder how we would ever get the men aboard, let alone a woman and two children; but it was all accomplished without accident, or even the wetting of a foot. As fast as the boats were unloaded they were cast adrift, to be destroyed against the ice pack a short distance under our lee where the waves were breaking masthead high.

It was no easier for others to leave their ships. Men imbue the vessels that carry them, womblike within their hulls, protecting them from the cold, hostile environment outside, with a kind of maternal love. "She," they invariably call these mother ships, feeling them to be immeasurably more than the sum of their planks and bolts, ropes and canvas. They know this from watching a ship make its way across tens of thousands of miles of ocean, shouldering aside storm swells and rogue waves with a solid, unshakable, seemingly instinctive devotion to plowing ahead, all the while protecting them—just as they might, for the most part, remember their mothers. *"With sad heart ordered all the men into the boats and with a last look over the decks abandoned the ship to the mercy of the elements,"* wrote Earle, first mate of the *Emily Morgan*, about their leave-taking on the afternoon of the fourteenth.

Earle decided to keep his group of four whaleboats from the *Morgan* going through the night (three more of the ship's boats had left earlier). With icy waves slopping into the open boats, breaking over the men (whose canvas or wool coats were perpetually soaked and freezing), dodging visible and submerged clumps of ice—while it was light—and trying to row and sail through a short, steep chop thrown up by the shallow depths beneath them, it was as desperate as a small-boat journey could be, and it only got worse, as Earle recorded:

> *As night approached the wind increased and heavy banks of cumuli came swelling up from the SE and soon enveloped us in a mantle of the blackest darkness. We were now in constant danger of coming in contact with the many fragments of ice floating between the land and the main pack.*
>
> *At 10.30 [p.m.] landed and gathering driftwood built a fire and made some strong coffee, this warmed us up a little. The wind increasing, we double-reefed our sails and shoved off at 11.30 into the darkness and rain; the navigation was difficult, and, as far as the boats were concerned, dangerous from the drift ice. The water did not exceed six feet in depth anywhere and in some places we went thumping over shoals. We kept the land well aboard—it is very low and we could see nothing of it at times.*

At one a.m. on the fifteenth, one of the *Morgan*'s boats hit a solid piece of ice, staving in its planks. The boat, and the others with it, were quickly run ashore, and in near-total darkness, occasionally using roman candle flares, the crew (well practiced from walrusing) nailed canvas over the smashed wood. They set out again an hour later. At eight in the morning, still ten miles north of Icy Cape, they landed for coffee and breakfast. They reached the cape at 10:30 a.m., where they found twenty-five or thirty other whaleboats, among them the *Morgan*'s remaining three, waiting out the wind, which by now had become a strong southwest gale. But Earle was anxious to reach the waiting ships before the wind grew even stronger, so, under his command, the *Emily Morgan*'s seven boats set out once more, rowing and beating under sail directly into the wind, first inside the ice, and later outside its protective barrier, plunging through what one whaling captain described as "the full force of a tremendous southwest gale and a sea that would have made the stoutest ship tremble." The seven stout ships waiting for the boats were indeed trembling; they had remained at anchor off a now highly dangerous lee shore in conditions that would ordinarily have long before sent them beating out to sea or running for shelter, but they held on. Two of them, the *Lagoda* and the *Arctic*, parted their chain anchor cables as they lay pitching into the storm waves. Both managed to reset their anchors. All through the fifteenth and sixteenth of September, tiny bobbing, storm-tossed whaleboats, singly and in ragged, strung-out groups, crabbing to windward under sail and oar, their passengers soaked and raw with cold, made their perilous way out to the ships. Earle and his boats reached the ships late in the afternoon of the fifteenth and were all taken aboard the *Europa*.

William Earle's account of his passage down the coast in the *Emily Morgan*'s whaleboats describes every other journey of this massive evacuation. Almost miraculously, between 150 and 200 whaleboats (each ship carried five on davits, and usually at least three others on deck) ferried 1,219 men, women, and children from the trapped fleet to the seven vessels waiting for them off Icy Cape. Not a single person was lost or badly injured, a testament not so much to luck but to the extraordinary seamanship and skill shown by every captain and every man.

The *Progress* took aboard a total of 221 people, including the Williams family, and two other captains and their wives and two children, one of them "a baby in arms." These last two families were probably Captain Edmund Kelley, wife, and child, from the *Seneca*, and Captain Robert Jones, wife, and child, who had been enjoying the plush accommodations aboard the Howlands' still-sparkling *Concordia*. The *Progress*'s captain, James Dowden, gave up his cabins to these three families. Aboard the *Europa*, Captain and Mrs. Benjamin Dexter, of the *Emily Morgan*, and Captain and Mrs. John Heppingstone, of the *Julian*, were taken in along with 276 other men. The remaining men were packed aboard the other five ships, like so many Irish immigrants, noted one whaleman.

Nathaniel Ransom and the *John Wells*'s boats also made it to the *Europa*. Like many others, Ransom had taken with him in his boat what he could of his personal belongings, including some prized reindeer coats he had obtained by trading with the Eskimos, but whether because these became soaked on the journey or because there was simply no room for them on the crowded ships, they were jettisoned at some point:

OFF ICY CAPE JUST AT PRESENT SEPTEMBER FRIDAY 15TH.
Strong breeze from S.W. I've just [come] aboard of Ship Europa Captain Mellen after being out in a hale & rainstorm pulling & sailing for last 24 hours I had to throw my bomb gun a box of bomb lances with a musked [musket] & lots of ammunition with several other things overboard my boat & all Cote[s] of Esquimaux garments.

Thirty-two whaleships had been abandoned. Many were old, and not all were in good condition, but the fleet's replacement value would have been in excess of $3 million. No meaningful modern equivalent can be calculated. The replacement value today of a fleet of thirty-two factory fishing vessels would be in the hundreds of millions of dollars. The loss of so many ships today, in a single event, would be reckoned a national disaster.

Seventeen

Aftermath

By September 17, all the refugees from thirty-two whaleships had been taken aboard the fleet's remaining seven vessels. Remarkably, there had not been a single loss of life, a testament to the extraordinary degree of seamanship shown by every man under the severest of tests.

They sailed for the Bering Strait, stopping for water and supplies at Plover Bay, at the southern end of the strait, then on to the Hawaiian Islands, reaching Honolulu by the end of October. From there, many of the captains and their families and crews sailed by scheduled passenger steamer to San Francisco, where, in early November, they boarded trains heading east. The Union Pacific and Central Pacific railroad companies had finished linking an unbroken transcontinental railway line less than two years earlier, in November 1869, often said to be the greatest engineering feat of the nineteenth century, the equivalent for its day of the moon landings a century later. The exhausted shipwrecked whalemen and their families, used to crossing oceans at six or seven miles per hour, tore across the continent, sometimes reaching speeds of sixty miles per hour. They marveled at the plunging California Sierras, the Rocky Mountains, the unending Great Plains (which reminded them of the vast featureless ocean, and ended after just a few days), and they experienced a profound alteration of their former perception of time and distance when they reached New York, a distance from San Francisco equivalent to an Atlantic crossing, in exactly seven days. The passage from New England to San Francisco by ship, which many of them had made, still took seven months by way of Cape Horn.

Nathaniel Ransom still carried with him the *John Wells*'s logbook and continued making regular daily entries, aboard ships and trains, beginning as always—the first instinct of a good seaman, and the first requirement of a logkeeper—with weather observations, until Tuesday, November 14, the day before he reached his home and "darling wife" in Mattapoisett:

THURSDAY 9TH. [OF NOVEMBER].
Pleasant weather passed quite a number of towns & villages. . . . I have felt quite like myself again today [that is, after suffering from a toothache for quite some time].

SUNDAY 12TH.
Nice weather passed through Chicago in afternoon. . . .

MONDAY 13TH.
Cloudy about noon arrived at Pittsburg. . . .

There would have been little visible weather to report from inside a train in the very early hours of a November morning, but Ransom's arrival in New York on November 14 did involve a short passage by boat, since the Pennsylvania Railroad line terminated at Jersey City, on the western shore of the Hudson River. The passengers boarded ferries to a Manhattan riverside terminal and from there took trains to the Grand Central Depot—none of which he had time to note, because he temporarily lost his bags:

TUESDAY 14TH.

We arrived at NY this morning at 7Am in time to get to Mattapoisett tonight but on account of my baggage not being here at the depot had to wait till midday. . . . Shall have to weather it out one more night—I've got the toothache of course—

It's no wonder his bags were misplaced. The recently completed Grand Central Depot (not the present structure, which was built between 1903 and 1913) had been open only a few weeks, and combined four lines, the New York Central, the Hudson River, the New York and Harlem, and the New Haven railroads, creating much chaos and confusion with luggage.

Ransom must have hurriedly written this last entry (above) in the *John Wells*'s logbook somewhere inside the depot—after sorting out his baggage problem, but before learning that he would in fact be out of New York and on his way to Massachusetts that afternoon. He was part of a large group from the shipwrecked fleet that was making its way from San Francisco to New Bedford together. Their progress was reported on November 16 by the *Republican Standard* of New Bedford, where many families eagerly awaited them:

The whole party of captains and officers from the shipwrecked fleet . . . came through together from San Francisco to New York by way of Omaha, Burlington, Chicago, Fort Wayne, Pittsburg, and the Pennsylvania Central route, making all connections and arriving in New York promptly on time, at 7 o'clock Tuesday morning, just one hour short of a week from the time they left San Francisco.

While the returning sons and husbands of New Bedford, Mattapoisett, Edgartown, New London, and elsewhere were welcomed and embraced by their families, second-guessers in whaling ports everywhere began to voice suggestions—just as the captains had anticipated—that the fleet had been abandoned too hastily. *The Friend*, the whaling community's newspaper in Honolulu, quickly responded strongly to these critics:

"WE LEFT NOT ONE MINUTE TOO SOON."

In conversation with a very sensible and reliable first officer [probably William Earle] of one of the lost ships in the Arctic, we asked him this question: "Did you not quit your vessel too soon, ought you not to have waited a little longer?" He replied with much decision, "We left not one minute too soon." This appears to be the unanimous opinion of all the masters, officers and seamen, with whom we have conversed.

We have heard an opposite opinion expressed by some who never saw the Arctic Ocean. It is an easy matter in Honolulu, with the thermometer at 80°, to criticise the actions of men who have faced danger and starvation under the shadow of icebergs, and while the icy barrier was momentarily pressing a fleet of ships on the barren shores of Siberia [*sic*]. We have no doubt that the owners and agents of whaleships and Insurance Companies in New Bedford, seated before a good coal fire, will express their *deliberate* opinion that the fleet was abandoned too soon. We have been permitted to read the private journal of one of the shipmasters, whose ship was saved, and it tells a story of anxiety that ought to silence all foolish censure of those shipmasters who were compelled to leave behind them their hard-earned wealth. The idea that thirty-three [*sic*] shipmasters and their crews abandoned their ice-bound vessels, except from stern and dire necessity is not to be entertained for one moment.

With so many lives at stake, the whaling captains had undoubtedly made the prudent decision. And yet, they may in fact have left too soon.

Thomas Williams had moved his family from Wethersfield, Connecticut, to the San Francisco Bay area after the Civil War, and on their return from Honolulu, Eliza and the younger children settled back into their home in Oakland. But Thomas immediately began making plans to return to the Arctic. With Samuel Merritt, the former mayor of Oakland, and others, he formed a salvage company. They bought and outfitted the whaleship *Florence*, and with a large crew that included his oldest son, Stancel, Williams sailed north again in May of 1872.

Others had the same idea, and a number of salvage ships joined the smaller but undeterred fleet of whaleships again trying to push through the ice in the Bering Strait in early summer. As they neared the whaling grounds, the whaleships and the salvors were met by Eskimos in their *umiak*s with great quantities of baleen for trade. They presumed these cargoes had been plundered from the abandoned whaleships.

Thomas Williams and his crew beat all the competing salvors to the fleet by traveling ahead inside the ice in whaleboats—a reversal of their escape. Near Wainwright Inlet they came upon the wrecks: ships lying on their sides in the shallows, their masts and spars broken, hulls crushed, timbers, rigging, barrels, boats, sea chests, and supplies littering the shore. Most of the ships were readily identifiable, even in their scattered pieces: Williams found parts of the *Monticello*'s bow and stern half a mile apart. A number of the ships, including the Howlands' beautiful *Concordia*, had been burned.

Astonishingly, there was a witness to the aftermath of the fleet's abandonment waiting to tell Williams and others what had happened after they had left. A boatsteerer from one of the ships had not gone with them in the whaleboats. He had stayed behind, planning to spend the winter inside one of the ships, to salvage what he could from them. His identity was not recorded, but what he told the men who met him on the shore in 1872 was soon known from Honolulu to New Bedford: two weeks after the whaleboats had escaped to the south, a heavy northeasterly gale—what everyone had been hoping and praying for— had sprung up and pushed out to sea most of the ice, freeing the ships. The greatest damage had then occurred from their being un-manned, smashing and grinding into each other and the leftover ice. The natives had subsequently looted what they could. Although many of the departing crews had smashed their liquor bottles so the Eskimos wouldn't find them, they had not thought to destroy their medicine chests. These had been found and opened, and some of the Eskimos had died after drinking the contents of their medicine bottles. These ships the Eskimos had burned. The winter appeared to have been a mild one, for the whalers and salvors found only small scattered ice. But the boatsteerer, who had felt his life in danger from the Eskimos, said $150,000 would not tempt him to spend another winter in the Arctic.

Thomas Williams floated and secured two ships, the *Minerva* and the *Seneca*, and filled his own and these two vessels with barrels of salvaged oil and many tons of baleen. He put his crews aboard the two ships and sailed south, the *Minerva* sailing by herself, the *Florence* tow-ing the *Seneca*. He was forced to cut the *Seneca* free during a gale, and the ship was lost, but the *Florence* and the *Minerva* returned to San Francisco with a cargo of oil and baleen worth $10,000—all that was realized from a potential catch, had all the ships returned to port with average cargoes, worth $1.5 million.

George Jr. and Matthew Howland had lost three of their ten ships, the *Concordia*, the *Thomas Dickason*, and the *George Howland*, and their cargoes, for which they had no insurance.

Eighteen

"How Hard It Is to Rise,
When You're Really, Truly Down"

I wish I knew why George and Matthew didn't quit the whale fishery entirely in 1871. George was 66 years old, Matthew 58; they were still rich men and had virtually unlimited opportunities to invest in forward-looking enterprises—textile mills, railroads, banks, real estate developments. . . . Was it sentiment? Did they honestly expect a return to the old prosperity; did they really believe there would be no more losses in the Arctic? . . . Whaling always was a kind of gambling, and after winning for five decades, their time had come to pay.

—LLEWELLYN HOWLAND III,
"Children of the Light" (1964)

Disasters that are more abstract, while no less damaging or terrify-ing, are more difficult to perceive than a crushed whaleship. Their true scale and ramifications may not be seen until they are well advanced. They take men by surprise in the middle of a normal day when they look up and find the world changed forever.

The *Whalemen's Shipping List and Merchants' Transcript* scarcely knew what to think about the state of its industry following the arctic disaster of 1871. It reported, in February 1872, under the headline "Review of the Whale Fishery for 1871": "We have to record another year of poor success in the whalefishery, both as concerns oil taken and pecuniary results." Poor results might occur in any year, but the pros-pects for the future had never looked so ominous: "Of the 34 vessels now in port, half are for sale."

Also for sale in New Bedford, but not selling, despite the enormous losses in the Arctic the previous summer, were thousands of barrels of oil, covering wharves and filling warehouses. Prices were depressed, and their owners were holding on to them, hoping for an improvement in the market. "With the uncertainty in [oil] prices, partly from substitutes [petroleum], and low prices of them, only good prices can be hoped for, and not counted upon."

Yet three weeks later, the newspaper peevishly dismissed the sum-mary of its own reports reprinted elsewhere: "The following which we clip from the Philadelphia Commercial List, shows how near home, an idea erroneous, may be disseminated:

THE WHALE-FISHERIES—A review of the whaling business for 1871 states that the past year was one of disaster and discourage-ment. The constant decrease of whaling vessels by loss, condemnation and sale is very ominous, and as no new vessels are added, it is believed that the trade will soon die out.

The *Whalemen's Shipping List* vigorously rebutted such dire conclusions—"We don't believe in the dying of whaling"—citing a confusing series of numbers meant to reveal the Philadelphia paper's ignorance of the difference between the sperm and right whale fisheries, and the returns from bone and oil sales. But a month later the *Shipping List* carried the following two articles:

A PARALYSED INDUSTRY—The depression of our ship building interest has continued so long that the race of hardy and intelligent mechanics whose works reflected credit upon the country, are now fast becoming extinct. Of course, in the present condition of business, no new hands engage in it, and the old ship-carpenters are rapidly adapting themselves to kindred trades which are still useful. Once we boasted of half a dozen or more yards. . . .

OPIUM EATING—We are told by one of our Apothecaries, who does a large and flourishing business, that the sales of opium amount to 20 p. cent more than they did ten years ago. It is a sad state of things if we are relinquishing rum for opium. . . .

In New Bedford, business was down, self-medication was up. In October 1872, the *Whalemen's Shipping List* lamented that another three New Bedford whaleships, the *Helen Snow*, the *Roscoe*, and the *Sea Breeze*, had been lost the previous August in the Arctic, and that the season there had again been a poor one, although "ships had done as well as usual walrusing."

Joseph Grinnell's Wamsutta Mills—four of them built and operating at a profit at the time of the disaster in the Arctic, and a fifth under construction, to open in 1875—saved New Bedford from complete economic collapse. While work along the waterfront and whaling's attendant service and product industries slowed and ground to a halt, many whalemen, particularly the Portuguese immigrants and their families living in the shanty neighborhoods along the river, found steadier work, even a growing demand for employment, in the mills. The city's poorer inhabitants had no investment or long family history in the whale fishery to tie them to it or keep them hoping, unrealistically, for an unlikely turnaround. They wanted only work and wages, and to get these without leaving home for years at a time was an added benefit.

No sudden, calamitous depression overtook New Bedford as a whole. Rather, there was a washing away, as if by a slow but inexorable tide, of an old order, and its concurrent replacement by a very different one. And in the course of this exchange, the nature and tone of New Bedford changed. It lost its elite position as a headquarters for a fabulously wealthy plutocracy and began to establish itself as a working-class city that was soon in the vanguard of the burgeoning textile industry. Just as whaling and the Industrial Revolution had fueled each other's growth, the development of the railroads and the use of mail-order catalogues, like Sears, Roebuck's, created a continent-wide market for cotton and textile goods—in the form of clothing for farmers and their families in the expanding West—while conveniently supplying New Bedford with a new industry, just as the old one withered. Workers' homes and whole new neighborhoods sprouted up in the immediate vicinities of the proliferating mills, while the genteel center of the town began to calcify and grow brittle. Large houses that had remained in families for generations were put up for sale.

. . .

THE HOWLAND BROTHERS did not know how to change. They noted what had happened; they were certainly aware of the general depression in their industry; yet they pressed on as before. They had never learned financial versatility. They were not businessmen in the truest sense, doing business for its own sake, or for the sake of making money. That had never been their primary concern. For two centuries their family had been engaged in a compact with God to slay the leviathan in the sea; wealth and station and power had derived from their unswerving adherence to this agreement. Efforts at diversification—their father George Howland's attempt to invest in other towns and other businesses, adventures motivated purely by financial interests—had ended badly, in failures all too human, and conspicuously lacking the wondrous returns of the whale fishery. And there remained good reasons for them to persevere at whaling: their ships—those that remained—were all paid for, and still earning a profit; sales of bone were still encouraging. They simply had no idea of the speed at which their world was passing away.

George Jr. was largely uninvolved, and little interested in the running of the business. Like Matthew's wife, Rachel, he used the family business and the social platform it gave him to perform good deeds. He was, as always, about town and the region with his civic responsibilities: a trustee of banks, of railroads, of Brown University, and he continued to enjoy the respect of others who believed him to be—as he correctly believed himself to be, in 1871—rich. He still saw no reason not to reaffirm what he had said a mere seven years before, toward the close of the Civil War: "'Can these improvements continue? And will science and art make the same rapid strides for the next fifty or one hundred years?' The only answer I can make is the real Yankee one: why not?"

It was Matthew who daily walked down the hill to the counting-house that stood at the head of Howland's Wharf, and there, bent over ledgers and inkwells, busied himself, as he had every day for more than forty years, with the numbers: the prices of whale oil, sperm oil, and "bone," the percentages of lays, the cost of provisions, of preserved meats, of whaleboats and oars and shooks. There were still great numbers of numbers, and in these he continued to absorb himself, taking comfort in the familiarity of routine.

And it was Matthew's line—his sons, warm and well fed on dry land, not men in tiny boats in peril from whales or icebergs—who, in a single generation, would play out the whale fishery's most vertiginous plunge from securest ivory tower to bottommost condition and, for one son, tragedy.

As circumstances constricted around him, Matthew grew increasingly absorbed in the careers of his three sons: Richard Smith Howland, twenty-three years old in 1871; Matthew Morris Howland, twenty-one; and William Dylwyn Howland, eighteen. Like his own father (and the fictional but authentically representative Caleb Wellworthy) he had groomed his sons to follow him in the whale fishery. They had been devoutly and purposefully educated: first, of course, at the weekly Meeting, then schooled at the Friends Academy, and, inevitably, in light of Uncle George's trusteeship, at Brown University in Providence. In 1874, Matthew dispatched Dick to California to act as their San Francisco agent. Morrie did not actually "go to sea" as a sailor but made several voyages between New Bedford, Honolulu, and San Francisco aboard Howland vessels. And young Willie went into the countinghouse with his father. Between the three of them, Matthew hoped, they would acquire a complete, complementary, and valuable experience to carry on the family business. For two years, as the boys confidently served out their apprenticeships, the seven remaining How-land whaleships sailed between New Bedford, Honolulu, San Francisco, and the Arctic. The whale fishery, Matthew still believed, was, and would remain, part of the natural order of things. Many agreed with him: "The [arctic] disaster," the *Boston Post* reported in November 1871, "was merely one of those deviations from natural laws against which all precautions are futile. Such an event would probably not occur again in a lifetime."

But it occurred again five years later. In 1876, twelve of the much smaller twenty-vessel fleet venturing into the arctic grounds that sum-mer were once again trapped by ice. This time, bearing in mind the change in conditions that had occurred after the crews left in 1871, and the possibilities for salvage, at least fifty men remained behind to spend the winter, as caretakers, aboard their ships. Only three were still alive when whaleships returned the following season. All twelve ships were lost. Four of them—the *Onward*, the *Java*, the *Clara Bell*, and the *St. George*—belonged to George Jr. and Matthew Howland. For them this was a far greater catastrophe than the disaster of 1871. Seven of their ten ships had been destroyed in five years. Now Matthew saw that the earth had tilted on its axis, throwing all natural and ordained laws out of balance, and the specific gravity of the whale fishery had unraveled.

His boys were forced to look increasingly to their own devices to make a living. Dick, who had bought a farm in Menlo Park, south of San Francisco, and stocked it with 200 hens, began to import "duck"—cotton from New Bedford's Wamsutta Mills, bought by Matthew and sent out to him to sell in the Bay Area. Morrie spent time in New York, dabbling as a trader in various commodities. And Willie went to work for Wamsutta management.

Late in 1878, another in an accelerating cascade of losses hit the family: "Hastings has failed," Matthew, Morrie, and Willie all wrote to Dick in September.

Hastings & Company—comprising George, John, and Waitsill Hastings, and partners—were oil and candle manufacturers, and their factory stood at the foot of Grinnell Street in New Bedford. The Howlands, and many others, sold them oil and traded with them. George Jr. and Matthew owned stock in what had been a seemingly unassailable bulwark of the whale fishery—of the very economy itself. The shock of such a failure, to the Hastingses, to the Howlands, and the business world at the time, was not unlike the failure of Bernard L. Madoff Investment Securities in 2008 (though there was no evidence of fraud in the Hastings operation). What had once been unassailably secure had dissolved like an apparition. The seismic tremor that passed through the Howlands' industry was of an unprecedented magnitude. Their world was breaking apart.

There was, too, a peculiarly unhinging sense of abandonment felt by the Quaker whaling merchants. They had felt themselves to be God's elect people. They had done great philanthropic deeds in His name, they had supported the emancipation of slaves, funded colleges; they had done His work on earth as diligently as perhaps no other group in postcolonial America. How could God so turn His back on *them*?

Matthew's boys were as unprepared as their father was for the dreadful loom of penury. "The business of America is business," said Calvin Coolidge during the giddy boom years of the 1920s; but this observation was more urgently, and physically, true fifty years earlier, in the second half of the nineteenth century, with the rise of the great enterprises of oil and the railroads, foreshadowing and laying the infrastructure for the unprecedented juggernaut of the automobile industry, which was already under way (Henry Ford's Quadricycle appeared in 1896) before the century's end. Failure in business then—as opposed to the widespread, equal-opportunity crash that soon followed Coolidge's remark, or, for that matter, the financial unraveling of 2008—was accompanied by a shame akin to a moral transgression. Now it stalked the Howlands. "Beneath the crust of solvency lay stark, unyielding terror," wrote Matthew's great-great-grandson Llewellyn Howland III. "It had, almost, a human character and shared the family table as a ravenous, unbidden guest." For Matthew, the only defense was to conserve those assets he still had with a caution that left him paralyzed. He kept his last three ships in port, afraid to send them to sea, but unwilling to sell them—for without ships there could be no whaling, and then what was he? And he held on to his real estate, stocks, and shares, always hoping for improvement.

His privileged (though not, thanks to Quaker austerity, lavishly pampered) sons had to reinvent themselves in adulthood as tradesmen, and they were woefully ill-equipped to do so.

"Sometimes I feel quite encouraged about the future and can almost see my way to establishing a good business," Dick wrote from California to his brother Willie, younger by five years, whom he was closer to than to Morrie—

> and then again it clouds over and things don't look so rosy. Taking it all together, however, I see no cause for despair. For I am learning all the time how to use money and perhaps I will one day get hold of enough to make a good start.

But the abrupt loss of security was devastating to him. As children do, he looked on what had befallen his father with an all-knowing hindsight, and felt with great resentment his own lack of preparedness for his present circumstances:

> Father . . . must remember that if the ships lost in the Arctic in 1871 had been insured, [he] would have been all right. . . .
>
> The great trouble of all of us is, we were brought up in ignorance of the problems of existence and were turned into life as green as leeks, then left to blunder toward the light without advice from anyone. My career was blighted by lack of insurance.

Matthew, in turn, was disappointed by his sons and their apparent inability to cope with their setbacks: "Father wrote me one of his utterly demoralized letters," Dick complained to Willie. "He said he was ready to despair about us."

Dick repeatedly wrote to his father, advising him to sell property, stocks, shares, and ships; Matthew wrote back asking him to say no more about it, that he, Matthew, was the better judge of his affairs.

Dick's mother, perhaps the gentler messenger, wrote to him: "We are trying to square things up, but there is no use forcing sales now. It would be ruinous. We must wait—just the hardest thing for some of us to do. . . . As for Christmas, I don't know whether we can raise much money. We are so poor now."

"Poor" was still, in 1878, a relative term.

Dick's anxiety about his father was a surrogate for his own concerns. His efforts at selling Wamsutta cloth were not supporting him and his family. Dick's 220 hens were paying his kitchen bills and encouraged him to think of expanding to 1,000, as well as adding cows and a vegetable garden. There was only one source to turn to for backing for this plan: "I've written Father about my idea of farming at Menlo and am collecting all the information I can get," he wrote to Willie. Nothing came of the expanded farm. Instead, alternately inspired and burdened by his family's great history of enterprise, he dreamed up moneymaking schemes, and—because of his family's supposed wealth—was approached by would-be entrepreneurs who had no idea how broke he really was.

I had a proposition made to me yesterday: to go into partnership with E. G. Pierce, the drayman, whom Morrie will know. He has built up his business until now he runs four heavy trucks, and he has a chance to extend it by . . . receiving grain and produce from Oregon and selling it . . . here. He says I can make $300 a month from $4,000.

Nothing came of Dick's draying dreams—the unrealized ingredients of a colorful historical novel: son of a whaleman goes into business with a teamster hauling produce up and down the West Coast through the years of explosive growth following the gold rush. But without ready capital, it was difficult to put any of his ideas into action. Some now seem speculative and fanciful—the gathering of egg albumen (for animal feed) from bird rookeries along the California coast—and might have lost the family even more money in the boom-and-bust cycles of the nineteenth century, during which the failure rate for new businesses, even sound ones, was high. But Dick was inventive and intelligent, and many of his ideas were practical and full of potential, such as coastal whaling, which would have required nothing more than the loan of one of his father's idle ships.

But Matthew was disinclined: "I cannot afford to lose 10 or 20 thousand dollars more. . . . It will not be prudent, to say the least, to fit out DESDEMONA at an expense of 12 to 15 thousand dollars for trading or whaling on the coast of California."

Dick's response to his father's caution was to stop writing home with accustomed regularity, and he could sound bitter in his letters to his brothers:

> From my early childhood I always rebelled against some portions of the life on Hawthorn Street. . . . Those grim Sundays and Quarterly Meetings and travelling Friends—the whole horrible system of Quakerism, in its attempt to crush out all natural feeling. . . . I don't want to be hard on Father and Mother. . . . They thought they were acting for the best. . . . But the theory was wrong and would have utterly crushed me, if I had not struck out for myself.

Matthew had a more harmonious relationship with his two younger sons. They remained closer to home, in both spirit and geography, and they asked less of their father.

Morrie, a popular, peripatetic socialite, flitted between his parents' home in New Bedford and Providence and New York City, making desultory connections as a trader of whaling-related and other merchandise (including mustard seed), to little effect. His diary (each of Matthew's boys kept one) shows that he was always more engaged in his social connections with old moneyed families:

> *Left home yesterday afternoon and reached New York this morning. Went to the Astor House for breakfast. . . .*
>
> *Just after dinner today a note came over from Isabel Rotch, asking me to go sailing. . . .*
>
> *This afternoon quite a large party went out on the MAGIC with Frank Weld. . . .*
>
> *Was busy all this morning preparing for my sailing party on the*

*TERESA. . . . Got into a comfortable place with Miss Hunter and spent
the time talking with her until our return. . . .*

*About noon time, got up from the office as early as I could and went
to the Delano's to play lawn tennis. . . .*

*All the usual set assembled at the Delano's. . . . After a little archery,
we separated.*

In November of 1879, Morrie, then twenty-nine, moved to New
York full-time to set himself up as a serious businessman:

*Left home today for New York, for the purpose of going into business there
as a metal broker. . . .*

*Having established myself in an office at 21 Cliff Street last week, I
began business today by leaving my card with the various purchasers of
lead. I was politely received by nearly all.*

Matthew wrote to Morrie almost daily, concerned for him, encouraging him, happy to see him finally making a real attempt at business,
and unable to refrain from offering him fretful advice:

Has thee sold that last lot of Mustard Seed yet; and the lot thee sold,
has thee received pay for it . . . ?

Thy letter to Mother has been received and we are very glad to
hear thee has really commenced making sales of lead. . . .

Why doesn't thee sell thy mustard seed? I would not keep it
much longer. . . .

How many tons of lead has thee sold thus far? It is now three
months since thee started. Can we judge of the next three months
by the past? I think, from what thee has told me, thee has not thus

far sold more than three or four different lots of lead. Do please continue to write and tell us all that transpires with thee. . . .

After a year in New York, Morrie was still not making his expenses. Matthew was floating him, anxious about the cost, but always, as for all his children, unguarded with his love:

Thee must try to keep thy expenses down all thee can, so they will not much exceed thy earnings. Does thee find any difficulty in keeping thy bank account [balanced]? It is very important *always* to have *something* in the bank. . . .

When we came home to tea last evening we missed thy company very much.

Another letter from Matthew to Morrie begins simply: "I have missed thee very much today."

In the fall of 1881, Matthew sold one of his last three ships, the *George and Susan*, built by his father and launched on his parents' wedding day in 1810. He got $9,500 for it, a good price in a depressed market for an aging (but obviously well-constructed) wooden ship that had paid for itself many times over. "Well!" he wrote Morrie. "She is gone from us after being in the family seventy years. It seems as though we are to part with everything of a material nature that is near and dear to us."

It was the industrious Willie, the youngest boy, who seemed the only one destined for any kind of financial stability, and, in time, he appeared to be making a real success by his own efforts, unaided by his father. In 1877, Willie took a low-level managerial position at the Wamsutta Mills, started by his uncle (by marriage), Joseph Grinnell. He apparently did well there, but the pay was low. "Dear Will works away bravely at the mill," Matthew wrote to Morrie. In 1881, Willie moved a few blocks south to the competing Potomska Mills. Here, too, he was well thought of, helping management draw up plans for a new mill, but he was ambitious and soon decided to start his own mill. His plan was to purchase an existing flour mill and convert it to cotton-yarn production, running 10,000 spindles. To do this, he began looking for subscribers for $125,000 worth of stock. Matthew was doubtful he could raise the money, for the new Acushnet Mills had just opened after raising $800,000. But Willie was dogged, and by then thoroughly experienced in the mill and textile business—and, of course, he was well connected. Perhaps because of the dilatory examples set by his brothers, he would surprise his father.

"It is rather lonesome in the office," Matthew wrote to Morrie. And, a month later: "I find it rather lonely in the counting room." The great house of Howland, the last of New Bedford's larger, older, historic whaling businesses, did not go out with a bang, but with the scratching of Matthew's pen in the empty Howland countinghouse, as he disbursed his remaining assets.

In February 1882, he sold his last two ships, the venerable *Rousseau* and the *Desdemona*, to the whaling firm of Swift & Allen, for $8,300. "It is a *very low* price," he wrote to Morrie, "but we did not think we could keep them longer." (It was a far better deal for Matthew than anyone knew. Whatever Swift & Allen's plans for them might have been, the ships never left New Bedford's waterfront again. They sat and rotted and sagged into the mud, a perfect symbol of whaling's decay.)

Matthew sold his Michigan Central Railroad stock, and then began dismantling his real estate holdings in New Bedford, rod by rod. And quietly: "Please tell R. Anthony as soon as thee can," he wrote to Morrie,

". . . [to] make me an offer for my lot (70 rods) and I will consider it, promising that no one shall know."

It was a comfort to note that "Will is driving about trying to obtain the subscription to his yarn mill and we think that so far he has done remarkably well. The subscriptions amount to very nearly $100,000, so that Willie is pretty sure it will go."

By late 1882, Matthew and his wife, Rachel, were also trying to sell their house (and block-wide, eminently divisible property) on Hawthorn Street, which they had built in 1840 and lived in for more than forty years. At the same time, Matthew was declining physically. "I should have written thee sooner, but have been very busy taking care of Father who has been quite ill," Rachel Howland wrote to Morrie in November 1882.

2nd day night he suffered extremely with what I suppose might be called a stoppage of the bowels. . . . I got the Doctor here and he staid three or four hours trying to allay the pain, which he finally accomplished by several doses of morphine injected into the arm. . . .

William Crapo [state representative, later president of the Wamsutta Mills] is still trying to get this place, but says he will not give over $30,000, while Father asks $40,000. What shall we do?

I think Father is very poorly indeed and very low spirited. What shall we do with him or for him? Thee must come and see him. . . .

Crapo has not treated us handsomely. . . . He seems to think he could just gobble us up and turn us out of house and home at his pleasure. And so the big fish eat up the little ones. . . .

Father has gone down to Meeting and I am alone. How often my heart aches to see more of thee.

The meetinghouse would have been as lonely as the Howland countinghouse. Like the whale fishery—in tandem with it, actually—New Bedford's Quaker community was diminishing in size and importance to the city. Schisms had sent many Quakers to other churches. The influx of outsiders and the broadening of New Bedford's ethnic population—initially because of whaling and, later, with the rise of the textile industry—left Old Lights George Jr. and Matthew Howland to walk around in their eighteenth-century garb, looking like anachronistic totems from a world that had all but disappeared. "The golden era of meetinghouse and countinghouse coincided," wrote historian Everett S. Allen. "And when the golden time was gone for one, it was gone for the other."

In 1883, Matthew had to borrow $4,000 from Willie to pay a debt—"Please do not say anything about it," he wrote to Morrie, asking him in the same letter for a loan of $300 for household expenses.

In September 1884, Matthew wrote to Morrie:

Willie informs us thee intends coming home next first day. We shall be very glad to see thee. I have been confined to the house since last 1st day with feet and legs much swollen. . . . The Doctor says I may drink a little Sherry, the very best. Could thee furnish me a small bottle and then bring it with thee. If not, perhaps we can get it here.

Leander Plummer died last evening.

In great haste, thy affectionately attached
Father

Shortly after he wrote that, "in great haste," Matthew himself was dead. Rachel was besieged by creditors. She moved in with Willie, his wife, Caroline, and their seven-year-old son, Llewellyn, while lawyers put the house and property on Hawthorn Street up for auction. Today, 81 Hawthorn Street, New Bedford, is occupied by professional medical offices. A plaque on the building gives the date of its construction and the names of its first two owners: "c. 1840; M. Howland; W. W. Crapo."

Over the course of their life, Matthew and Rachel gave away, largely though her philanthropic endeavors, more than half their income.

During his last two years, Matthew's deepening impoverishment and ill health were offset by the thrill of watching his youngest son's dream come to fruition. By November 1882, Willie had, against steep odds, raised his capital, converted the flour mill, fired up his steam-driven spindles, and was doing business as the New Bedford Manufacturing Company.

From the beginning, the mill was a conspicuous success. After two years of operation, its stock, when it could be purchased, was selling for $110–$118 per share, compared with $85 and $87 per share, respectively, for stock in the larger, more established Wamsutta and Acushnet mills. Willie seemed to have a golden touch. The hallmark of his business was the smoothness of its labor relations. His mother, Rachel, had filled him with a strong sense of fair play and with advanced, frankly idealistic notions of workers' rights, and Willie sincerely tried to provide the best for his employees. He paid them more than the other mills, and when strikes stopped production at Wamsutta, Potomska, and Acushnet, the New Bedford Manufacturing Company continued running. Working for his father, Willie had learned austerity in business, but he had also seen Howland ships sent to sea equipped with the finest gear, food, and men, and the results of running a quality operation. As a consequence of both these influences, his product was superior, and his sales were commensurate. He had no trouble raising a further $350,000 to build a brand-new mill in 1888, the Howland Mill, doing business as the Howland Mills Corporation. In 1892, he founded, along with William Rotch, a descendant of New Bedford's other premier whaling family, the Rotch Spinning Company.

With the capital he was now able to raise, Willie launched an ambitious scheme to create Howland Village, a 150-acre company housing park for his workers. He hired the Boston architectural firm of Wheelwright and Haven to produce three different house designs in a Dutch Colonial style, each varying in window, roof, ornament, and other details. The first fifty houses in Howland Village were built by 1889 (fifty-eight years before groundbreaking at Levittown, Long Island, New York). These were not cramped worker bungalows: thirty-five of the houses had five bedrooms, the remainder, three bedrooms; all had indoor plumbing, bathrooms with toilets and tubs, rare luxuries for the 1880s. Howland Village was sited on a hill west of the mills, with winding roads, and the houses and their lots were laid out in a pleasing, nonuniform effect. Rents for the houses ranged between $8.50 and $10 per month, for both skilled and unskilled Howland workers, who were earning between $50 and $80 per month.

By the 1890s, New Bedford had turned away from the sea. Its ships lay for sale and rotting along its depressed waterfront. Its industry looked landward over the rising, flourishing brick mills, and the railroads were now carrying raw materials into the city and its cottons and yarns away to market. With 1,000 workers operating 78,000 spindles in 200,000 square feet of floor space in two plants, the Howland Mills Corporation ranked third in size of New Bedford's textile mills, and was thought to be on its way to overtaking the Wamsutta and Potomska mills by the end of the century.

Willie's commitment to the welfare of his workers was tested and proven through the depression that gripped the American economy and created strife between capital and labor during the early to middle 1890s. In 1892, a state law reduced the working hours of mill employees from sixty to fifty-eight hours a week; while the other mills in New Bedford reduced their workers' pay, Willie kept pay rates at their former levels. In August 1894, the New Bedford Manufacturers Association, of which Willie was a member, recommended a 10 percent wage cutback for the city's 10,000 textile employees. The textile unions called for a citywide strike. Willie attempted to reach an agreement between the workers and the manufacturers, and when asked by the *New Bedford Evening Standard* what he would do if that failed, he replied that he would continue to run his mills at the former pay rates and do nothing that would disrupt "the smooth and friendly relations we have in our mills at present." When his efforts to break the strike failed, Willie kept his word. While the Wamsutta, Potomska, Acushnet, and other mills and related concerns remained closed for the next two months, the Howland mills continued at full operation, their employees still earning their old pay rates. Even when the State Board of Arbitration and Conciliation finally reached a compromise agreement with the unions for a five-percent pay cut, workers at the Howland mills continued to receive their prestrike pay. The *New Bedford Evening Journal* reported that Willie was "almost worshipped" by his employees, who subsequently presented him with a framed address in appreciation of his stand.

William Howland was seen, not only in New Bedford, but around the country, as a model employer. The Cleveland *Plain Dealer* featured an article describing the wages, housing, annual steamboat excursion to Martha's Vineyard enjoyed by Howland workers, and Willie's plans for their further benefit, which included a cooperative insurance scheme, and expansions at Howland Village that would provide a gymnasium, library, and an evening school for his employees and their families. "A few more such ventures as this and we shall see the beginning of the end of the great struggle between capital and labor," concluded the article.

New Bedford's newspapers frequently noted that "the most cordial relations have always existed" at the Howland mills; they compared the "air of comfort, contentment, and prosperity" in Howland Village with the "squalor" of the housing provided to Potomska mill employees, and described Willie as a "sagacious manufacturer, a man who has long shown it to be his belief that it is good business to treat the help fairly and liberally." The Quaker ethic, learned from his parents and grandparents, and in his father's countinghouse, seemed to be paying off for Willie in his great enterprise.

But the downturn in the American economy, and its effect on the textile market, could not be averted through goodwill. On April 15, 1897, the *New Bedford Evening Standard* reported irregularities in the finances of two New Bedford mills, the Bennett and Columbia mills, Howland competitors. It was soon revealed that management of both companies had paid out excess dividends, made false reports to state officials, banks, and stockholders, and embezzled hundreds of thousands of dollars. On April 16, both mills were placed in receivership. On April 23, William Howland requested a loan of $200,000 from New Bedford's National Bank of Commerce to cover his own mills' debts that were about to fall due. There had also been rumors of financial difficulties at the Howland mills, which Willie's request seemed to bear out. Notwithstanding that the bank had been founded by his father, Matthew Howland, and that Willie himself was on its board of directors, the business climate in New Bedford had suddenly grown wintry, and bank officials now asked to see the Howland books.

Willie returned to his office. His bookkeeper, Harry M. Pierce, later reported their conversation to the *Evening Standard*: "Well, Harry, the game's up," Howland told him. "The bank has refused to let us have any more money, and they want to put a man on the books to see if I'm a thief. It's too much for me, and all that's left for me to do is go and hang myself." Pierce tried to calm his employer, and then Willie said he was going out for a walk.

He was not seen again for thirteen days, until May 6, when his body was discovered floating under the wharves along the waterfront. He was forty-four.

The New Bedford Manufacturing Company, the Howland Mills Corporation, and the Rotch Spinning Company were all declared bankrupt and put into receivership. The mills were reorganized. Within a year, the employees of the former Howland mills had joined the city's other textile workers in a long and bitter strike. The renters in Howland Village were turned out and the houses sold, and New Bedford's workers' utopia vanished forever.

Virtually all of the shareholders Willie had successfully persuaded to invest in his mills had been his immediate family—his mother and father, Dick, and Morrie—other Howland relatives, and lifelong friends. Like New Bedford's whaling interests, the mills and their stock had been owned by the city's oldest, most venerable families. The failure—and the deepening troubles overtaking the city's other mills—had, like whaling's failure, struck deepest at the core of New Bedford's once brilliant plutocracy.

WILLIAM HOWLAND LEFT BEHIND a wife and two sons, and a gold Patek Philippe pocket watch. The watch was found on him when his body was recovered. Its ruined original works were replaced by a less expensive mechanism.

Willie's son, Llewellyn Howland, eventually passed that watch on to his grandson, Matthew Howland's great-great-grandson, Llewellyn Howland III. A few days before that young man left home to start his freshman year at Harvard in the 1960s, the elder Llewellyn called him over to his house. He wished him luck, offered a few words of general advice, and then told him about the end of his own abbreviated single year at Harvard:

When your great-grandfather died, I, of course, had to leave Cambridge and come right home. It was a nasty April day, raining, grey, bitter. I hated to leave Cambridge and I hated the stink of the New Haven cars and I hated the dreadful stretch of tenements by the track and the soot and the dirt. And when I looked out and saw the old men picking garbage in South Boston and the ragged children playing in the streets, God! how it frightened me to see them there. The squalor of it. The hopelessness of being poor. . . . Well, I've been fortunate, the family has been fortunate. But don't ever forget, don't ever forget what it would mean, being in those people's place. How hard it is to rise, when you're really, truly down.

Barrels of unsold whale oil on the New Bedford waterfront.
(Courtesy New Bedford Whaling Museum)

Epilogue 1

William Fish Williams made a fourth whaling voyage with his father as captain, shipping aboard the *Florence*, as a boat-steerer, from December 25, 1873, to November 12, 1874, sailing from San Francisco to the Sea of Okhotsk and back. At the end of that voyage, Willie, aged fifteen, decided he had had enough of the sea and wanted instead to become an engineer. He entered the School of Mines at Columbia University, in New York, in 1878, and in 1881 earned the degree of civil engineer. In 1882 he earned the further degree of engineer of mines. He worked as a mining engineer, far from the sea, in several places in the United States, but eventually settled in New Bedford, where he became the first city engineer. He wrote several accounts of his voyages as a boy aboard whaling ships. Williams died at home in New Bedford in 1929, at the age of seventy.

. . .

His father, Captain Thomas William Williams, continued whaling in the Arctic until 1879. That summer, on his last voyage, aboard the bark *Francis Palmer*, he carried on deck a small steam launch in which he chased whales at speed through the ice. "He would be gone for days at a time," wrote his son Willie, "and suffered hardships from exposure, poor food, and water, beside worries which broke his health." He died at home in Oakland the following summer, in August 1880.

Eliza and her daughter Mary returned to Wethersfield, Connecticut, where Eliza died in 1885.

Matthew's son, Dick—Richard Smith Howland—finally found the right outlet for his talents. In 1884, his wife Mary's uncle died and left her a large amount of stock in the profitable Providence Journal Company, publisher of the *Journal* and *Bulletin* newspapers in Providence. Dick, Mary, and their five children returned east to the city in 1885, and eventually Dick became manager of the Providence Journal Company. According to the centennial history of the *Journal*, published in 1962, his twenty-year stint as manager was a happy one. Circulation and income climbed.

Morrie never made a success as a businessman. He accepted Dick's offer of a job as the *Journal*'s book review editor. Dick also moved his mother, Rachel, to Providence, where she lived until her death in 1902. In 1905, Dick left his position at the Providence Journal Company and moved to Asheville, North Carolina, where he bought local railroad, quarrying, and textile stocks. With Dick gone, Morrie was let go from the *Journal* and joined his brother in Asheville, as his bookkeeper. The two retired and died in Jacksonville, Florida.

George Howland, Jr., died in 1892, outliving his younger half brother, Matthew, by eight years, and his wife, Sylvia, by two. Four years before his death he was forced to sell his mansion on Sixth Street, in which he had lived for more than half a century. He died penniless, but he had seen worse than the loss of his wealth. George's three children, sons, had all died before him, two as infants, and the third at the age of twenty-eight, in 1861, more than thirty years before his father.

Epilogue 2

In the wake of the closure of a BP oil field in Prudhoe Bay,
Alaska, oil prices shot up to $77 a barrel on Wednesday. . . .
The Prudhoe Bay oil field was discovered in 1968, and
began pumping in 1977. That first year, up to 1.5 million
barrels a day were pumped from the site. Now the site is
what is called a mature field and is far less productive,
pumping a maximum of about 400,000 barrels a day into
the Trans-Alaska Pipeline. . . . The future of oil production
at Prudhoe Bay, the largest oil field in the United States,
is tangled in issues like depletion of the fields, and global
pressure to find alternate sources.

The New York Times, *August 11, 2006*

In August 1886, as William Howland was expanding his mills in New Bedford, a twenty-three-year-old adventurer and part-time whaleman named Charlie Brower, a New Yorker by birth, was heading east with a group of ten men from Point Barrow in two small whaleboats. They were exploring the feasibility of small-boat whaling from a fixed base on Point Barrow for the Pacific Steam Whaling Company, based in San Francisco. Brower and the others had traveled north by steamer and been dropped off at the company's Point Barrow "station"— a shack above the beach. The company believed that newer, less exploited whaling grounds lay to the east of Point Barrow, along the Beaufort Sea coast of Alaska's northern shore, where few whaleships had ventured.

Heading eastward around the point by oar and sail in their small whaleboats, they camped the first night on an island between the sea and Elson Lagoon, close to the spot where Jared Jernegan's whaleship *Roman* had sunk fifteen years earlier. In addition to the wreckage of countless whaleships that littered the shore and barrier islands around Point Barrow, Charlie Brower and his men also found human skeletons and bodies in various stages of decomposition and preservation— probably some of the fifty men who remained behind with their trapped ships in the winter of 1876–1877, and had disappeared by the next summer.

After several days of hard rowing and beating to windward, camping ashore each night, the two boats were stopped by a storm at Cape Simpson, forty miles east of Point Barrow. The men aboard had seen no whales, and were discouraged. While the weather kept them pinned ashore, Brower and another man, Patsy Grey, headed inland over the marshy tundra with guns, hoping to shoot something to eat. Climbing over the top of a low rise of ground, they saw a small lake stretching out below them. It looked oddly black. They walked down to the edge of the lake. Liquid at its center, the "water" at their feet appeared to be "an asphalt-like substance."

Oil, thought Brower. Grey disagreed, having never heard of such a thing. Brower had: his luckless father had unaccountably gone bust in the wild early days of the Pennsylvania oil fields. Brower lit a match and lowered it to the asphalt. "It burned with intense heat and lots of greasy smoke," he later wrote.

They walked on around the small burning lake. Half a mile farther they reached a much larger "oil lake," where they saw the black carcasses of caribou and eider ducks trapped on its surface. Brower and Grey had discovered the seeping surface of the vast oil reserve that lay beneath the northern rim of Alaska, which would eventually be tapped from Prudhoe Bay, 120 miles to the east of where the two men stood. Apart from blundering caribou and eider ducks, it would lie undisturbed for another eighty years.

The whaleboats had come as far as they could go. Provisions were running low. When the storm passed, the whalemen sailed west again, back to Point Barrow.

Acknowledgments

A litany of inadequate expression:

I can't sufficiently thank my longtime literary agent, Sloan Harris. He is pragmatic, scrupulously honest, a gentleman, and a friend. Every book I've written owes him a great debt. Kristyn Keene has also been unfailingly helpful. I also want to thank Liz Farrell and Josie Freedman at ICM.

At Putnam, I'm extremely grateful to Ivan Held for his faith in this book. Dan Conaway, my editor on two previous books, championed this one and then moved away, and I've missed you, Dan. I've been fortunate to have the sage editorial skill of Rachel Kahan, who took the book over from Dan, and its finished shape bears her contribution and commitment. I want to thank Rachel Holtzman for her enthusiasm, and Lauren Kaplan for her help. This book has benefited greatly from the knowledge, judgment, eye, and ear of its extraordinary copy editor, Ed Cohen.

The generous contribution, suggestions, and friendship of Llewellyn Howland III have meant a great deal to me and to this book. I can't thank you enough, Louie. I want to thank Polly Saltonstall for introducing me to Louie.

Mike Dyer, curator at the New Bedford Whaling Museum, read the manuscript and made valuable suggestions. Laura Pereira, Kate Mello, Maria Batista, and Michael Lapides of the New Bedford Whaling Museum were also helpful.

Thank you, Jan Keeler, for your supply of clippings, knowledge, and enthusiasm.

Paul Cyr at the New Bedford Public Library was helpful.

John Bockstoce's work on American whaling in Alaskan waters and in numerous publications, especially the book *Whales, Ice, and Men*, is unparalleled, and I'm grateful for his comments and observations.

Phil Hardy, Chris Whann, and Susannah Mintz were valued mentors at Skidmore College.

In Tucson, Stephanie Pearmain, Aurelie Sheehan, Larry Cronin, and Marla Reckart.

For their friendship and encouragement, with this inadequate mention, I want to thank Kelly Horan; Robert and Penny Germaux; Jennie, Oskar, and Katya von Kretschmann; Peter Birch and Barry Longley; David and Anita Burdett; Jennifer Haigh; Kat Laupot; Bill and Jan Conrad; Robert and Sarah Reilly; Richard Podolsky; Robert and Su. Sane Hake; W. Hodding Carter; Bennet Scheuer; Amita Jarmon; Tom and Sasha Laurita; and their families.

I'm more grateful than I can say for the love and support and generosity of Roberta Franzheim and Josephine Franzheim.

Thanks enduringly to my sister Liz Sharp, Tony Sharp, Annie Nichols, Matt deGarmo, Cynthia Hartshorn, my mother Barbara Nichols. This book would not have been written without the love and support of my brother, David Nichols.

Hopefully you all know.

And my beautiful son, Gus, for every minute.

Sources

Allen, Everett S. *Children of the Light*. Boston: Little, Brown, 1973.

Ashley, Clifford W. *The Yankee Whaler*. Boston: Houghton Mifflin, 1926.

Bockstoce, John. *Arctic Passages*. New York: Hearst Marine Books, 1991.

———. *Whales, Ice, and Men*. Seattle: University of Washington Press, 1986.

Bowditch, Nathaniel. *American Practical Navigator*. Washington, D.C.: Department of Defense, Defense Mapping Agency, 1977; originally published 1802.

Brower, Charles. *Fifty Years Below Zero*. New York: Dodd, Mead, 1942.

———. *The Northernmost American: An Autobiography* (manuscript, Dartmouth College).

Bullen, Frank T. *The Cruise of the Cachalot*. London: Smith, Elder, 1898.

Burch, Ernest S., Jr. *Alliance and Conflict*. Lincoln: University of Nebraska Press, 2005.

———. *The Iñupiaq Eskimo Nations of Northwest Alaska*. Fairbanks: University of Alaska Press, 1998.

———. *Social Life in Northwest Alaska*. Fairbanks: University of Alaska Press, 2006.

Chyet, Stanley F. *Lopez of Newport*. Detroit: Wayne State University Press, 1970.

Davis, L., R. Gallman, and K. Gleitner. *In Pursuit of Leviathan*. Chicago: University of Chicago Press, 1997.

de Jong, C., and F. Schmitt. *Thomas Welcome Roys*. Newport News, Virginia: The Mariners' Museum, 1980.

Dexter, Lincoln A., ed. *The Gosnold Discoveries in the North Part of Virginia, 1602*. Sturbridge, Massachusetts: Universal Tag, 1982.

Dolin, Eric Jay. *Leviathan*. New York: W. W. Norton, 2007.

Druett, Joan. *Petticoat Whalers*. Hanover, New Hampshire: University Press of New England, 2001.

Ellis, Leonard Bolles. *History of New Bedford*. Syracuse, New York: Mason, 1892.

Emery, William M. *The Howland Heirs*. New Bedford, Massachusetts: E. Anthony and Sons, 1919.

Erikson, Kai T. *Wayward Puritans*. New York: John Wiley & Sons, 1966.

Frank, Stuart M., ed. *Meditations from Steerage: Two Whaling Journal Fragments*. Sharon, Massachusetts: The Kendall Whaling Museum, 1991.

Garner, Stanton, ed. *The Captain's Best Mate*. Providence, Rhode Island: Brown University Press, 1966.

Haley, Nelson Cole. *Whale Hunt*. Mystic, Connecticut: Mystic Seaport Museum, 2002.

Howland, Franklyn. *The Howlands of America*. New Bedford, Massachusetts: E. Anthony and Sons, 1885.

Howland, Llewellyn, III. "Children of the Light" (unpublished manuscript, 1964).

Leavitt, John F. *The Charles W. Morgan*. Mystic, Connecticut: Mystic Seaport Museum, 1998.

Macy, Obed. *The History of Nantucket*. Boston: Hilliard, Grey, 1835.

McCabe, Marsha, and Joseph Thomas. *Not Just Anywhere*. New Bedford, Massachusetts: Spinner, 1995.

McMullin, Thomas Austin. "Lost Alternative: The Urban Industrial Utopia of William D. Howland." *The New England Quarterly*, 55 (March 1982).

Miller, Pamela A., ed. *And the Whale Is Ours*. Boston: David R. Godine, 1979.

Morison, Samuel Eliot. *The Oxford History of the American People*, vols. 1 and 2. New York: Oxford University Press, 1965.

Pease, Zephaniah W., ed. *Life in New Bedford a Hundred Years Ago: The Diary of Joseph Anthony*. New Bedford, Massachusetts: The Old Dartmouth Historical Society, 1922.

Philbrick, Nathaniel. *Mayflower*. New York: Viking, 2006.

Poole, Dorothy Cottle, and Captain Jared J. Jernegan II. *The Dukes County Intelligencer* (Edgartown, Massachusetts), 14, no. 2 (November 1972).

Railton, Arthur R. "Jared Jernegan's Second Family," *The Dukes County Intelligencer* (Edgartown, Massachusetts), 28, no. 2 (November 1986).

Ricketson, Daniel. *The History of New Bedford*. New Bedford, Massachusetts: Self-published, 1858.

Rogers, Francis M. *Atlantic Islanders of the Azores and Madeira*. North Quincy, Massachusetts: Christopher Publishing House, 1979.

St. John de Crèvecoeur, J. Hector. *Letters from an American Farmer and Sketches of Eighteenth-Century America*. London: Penguin, 1981.

Slack, Charles. *Hetty: The Genius and Madness of America's First Female Tycoon*. New York: HarperCollins, 2004.

Sparkes, Boyden, and Samuel Taylor Moore. *The Witch of Wall Street: Hetty Green*. New York: Doubleday, Doran, 1935.

Stackpole, Edouard A. *Nantucket in the Revolution*. Nantucket, Massachusetts: The Nantucket Historical Association, 1976.

———. *The Sea-Hunters*. New York: J. B. Lippincott, 1953.

Starbuck, Alexander. *History of the American Whale Fishery*. Washington, D.C.: Government Printing Office, 1878.

Sturtevant, William, and David Damas, eds. *Handbook of North American Indians*, vol. 5 (Arctic). Washington, D.C.: Smithsonian Institution, 1984.

Taber, Mary J. *Just a Few Friends*. Philadelphia: John C. Winston, 1907.

Tarbell, Ida M. *The History of the Standard Oil Company*. New York: McClure, Phillips, 1905.

Tolles, Frederick B. "The New-Light Quakers of Lynn and New Bedford," *The New England Quarterly*, 32, no. 3 (September 1959).

Tucker, George Fox. *A Quaker Home*. Boston: George B. Reed, 1891.

United States Department of Commerce. *United States Coast Pilot*, vol. 9 (Pacific and Arctic Coasts), 7th ed. Washington, D.C.: U.S. Government Printing Office, 1964.

———. *United States Coast Pilot* (Alaska, part 2). Washington, D.C.: Government Printing Office, 1916.

Whiting, Emma Mayhew, and Henry Beetle Hough. *Whaling Wives of Martha's Vineyard*. Boston: Houghton Mifflin, 1953.

Williams, Harold, ed. *One Whaling Family*. Boston: Houghton Mifflin, 1964.

Yergin, Daniel. *The Prize*. New York: Simon & Schuster, 1992.

NEWSPAPERS

New Bedford *Republican Standard* (New Bedford, Massachusetts).

New Bedford *Evening Standard* (New Bedford, Massachusetts).

Whalemen's Shipping List and Merchants' Transcript (New Bedford, Massachusetts).

The Friend (Honolulu).

LOGBOOKS

Elizabeth Swift (New Bedford Whaling Museum).
Gay Head (New Bedford Whaling Museum).
Henry Taber (New Bedford Whaling Museum).
John Wells (New Bedford Whaling Museum).
Seneca (New Bedford Whaling Museum).
Thomas Dickason (New Bedford Whaling Museum).